EUL VERLAG

Reihe: Quantitative Ökonomie · Band 166

Herausgegeben von Prof. Dr. Eckart Bomsdorf, Köln, Prof. Dr. Wim
Kösters, Bochum, Prof. Dr. Winfried Matthes †, Wuppertal, Prof. Dr.
Mark Trede, Münster, Prof. Dr. Ansgar Belke, Essen, und Prof. Dr.
Markus Pütz, Lahr

Dr. Valentin Braun

Dynamic Copulas for Finance

An Application to Portfolio Risk Calculation

Bibliografische Information der Deutschen Nationalbibliothek

Die Deutsche Nationalbibliothek verzeichnet diese Publikation
in der Deutschen Nationalbibliografie; detaillierte bibliografische
Daten sind im Internet über <http://dnb.d-nb.de> abrufbar.

Dissertation, Goethe-Universität Frankfurt am Main, 2011

ISBN 978-3-8441-0040-2
1. Auflage Juni 2011

© JOSEF EUL VERLAG GmbH, Lohmar – Köln, 2011
Alle Rechte vorbehalten

JOSEF EUL VERLAG GmbH
Brandsberg 6
53797 Lohmar
Tel.: 0 22 05 / 90 10 6-6
Fax: 0 22 05 / 90 10 6-88
E-Mail: info@eul-verlag.de
http://www.eul-verlag.de

**Bei der Herstellung unserer Bücher möchten wir die Umwelt schonen. Dieses
Buch ist daher auf säurefreiem, 100% chlorfrei gebleichtem, alterungsbestän-
digem Papier nach DIN 6738 gedruckt.**

Vorwort

Die vorliegende Arbeit entstand im Rahmen meiner Tätigkeit als wissenschaftlicher Mitarbeiter und Doktorand an der Johann Wolfgang Goethe-Universität Frankfurt. Vielen Personen bin ich zu Dank verpflichtet, die mich während meiner Promotionszeit unterstützt und zum Gelingen meiner Arbeit beigetragen haben. Diese Dissertation hätte nicht ohne die Unterstützung meiner Familie entstehen können. Zu außerordentlichem Dank bin ich meiner Frau Maria Luisa Navarro-Braun verpflichtet. Sie hat mich in einer Zeit, in der es auf unermüdliches Engagement ankam, entscheidend motiviert. Ebenso hilfreich waren ihre sprachlichen Änderungsvorschläge, die den Lesefluss dieser Monographie maßgeblich verbesserten. Ihr widme ich diese Arbeit, die ohne ihre uneingeschränkte Hilfe und große Geduld nicht hätte erstellt werden können. Meine Eltern Marlene Schlickenrieder-Braun und Dr. Wolfgang Braun haben meine Ausbildung ermöglicht und mir vielfältige Gestaltungsräume eröffnet. Ich danke ihnen zutiefst für ihre finanzielle Unterstützung und die vielen motivierenden Worte. Des Weiteren danke ich meinem Doktorvater, Herrn Prof. Dr. Andreas Hackethal, für den nötigen wissenschaftlichen Freiraum zur Entwicklung und Umsetzung meiner Ideen. Ebenso danke ich Herrn Prof. Dr. Holger Kraft für die Übernahme des Koreferats. Die Zusammenarbeit mit Martin Grziska von der LMU München hat entscheidend zum Erfolg meiner Forschung beigetragen. Gemeinsam haben wir neue Ideen diskutiert und ihre Umsetzung vorangetrieben. Daneben wird mir die kollegiale und freundschaftliche Atmosphäre während der Promotionszeit in angenehmer Erinnerung bleiben. Dafür gilt mein Dank allen ehemaligen Kollegen.

Valentin Braun

Frankfurt am Main, Mai 2011

Contents

List of Tables

List of Figures

Abbreviations

ac	Archimedian Copula
AD	Absolute Difference
ADCC	Asymmetric Dynamic Correlation Coefficient
CvaR	Conditional Value at Risk
DCC	Dynamic Correlation Coefficient
DoF	Degree of Freedom
dp	Dynamic Process
dw	Dynamic Weight Indicator
GoF	Goodness-of-Fit
KS	Kolmogorov-Smirnov Test Statistic
LB	Ljung-Box Test Statistic
LL	LogLikelihood
log	Logarithmus
MLE	Maximum Likelihood Estimation
NIC	News Information Curve
Pr	Probability
RS	Regime-Switch
SL	Significance Level
VaR	Value at Risk
YTM	Yield-to-Maturity

List of Symbols

α	ARCH Coefficient
β	GARCH Coefficient
δ	Conditional Copula Density
ε	Residual
η	Standardized Residual
η^-	Negative Standardized Residual
γ	Leverage Coefficient
Γ	Gamma Distribution
ι	Dynamic Archimedian Copula Parameter
κ	(E)GARCH Process Constant
Λ	Logistic Transformation
λ_1	Autoregressive Process Coefficient
λ_2	Moving Average Process Coefficient
μ	Mean
ν	Degree of Freedom
$\odot$	Hadamard Product
ω	ARMA Process Constant
$\otimes$	Kronecker Product
ϕ	Generator Function
Φ	Standard Normal Distribution
Φ_R	Multivariate Standard Normal Distribution
ψ	Inverse Generator Function
ρ	Kendall's Rank Correlation Coefficient
σ	Standard Deviation
Σ	Unconditional Covariance Matrix
θ	Copulaparameter
ϖ	Skewness
ς	Unconditional Return Standard Deviation
Ξ	Threshold
ζ	Regime Probability
a	Dynamic Copula Autoregressive Coefficient
ar	Autoregressive Lag
BP	Bond Price
b	Dynamic Copula Moving Average Coefficient
C	Copula Function

c	Copula Density
ck	Cokurtosis
cs	Coskewness
d	Dimension
E	Expectation Function
F	Distribution Function
f	Density Function
$\mathbf{G}$	Godambe Information Matrix
g	Dynamic Correlation Coefficient Asymmetry Parameter
GED	Generalized Error Distribution
k	Dynamic Copula Process Constant
L	Lagrange Function
ln	Natural Logarithmus
LS	Log-Series Distribution
m	Median
$\mathbf{M}$	Score Function Covariance Matrix
M	Mixture Distribution
ma	Moving Average Lag
N	Normal Distribution
$\mathbf{P}$	Transition Probability Matrix
p	ARCH Lag
$\mathbf{Q}$	Conditional Covariance Matrix
q	GARCH Lag
$\mathbf{R}$	Korrelation Matrix
r	i.i.d. Random Vector
rm	Reference Maturity
SM	Standardized Moment
St	Stable Distribution
$Stud-t$	Student's-t Distribution
s	State Variable
sc	Score Function
$skew-t$	Skewed t-Distribution
T	Sample Size
$\mathbf{U}$	Uniformly Distributed Random Variable Matrix
U	Uniform Distribution
v	Dynamic Correlation Coefficient GARCH Parameter
w	Weight
$\mathbf{X}$	Return Matrix
x	Vector of Returns
z	Dynamic Correlation Constant

Chapter 1

Introduction and Thesis Structure

1.1 Introduction

Modern financial markets exhibit a variety of characteristics which are difficult to comprise with commonly applied statistical methods. On the univariate level, financial returns are often non-normally and non-symmetrically distributed. GARCH models are very powerful tools to capture the features of the univariate time series. On the multivariate level, time-instable dependencies are well observed phenomenon. However, their proper quantification has not been solved yet. In order to describe the characteristics of portfolios which contain multiple assets precisely, both aspects are equally important as their combination defines the joint distribution and hence the portfolio risk. Thus, the development of statistical methods which improve the accuracy of joint distributions is a central aspect of modern research.

So far, the multivariate Normal distribution is commonly applied to represent the joint distribution of financial assets. This assumption requires the univariate return series to follow a Normal distribution. Empirically this feature has been disproven. Additionally, the multivariate Normal distribution is symmetrical and not able to capture tail dependencies. Hence, empirically observed joint extreme events are neglected or at least severely underestimated. To account for tail dependence, this setup is sometimes extended to the multivariate Student's-t distribution. Nevertheless, this framework relies on the assumption that the univariate time series follow Student's-t distributions with an identical degree of freedom. Again, the multivariate Student's-t distribution models only symmetric dependencies.

Empirical work contradicts those assumptions. King, Wadhwani and Hamao et al. (1990), Engle and Susmel (1993), Kofman and Martens (1997), Longin and Solnik (2001), Ang and

1

Chen (2002), Bae et al. (2003), Forbes and Rigobon (2003), Hong et al. (2007), Statman and Scheid (2008) and many more present evidence of asymmetric dependencies in financial markets. All authors come to the same conclusion: markets rise independently but drop simultaneously. Hence, financial markets are less dependent in phases of economic growth than in times of economic downturns. Severe negative returns of various assets occur more frequently together than positive returns of the same amplitude. This asymmetric dependence generates joint distributions featuring long left but fatter and shorter right tails (Fama (1976), Brown and Warner (1985), Lo and MacKinlay (1988)). Consequently, multivariate Normal or Student's-t distributions are not an adequate measure to represent the joint distribution of financial assets.

In regards to the univariate time series, Schwert (1989), Brandt and Kang (2004), Mele (2007) and Liu (2007) show evidence that financial market returns exhibit volatility asymmetries, heteroskedasticity and asymmetric distributions. Volatility asymmetry describes the nature of modest reaction to good news and overreaction to bad news, resulting in dramatic asset value declines. Heteroskedasticity refers to the phenomenon of clusters of high volatility and clusters of low volatility. In addition, financial time series often feature skewed distributions and consequently their allocation via the multivariate Normal or Student's-t distributions is inaccurate. Engle (1982) and Bollerslev (1986) introduce ARCH and GARCH models to capture the characteristics of the univariate time series. Yet, Granger (1969) found that shocks in one time series impact other time series as well: "A time series X_t is said to cause another series Y_t if and only if past values of X are useful in predicting Y_t when the past values of Y have also been taken into account." Due to the fact that most financial portfolios comprise more than one asset, the Granger causality unfolds the importance of a precise dependence measure.

Therefore, modern research focuses on the development of model frameworks which simultaneously account for the characteristics of the univariate time series and their multivariate dependence structures. A precise combination of the univariate and multivariate characteristics is extremely important to determine accurate multivariate distributions which define portfolio default probabilities. Thus, this line of research is especially important for financial institutions and insurances as their portfolios contain multiple assets.

Lately, Copulas have gained an increase in interest as an alternative to model multivariate joint distributions. The basic Copula concept was developed by Sklar (1959). It allows to separate the joint distribution function into two parts: The univariate distribution functions which describe the features of the individual time series and the Copula function which solely captures their dependence structure. According to the Sklar theorem (1959), both parts of the joint distribution are analyzed independently. Firstly, the univariate models are calibrated. They are not limited to a unique family and are estimated independently. Secondly, the joint distribution function is constructed via the Copula, aggregating the univariate distributions. The Copula choice is arbitrary and independent from the univariate models. This procedure results in a wide variety of very flexible joint distribution functions which are able to capture asymmetric dependencies as well as asymmetries in the univariate distributions. These features are a tremendous improvement compared to the joint Normal and Student's-t distributions.

Copulas have been well defined functions since their introduction in the 1950's, but they were first applied to finance at the beginning of the 21st century. For example, Bouye et al. (2000, 2001), Embrechts et al. (2003), Mendes and Souza (2004) and Kole et al. (2006) were some of the pioneers who utilized Copulas to measure the dependencies of financial markets. Their main focus was to quantify accurate non-normal joint distributions in order to estimate precise portfolio shortfall probabilities. Especially in the area of risk management, Copula theory and its application to financial data has attained an increase in interest. Copulas are utilized to describe the dependence structures of time series to determine market and credit risk. As mentioned earlier, the greatest advantage of this concept is the separation of the univariate models from the Copulas. Due to the large variety of possible Copula functions, I am able to investigate and modulate asymmetric dependencies. There exist Copula functions which feature stronger dependencies in the left than in the right tail of the joint distribution and vice versa; A very interesting and important characteristic in regards to financial markets. Nelsen (2006) gives a very detailed introduction to symmetric and asymmetric Copula functions.

Although Copulas represent the dependencies of financial markets more accurately than linear correlation matrices, a major drawback remains. There are plenty of bivariate Copulas, but their multivariate options are limited. Basically, there are two Copula families which are extendable to multiple dimensions: the Archimedian and the Elliptical Copulas. Multidimensionality is a major aspect for portfolio theory and therefore those two Copula families set the basis for this thesis. Both families have their advantages and disadvantages. The Archimedian Copulas model asymmetric dependence structures but comprise any information via a single parameter. Thus, this skeleton is limited to capture linkages of multiple time series with similar characteristics. The Elliptical family features parameter plurality but models dependencies symmetrically. More research is necessary to determine how to model asymmetric dependencies of

3

multiple time series, properly. One possibility to overcome the shortage of multivariate choices is to combine different multivariate Copulas into a Mixture Copula (Hu (2006)). This construct produces "new" Copulas which replicate the dependence structure of multiple securities more accurately than single Copulas.

Even though Mixture Copulas amend dependence modeling tremendously, the Mixture weights and the individual Copula parameters remain static. In contrast, the dependence structures of financial assets are not time-stable but they change in shape and intensity. Consequently, Static Mixture Copulas are not able to comprise sudden and constitutive switches of financial markets' interaction, completely. Yet, two lines of literature have just started to focus on this issue, leaving a broad range for improvements. The first research area divides the dataset into different dependence regimes and estimates different Copula models for each regime (Pelletier (2006), Rodriguez (2007), Garcia and Tsafak (2007)). This procedure is labeled Regime-Switch (RS) Copulas. I stick to the framework proposed by Chollete et al. (2009) but extend the Copula choices within the regimes to the class of multivariate Mixtures. Thus, I enhance the model flexibility to capture the characteristics of intense and weak dependence phases. In the RS Copula framework, the Copula families and parameters are constant within one regime but vary across regimes. Engle and Sheppard (2001) introduce a more flexible dependence skeleton, their dynamic correlation coefficients (DCC), which sets the basis for the second literature field. In their framework, the correlation parameters follow a GARCH-like process and therefore constantly adapt to changes in the dependence structure. While favorable components of their approach are its multidimensionality and flexibility, it is limited to model symmetric dependence. In 2006 Capiello et al. implemented a leverage factor into this framework to account for asymmetric correlation response. This yielded the asymmetric dynamic correlation coefficients (ADCC). Nevertheless, linear correlation coefficients remain the basis, neglecting tail or asymmetric dependencies. In order to capture asymmetric dependencies whose intensities swing over time, Patton (2006) introduces his skeleton of conditional Copulas. The parameters follow an ARMA-like process, but this setup is limited to the bivariate case.

Despite tremendous amendments in regards to dependence modeling, the most significant question remains: How to capture the characteristics of time-instable asymmetric dependencies in a multivariate setup? Ausin and Lopes (forthcoming 2010) implement Engle and Sheppard's (2001) DCC framework into the Student's-t Copula skeleton. In cooperation with Martin Grziska, I integrate Capiello et al. (2006) ADCC into the Student's-t Copula. Both approaches result Dynamic Student's-t Copulas which model tail dependence, are well defined for multiple dimensions and their parameters follow stochastic processes. Additionally, our setup accounts for asymmetric correlation response. Nevertheless, both dynamic models are based on the symmetric Student's-t Copula and are therefore unable to comprise asymmetric dependencies. Patton (2007) appeals to extend the existing bivariate dynamic asymmetric dependence models to multiple dimensions. In allusion to Patton (2006), Hafner and Manner (2009) define an autoregressive process for the Copula parameters. Theoretically, their approach is applicable to any Copula and any dimension, but it is computationally extensive. Independent from their work, I propose multivariate Dynamic Archimedian Copulas whose parameters follow well defined ARMA processes. Similar to Patton (2006), this approach comprises time-instable asymmetric dependencies, but it is dimensionally unlimited. In a similar manner, I construct a stochastic process for Hu's (2006) Mixture approach resulting in a Dynamic Mixture Copula. The advantage of the proposed construct is twofold. Different portions of the data are represented through different Dynamic Copulas whose parameters evolve over time. Additionally, the weights within the Dynamic Mixture skeleton are time-flexible.

The contribution of this thesis to existing Copula theory is threefold. Firstly, the ADCC framework is integrated into Elliptical Copulas to model time-instable parameter intensities. Secondly, a stochastic process is proposed to model the parameters of multivariate Archimedian Copulas. This preserves the asymmetries in the dependence structure but simultaneously allows the parameter intensities to swing. Thirdly, a Dynamic Mixture framework is introduced, enhancing the model flexibility to adapt to data containing time-instable dependencies. The three approaches are extensions to the current Copula literature and contribute to solve the question: How can time-instable multivariate asymmetric financial market dependencies be modeled?

The empirical application of the proposed models contributes to three areas of financial research. Firstly, I analyze if Stock market comovements follow a recurring pattern. Furthermore, the interaction of the time-flexible Copula parameters with the underlying Stock prices and volatilities is investigated. This reveals the drivers for tightening and loosening dependencies. Although plenty of empirical studies have documented the asymmetric dependence patterns of Stock markets, there exist only few surveys on international Bond markets. I examine if there are simple relations between Bond yields and the Bond yield dependencies or between Bond yield volatilities and the Bond yield dependencies. Additionally, I examine whether changes in the Bond yield dependencies follow a unique and recurring pattern or if they are driven by fundamentals. Although most financial portfolios contain more than one security type, I am not aware of any studies which investigate shifts in the dependencies of various asset classes. Therefore, I analyze diversification effects among multiple asset classes and compare them to the effects of global diversification within a single asset class. The comovements of the Dynamic Copula parameters with the appropriate financial markets exhibit the causes for shifts in the dependence structure. In allusion to Guidolin and Timmermann (2007), I test whether increasing volatility levels tighten dependencies. The interaction of volatility and dependence defines portfolio risks. Therefore, this relation is especially important and significantly impacts the optimal portfolio construction.

Secondly, out-of-sample portfolio risk forecasts amplify the advantages of Dynamic Copulas. Portfolio shortfall probabilities are predicted on basis of Static, Regime-Switch and Dynamic Copulas but the marginal models remain the same. The dominant accuracies of the Dynamic Copula based predictions prove the necessity to grasp time-flexible dependence patterns. Those analyses also quantify possible portfolio risk forecast exceedances caused by misspecified dependencies.

Thirdly, optimal portfolios are constructed via the Mean-Variance and the Mean-CVaR procedures on basis of simulations from Static, Regime-Switch and Dynamic Copulas. The Mean-CVaR algorithm explicitly accounts for portfolio skewnesses which are aggravated by asymmetric dependencies. The Dynamic Copulas capture the asymmetric interactions of financial markets very precisely and therefore enhance the portfolio selection. In return, the security selection procedures accentuate the impact of misspecified dependence structures on the optimal portfolio choices.

1.2 Thesis Structure

This thesis contributes to the research area of multivariate time-instable dependence models. It is divided into a theoretical part which proposes multivariate Dynamic Copulas and an empirical section which employs various dependence models to detect the most advantageous approach. The chapters are arranged as follows:

Chapter 2 gives an introduction to the univariate GARCH models because they set the basis for the multivariate Copulas. Therefore, an advertent and precise calibration of the marginal models is inalienable to avoid adulterations of the Copula calibrations. Two model choices are utilized to capture the volatility characteristics of the univariate time series, precisely: The symmetric GARCH and the asymmetric EGARCH. In addition, the time series are filtered via ARMA models to guarantee an exact fit.

Chapter 3 presents the theoretical foundations of Copulas. At first, the multidimensional Static Archimedian and Elliptical Copulas are described. Further, their possible combinations in Hierarchical and Mixture frameworks are discussed. Second, the theoretical foundation of the Regime-Switch Copulas is illustrated. Third, a dynamic process is defined for the Archimedian Copula parameters. Fourth, the Capiello et al. (2006) ADCC frame is integrated into Elliptical Copulas to model their parameters time-flexible via a well defined stochastic process. Finally, the multivariate Dynamic Copulas are integrated into a Dynamic Mixture structure. The Mixture weights follow a well defined ARMA process, introducing additional flexibility. The proposed Dynamic Copulas are given for the multivariate case.

Chapter 4 presents the descriptives of the datasets which are utilized for the empirical analyses (Bond yields only, Stocks only, Multi Asset Classes) and the parameter estimates for the GARCH models. On basis of the filtered residuals, the different Copulas are estimated and their according parameters are illustrated. The time-flexible Copula estimates reveal information about changes in the dependence structures and the according economic drivers. I focus on three major economic shocks in this context: The 1999 Euro introduction, the 2001 terror attacks and the 2008/2009 credit crunch.

Chapter 5 examines the interaction of dependencies, volatility levels and returns. The proposed models are utilized to revise the linkages between dependencies and volatilities and the linkages between dependencies and returns of financial markets. The interactions of dependencies, volatilities and returns are a key factor to compute accurate portfolio risks. Therefore, the impacts of the volatility levels and the returns on the RS Copula regime probabilities are examined. Additionally, the correlations of the Dynamic Copula parameters with the according volatilities and returns are computed. The same analyses are conducted for Bond yield, Stocks and Multi Asset Classes datasets. Furthermore, the interactions of the univariate volatilities and returns are examined.

Chapter 6 conducts out-of-sample risk forecasts on portfolio level. Any Copula simulations are nested with the same univariate volatility forecasts. Hence, differences in the portfolio risk predictions are only due to variations of the Copula models. This setup allows a fair and direct comparison of the Copula skeletons and their impacts on the forecast accuracies. This analysis is conducted for one Bond yields only, one Stocks only and one Multi Asset Classes portfolios.

Chapter 7 allocates portfolios on basis of the Stocks only and the Multi Asset Classes data. Four Stock return datasets are simulated with identical univariate characteristics but different dependence structures. The returns of the first Stocks dataset are linked via a linear correlation matrix. The second to the fourth Stocks datasets contain the dependencies from the "best-fit" Copulas of each type. In the same manner, four Multi Asset Classes datasets are simulated. Finally, portfolios are allocated via the Mean-Variance and the Mean-CVaR procedures on basis of the eight datasets. The significant differences in the optimal portfolio shares amplify the impact of misspecified dependence patterns.

Chapter 8 draws conclusions on the findings and gives an outlook on future research.

Chapter 2

GARCH Theory

2.1 Introduction

Volatility is a key component in the areas of asset and risk management, asset pricing and significantly impacts the security selection process. Although the majority of researchers agrees on the predictability of volatility, they differ in the question how to model and forecast volatility. Throughout the years a wide variety of studies concerned with financial volatility was published. Some authors examine the volatility characteristics empirically motivating others to propose new models to capture those characteristics. The most interesting volatility feature detected by empirical analyses is its asymmetric response characteristic (Christie (1982), French, Schwert and Stambaugh (1987), Schwert (1990) and Baillie and Myers (1991)). Consequently, volatility models which account for this important feature have been developed. The most prominent asymmetric volatility model is the EGARCH, introduced by Nelson (1991). His work provides a theoretical skeleton for the differing impact magnitudes of good and bad news on volatility. Engle and Ng (1993) introduce News Impact Curves (NIC) which analyze the impact structure of news on the volatility for various GARCH models.

A review of the applications that rely on conditional volatilities amplifies the importance of correct volatility estimates. In case of Stocks valuation, Merton (1980) shows that the predictable market volatility directly impacts the expected market return. His findings are supported by French, Schwert and Stambaugh (1987). In addition, Schwert and Seguin (1990) provide evidence that market volatility drives individual Stock volatilities. The field of risk management is closely related to Stocks valuation and hence accurate volatility estimates are a key factor.

The next section presents the properties of GARCH and EGARCH models and possible variations of the assumed return distributions. The news impact curves are utilized to illustrate the characteristics of both models.

2.2   GARCH Models

Frequently observed features of financial time series are their skewed return distributions and volatility clustering. Researchers have put much effort towards capturing those features in an adequate framework. Engle (1982) set the basis for volatility modeling with the introduction of his AutoRegressive Conditional Heteroskedasticity concept (ARCH). The basic idea behind his invention is to cluster volatility. Future volatility is thought to depend on the latest historic observations. Thus, observed high volatility levels lead to distinct future volatility and vice versa. As a consequence, volatility occurs in clusters of high and low levels. In its general form the ARCH(p) model is defined as:

$$\sigma_t^2 = \kappa + \sum_{i=1}^{p} \alpha_i \varepsilon_{t-i}^2. \tag{2.1}$$

Hence, the volatility (σ^2) depends on a constant term (κ) and lagged disturbances (ε_{t-i}). $\alpha_1, ..., \alpha_p$ indicate the lag parameters. It appears logical to expect that the latest news impact the current volatility most. Under this assumption, $\alpha_i < \alpha_j$ for $i > j$. Consequently, shocks that occurred more than i periods ago have no impact on the current volatility, at all.

An extension to the ARCH framework was developed by Bollerslev (1986), named Generalized ARCH model (GARCH(p,q)):

$$\sigma_t^2 = \kappa + \sum_{i=1}^{p} \alpha_i \varepsilon_{t-i}^2 + \sum_{j=1}^{q} \beta_j \sigma_{t-j}^2. \tag{2.2}$$

Volatility in this process is not only dependent on the history of the observed time-series but also on the history of the filtered volatility. The according lag parameters are labeled $\beta_1, ..., \beta_q$. Bollerslev et al. (1992) indicate that the application of a GARCH(1,1) model is most efficient. Therefore, I stick to one lag only for the rest of this thesis. With respect to volatility clustering, this framework offers several advantages over Engle's original ARCH model. However, its basic setup assumes symmetrically distributed returns. Hansen (1994) introduced the skew-t distribution to the ARCH process. This idea is easily transferable into the GARCH procedure and enhances its ability to model financial time series more accurately. Possible distribution choices for the innovations in the ARCH and GARCH models are:

$$
\varepsilon_t \sim \begin{cases} N(\mu, \sigma) \\[4pt] GED(\mu, \sigma, v) \\[4pt] Stud - t(\mu, \sigma, v) \\[4pt] skew - t(\mu, \sigma, v, \varpi), \end{cases}
$$

with mean μ, standard deviation σ, degree of freedom v and skewness parameter ϖ.

Although Hansen's extension to the original ARCH and GARCH models enhances volatility modeling tremendously, those processes still reveal a major shortcoming: The news impact on volatility is assumed to be symmetric. Therefore, both models embrace the same impact of positive and negative news on volatility. In contrast, empirical observations exhibit a smaller impact of unexpected price increases (positive news) than of unexpected price drops (negative news) on volatility. This leverage or asymmetric effect is confirmed by French, Schwert, and Stambaugh (1987), Brandt and Kang (2004), Mele (2007), Liu (2007) and many more.

Nelson (1991) enhances the symmetric GARCH model to capture asymmetries via a "leverage effect". This approach is named Exponential GARCH model (EGARCH(1,1)) and defines the conditional variances, σ_t^2, as an asymmetric function of lagged disturbances ε_{t-1}:

$$
ln(\sigma_t^2) = \kappa + \alpha \frac{|\varepsilon_{t-1}|}{\sigma_{t-1}} + \gamma \frac{\varepsilon_{t-1}}{\sigma_{t-1}} + \beta ln(\sigma_{t-1}^2), \tag{2.3}
$$

where γ captures the leverage effect. If γ is negative, negative shocks have a greater impact on volatility than positive shocks and vice versa, but positive variances are always guaranteed. Engle and Ng (1993) developed the News Information Curve (NIC) which illustrates the differences of the GARCH and EGARCH models. It measures the impacts of new information on the volatility estimates. The NIC for the GARCH(1,1) model is defined as:

$$
\sigma_t^2 = A + \alpha \varepsilon_{t-1}^2, \tag{2.4}
$$

11

where σ_t^2 is the conditional variance at time t and ε_{t-1} is the disturbance at time $t-1$. $A = \kappa + \beta \varsigma^2$ where ς is the unconditional return standard deviation. The NIC for the EGARCH(1,1) model is defined as:

$$\sigma_t^2 = A \, exp \left[\frac{\gamma + \alpha}{\varsigma} \varepsilon_{t-1} \right], \; for \; \varepsilon_{t-1} > 0 \tag{2.5}$$

$$\sigma_t^2 = A \, exp \left[\frac{\gamma - \alpha}{\varsigma} \varepsilon_{t-1} \right], \; for \; \varepsilon_{t-1} < 0, \tag{2.6}$$

where $A = \varsigma^{2\beta} exp \left(\kappa - \alpha \sqrt{\frac{2}{\pi}} \right)$.

Figure 2.1 – News Impact Curves of a GARCH and an EGARCH model. The solid line presents the News Impact Curve for the GARCH model. The dashed line presents the News Impact Curve for the EGARCH model.

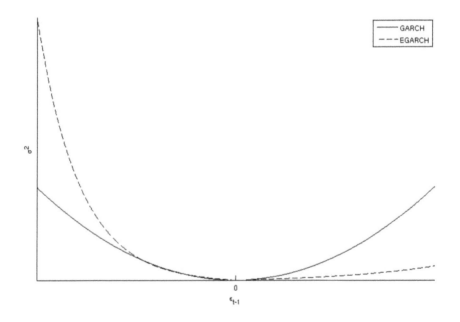

Figure 2.1 presents the NIC for the GARCH(1,1) and for the EGARCH(1,1) models. It is obvious that only the EGARCH framework distinguishes the influence of good and bad news on volatility. Engle and Ng (1993) give a good overview on the GARCH model variations which follow Nelson's (1991) concept to account for asymmetric volatility responses. Nevertheless, the basic idea remains the same: Volatility is influenced asymmetrically by good and bad news.

Therefore, I stick with the symmetric GARCH(1,1) and the asymmetric EGARCH(1,1) approaches throughout this thesis.

Well specified univariate models set the basis for accurate dependence measures. Thus, I filter the return series with an ARMA(ar,ma) process before I apply the volatility models:

$$x_t = \mu_t + \eta_t \sigma_t \tag{2.7}$$

$$\mu_t = \omega + \sum_{i=1}^{ar} \lambda_{1,i} x_{t-i} + \sum_{j=1}^{ma} \lambda_{2,j} \varepsilon_{t-j}, \tag{2.8}$$

where η are the standardized residuals, ω is the constant and λ_1 and λ_2 are the lag parameters of the AR and the MA terms. For well defined ARMA processes, I limit $\sum_{i=1}^{ar} |\lambda_{1,i}| < 1$ and $\sum_{j=1}^{ma} |\lambda_{2,j}| < 1$ to account for stationarity and invertibility. A more detailed description of ARMA processes and their constraints is given in Tsay (2005). Overall, I filter the univariate return series with an one-step ARMA(ar,ma)-GARCH(1,1) and an one-step ARMA(ar,ma)-EGARCH(1,1) processes and identify the most appropriate setup via the Bayesian Information Criteria (BIC). The standard errors are calculated according to White (1982). His quasi maximum likelihood estimation combines the second derivative and the outer product matrix of the information matrix to compute the standard errors. Thus, the estimated standard errors are more robust in case of false density estimations. The selected GARCH procedures filter white noise residuals for each individual return series, but do not comprise any information about their coherences. Yet, Granger (1969) found that shocks in one time series impact other time series as well. In order to prevent the neglection of asymmetric dependence structures, I quantify the interrelation of the filtered standardized residuals via Copulas.

Chapter 3

Copula Theory

3.1 Copula Basics

This section gives a short introduction to Copula theory. The basis for Copulas is defined by Sklar's theorem (1959):

Let F be a joint distribution with marginal distributions $F_1, ..., F_d$. Thus there exists a d-dimensional Copula $C : [0, 1]^d \rightarrow [0, 1]$ such that for all $x_1, ..., x_d \in \bar{\mathbb{R}}^d$,

$$F(x_1, ..., x_d) = C(F_1(x_1), ..., F_d(x_d)).$$ (3.1)

If all marginals $F_1, ..., F_d$ are continuous the Copula is unique. Vice Versa, if C is a Copula and $F_1, ..., F_d$ are marginals then (3.1) yields a d-variate distribution with marginals $F_1, ..., F_d$.

Based on this theorem, a wide variety of Copulas has been developed. Nelsen (2006) provides a detailed compilation of the existing Copula functions. This thesis focuses on two specific families from the wide range of possible Copula functions which are extendable to multivariate dimensions. First, the Archimedian Copulas which are characterized by a single parameter and are limited to model positive dependence. However, their ability to capture asymmetries in the dependence structure is a very worthy feature in regards to financial time series. Second, I focus on Elliptical Copulas which contain the Gaussian and Student's-t Copulas. Although both are limited to model symmetric dependence, their parameter plurality is an advantageous feature. Both Copula families are well defined parameterized functions which are adapted to data via maximum likelihood estimations (MLE). Consequently, simulations are easily implementable; A very useful tool for financial research.

3.2 Multivariate Static Copulas

3.2.1 Static Archimedian Copulas

Archimedian Copulas are characterized by their ability to capture any information about the d-dimensional dependence structure in the univariate generator function ϕ. The generators are capable of constructing d-dimensional Archimedian Copulas but limited to model positive dependencies (Nelsen (2006)). At first glance, this looms a great disadvantage, but as mentioned earlier, positive dependence relishes greater relevance in economics. Kimberling (1974) gives sufficient and necessary conditions for a strict generator ϕ to generate d-dimensional Archimedian Copulas:

Let $\phi : [0,1] \rightarrow [0,\infty]$ be a continuous strictly decreasing function such that $\phi(0) = \infty$ and $\phi(1) = 0$. Thus $\phi^{-1} : [0,\infty] \rightarrow [0,1]$ denotes the inverse of ϕ with the same attributes, but $\phi^{-1}(0) = 1$ and $\lim_{s \to \infty} \phi^{-1}(s) = 0$.
The function $C : [0,1]^d \rightarrow [0,1]$ is defined as a d-dimensional Archimedian Copula

$$C(u_1,...,u_d) = \phi^{-1}\left(\sum_{i=1}^{d} \phi(u_i)\right) \tag{3.2}$$

iif ϕ^{-1} is completely monotonic on $[0,\infty)$.

According to Bernstein's theorem (Joe (1997)) the inverse of the generator function ϕ^{-1} can be expressed as a Laplace-Transform ψ of non-negative random variables H with mixture distribution M:

$$\phi^{-1}(s) = \psi(s) = E\left(e^{-Hs}\right) = \int_0^\infty e^{-hs} dM(h), \ s \geq 0. \tag{3.3}$$

This thesis only considers Copula functions which are well defined for multiple dimensions. In case of the Archimedian Copulas this restriction limits me to the Clayton, Frank and Gumbel Copulas. Detailed descriptions of their functions are given in table 3.1.

There are two well defined methodologies to simulate data from a multivariate Archimedian Copula. The conditional inversion method which can be applied to any Copula function, regardless of its family. Its basic procedure consists of three steps: First, simulate i.i.d uniform data $(r_1,...,r_d)$; Second, set $u_1 = r_1$; Third, evaluate r_i via the inverse of the conditional Copula function for $i = 2,...,d$ $(u_i = C^{-1}(r_i|u_1,...,u_{i-1}))$. This procedure generates the uniformly distributed simulations, $\mathbf{U}^{n \times d} \sim U[0,1]$, which contain the dependence structure of the Copula C.

16

Table 3.1 – Archimedian Copulas. The first column gives the names of the Copulas. The second column presents the according Copula functions (C). The third and fourth columns present the Copula generator functions ϕ and its Laplace transform ψ. The last column presents the mixture distribution function (M) where LS is the Log-Series distribution and St denotes the Stable distribution.

Copula	$C(u_1, ..., u_d)$	$\phi(u)$	$\psi(s)$	M
Clayton	$\left[\sum\limits_{i=1}^{d} u_i^{-\theta} - d + 1 \right]^{-\frac{1}{\theta}}, \theta > 0$	$\frac{1}{\theta}\left(u^{-\theta} - 1 \right)$	$(1+s)^{-\frac{1}{\theta}}$	$\Gamma\left(\frac{1}{\theta}, 1\right)$
Frank	$-\frac{1}{\theta} \ln\left[1 + (e^{-\theta} - 1) \prod\limits_{i=1}^{d} \frac{e^{-\theta u_i} - 1}{e^{-\theta} - 1} \right], \theta > 0$	$\ln\left[\frac{e^{-\theta u} - 1}{e^{-\theta} - 1} \right]$	$-\frac{1}{\theta} \ln\left[(e^{-\theta} - 1) e^{-s} + 1 \right]$	$LS\left(e^{-\theta}\right)$ over $\mathbb{N}$
Gumbel	$\exp\left[-\left[\sum\limits_{i=1}^{d} (-\ln(u_i))^{\theta} \right]^{\frac{1}{\theta}} \right], \theta \geq 1$	$[-\ln(u)]^{\theta}$	$\exp\left(-s^{\frac{1}{\theta}} \right)$	$St\left(\frac{1}{\theta}, 1, \gamma, 0\right)$

17

A detailed introduction to this simulation method is given in Hoermann et al. (2004). However, this procedure turns inefficient due to its recursive character.

Based on equation 3.3, Marshall and Olkin (1988) develop a procedure to simulate $\mathbf{U}^{n \times d}$ from the Archimedian Copulas via their Laplace transforms. Again, this simulation procedure requires three steps: First, generate a realization of the random variable H from the distribution M under the condition that its Laplace transform ψ is the inverse of the Copula generator function ($\psi = \phi^{-1}$). Table 3.1 presents the distributions of the random variable and the according inverse generator functions for the Archimedian Copulas; Second, generate i.i.d uniform data $(r_1, ..., r_d)$; Third, calculate $u_i = \psi\left(\frac{-ln(r_i)}{h}\right)$, for $i = 1, ..., d$. The fact that Marshall and Olkin's (1988) algorithm does not require any derivatives and is not recursive enhances the simulation speed, tremendously. Therefore, I apply this procedure to generate random numbers from the Archimedian Copulas.

3.2.2 Static Elliptical Copulas

Elliptical Copulas are often called implicit Copulas due to their affiliation from well known multivariate distributions with steady marginal distributions. Examples are the multivariate Gauss or the multivariate Student's-t distributions. Their greatest advantages are their parameter plurality and their abilities to extend to multiple dimensions, easily (Hult and Lindskog (2002), Nelsen (2006)). The multivariate Student's-t Copula is defined as

$$C(u_1, ..., u_d; v, \mathbf{R}) = t_{v,\mathbf{R}}\left(t_v^{-1}(u_1), ..., t_v^{-1}(u_d)\right) \tag{3.4}$$
$$= \int_{-\infty}^{t_v^{-1}(u_1)} \cdots \int_{-\infty}^{t_v^{-1}(u_d)} \frac{\Gamma\left(\frac{v+d}{2}\right) |\mathbf{R}|^{-\frac{1}{2}}}{\Gamma\left(\frac{v}{2}\right)(v\pi)^{\frac{d}{2}}} \left(1 + \frac{1}{v}x'\mathbf{R}^{-1}x\right)^{-\frac{v+d}{2}} dx_1 \cdots dx_d,$$

where t_v^{-1} represents the univariate quantile function of the Student's-t distribution with v degrees of freedom and $t_{v,\mathbf{R}}$ is its according multivariate distribution function with degrees of freedom v and correlation matrix $\mathbf{R}$. This parameterization concedes the Student's-t Copula distinct flexibility to fit to data with strong tail dependence and to model higher dimensions. Compared to the family of Archimedian Copulas, the Student's-t Copula exhibits the disadvantage of symmetric tail dependence. However, it compensates this shortfall with its ability to model negative dependencies in d dimensions. The Gaussian Copula is included in this family

18

as a special case $(v \to \infty)$, but constrained in its flexibility in matters of its exclusive parameterization via the correlation matrix $\mathbf{R}$:

$$C(u_1,...,u_d;\mathbf{R}) = \Phi_{\mathbf{R}}\left(\Phi^{-1}(u_1),...,\Phi^{-1}(u_d)\right), \tag{3.5}$$

where Φ^{-1} represents the quantile function of the univariate standard normal distribution and $\Phi_{\mathbf{R}}$ the multivariate standard normal distribution function with correlation matrix $\mathbf{R}$. By definition, $\mathbf{R}$ must be positive definite.

3.2.3 Static Canonical-Vine Copulas

Bedford and Cooke (2002) introduced Canonical-Vine Copulas in statistics and Aas et al. (2009) were the first to apply them to finance. Canonical-Vine Copulas are constructed hierarchically resulting great flexibility to adapt to empirical data. The main idea is to combine several bivariate Copulas in a cascade. Figure 3.1 illustrates the Canonical-Vine Copula graphically.

Figure 3.1 – Canonical Vine Copula

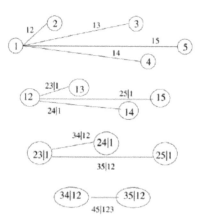

Hence, multidimensional problems can be examined with bivariate Copulas via pair-Copula decompositions. This is a great advantage because a huge number of bivariate but only a limited number of multidimensional Copulas exist. Additionally, Canonical-Vine Copulas are not limited to consist of multiple bivariate Copulas of the same type, but they are flexible enough to combine several different bivariate Copula families. A well known feature of a joint density function of d variables $(x_1, ..., x_d)$ is the possibility to decompose its density iteratively conditional as:

$$f(x_1, ..., x_d) = f_1(x_1) \cdot f(x_2|x_1) \cdot f(x_3|x_1, x_2) \cdots f(x_d|x_1, ..., x_{d-1}). \tag{3.6}$$

According to the Sklar theorem (Equation 3.1) it is possible to further decompose the joint density function into the conditional densities and conditional pair-Copula functions. Thus, the first Copula function c_{12} links the first and second variables (x_1, x_2)

$$f(x_2|x_1) = c_{12}(F_1(x_1), F_2(x_2)) \cdot f_2(x_2)$$

and the second conditional density is given by

$$f(x_3|x_1, x_2) = c_{23|1}(F_{2|1}(x_2|x_1), F_{3|1}(x_3|x_1)) \cdot f(x_3|x_1),$$

where $c_{23|1}$ denotes the conditional Copula of x_2 and x_3, given x_1. According to the first conditional density function, $f(x_3|x_1)$ can easily be substituted and results

$$f(x_3|x_1, x_2) = c_{23|1}(F_{2|1}(x_2|x_1), F_{3|1}(x_3|x_1))c_{13}(F_1(x_1), F_3(x_3)) \cdot f_3(x_3).$$

This results one unconditional, f_3, and two conditional density functions, $f(x_2|x_1)$ and $f(x_3|x_1, x_2)$. According to equation 3.6, I combine the previous expressions and receive the joint density function. It consists of the conditional Copulas and the unconditional density functions:

$$f(x_1, x_2, x_3) = c_{23|1}(F_{2|1}(x_2|x_1), F_{3|1}(x_3|x_1))c_{13}(F_1(x_1), F_3(x_3))c_{12}(F_1(x_1), F_2(x_2)) \cdots$$
$$f_1(x_1) \cdot f_2(x_2) \cdot f_3(x_3).$$

Following the previous steps iteratively, I can decompose any conditional density function into conditional bivariate Copulas and the unconditional density functions. Consequently, the general density function decomposition for d variables is given by

$$f(x_1, ..., x_d) = c_{1...d}(F_1(x_1), ..., F_d(x_d)) \cdot f_1(x_1) \cdots f_d(x_d).$$

Finally, I outlay Joe's (1996) decomposition of the conditional pair-Copulas:

$$F(x|y) = \frac{\partial C_{x,y_j|y_{-j}}(F(x|y_{-j}), F(y_j|y_{-j}))}{\partial F(y_j|y_{-j})},$$

where y_{-j} denotes the vector y excluding the component y_j. It is obvious that the first variable plays a special role in this concept. Any other variables are conditioned on the first variable. I arbitrarily choose variable x_1 for this position, although any other choice is legitimate, as well. Hence, in this setup variable x_1 sets the basis for all conditional Copulas. During the estimation procedure, I first calibrate the bivariate Copulas of x_1 with any other variable. Thereafter, I condition on x_1 and estimate all bivariate conditional Copulas of x_2 with all other variables, etc. For a d dimensional variable set the joint density corresponding to the d dimensional Canonical-Vine Copula is:

$$f(x_1,...,x_d) = \prod_{k=1}^{d} f_k(x_k) \prod_{j=1}^{d-1} \prod_{i=1}^{d-j} c_{j,j+1|1,...,j-1}\left(F\left(x_j|x_1,...,x_{j-1}\right), F\left(x_{j+i}|x_1,...,x_{j-1}\right)\right). \quad (3.7)$$

3.2.4 Static Mixture Copulas

In order to combine the parameter plurality of Elliptical Copulas with the asymmetric features of Archimedian Copulas I give a short introduction to Static Mixture Copulas. Hu (2006) demonstrates the flexibility of this construct and its ability to adequately represent the empirical dependence patterns. The Mixture Copula consists of n Copulas of any kind but of d dimensions:

$$C(u_1,...,u_d; w_1,...,w_n, \theta_1,...,\theta_n) = \sum_{j=1}^{n} \left[w_j C_j(u_1,...,u_d, \theta_j)\right], \quad (3.8)$$

where $\theta_1,...,\theta_n$ are the Copula parameter sets and the Mixture weights (w) are constrained to $\sum_{j=1}^{n} w_j = 1$. Its advantage over a single Static Copula is obvious. The Mixture Copula consists of various Copulas which exhibit different features. One example is the combination of one symmetric and one asymmetric Copula. In this case, two different Copulas describe the dataset's dependence structure, according to their shares in the Mixture construct. Consequently, each Copula is adjusted only to the portion of the data they represent. Splitting the dependence structure in this manner allows to calibrate the parameters more precisely, as they only have to match their data portions. In contrast, the application of a single Copula requires its parameters to capture the dependence of the complete dataset, resulting greater compromises and inaccuracy in the adjustment. The according Mixture Copula simulations consist of weighted simulations

21

which are drawn from the underlying Copulas. In this example, the symmetric Copula would generate the portion w_s and the asymmetric Copula would generate the portion w_a of the Mixture simulations. Figure 3.2 illustrates the Mixture concept graphically. The four figures on the left side present the contour plots and densities of a Gaussian Copula and a Clayton Copula. On the right side both Copulas are combined into a Mixture Copula. The resulting Mixture Copula's advantages are obvious; parameter plurality and asymmetric dependence features.

Although Static Mixture Copulas improve the preciseness of dependence representation, their parameters and shapes remain constant. Thus, Static Mixture Copulas are not able to seize severe and permanent shifts in the dependence structure, over time. Accordingly, simulations are conducted with identical Copula parameters and Mixture weights regardless of mutations in the dependence structure.

3.3 Multivariate Regime-Switch Copulas

I model dependence with Regime-Switch (RS) Copulas to account for changes in its structure. In this manner I follow Pelletier (2006), Garcia and Tsafak (2007) and Chollete et al. (2009) who allow different dependence regimes which vary in shape and/or intensity. Thus, I am able to allocate different Copula types to phases of intense and weak dependence. In this framework, the Copula families and parameters are constant within one regime but vary across regimes. The Markov switching process defines the regime probabilities. In other words, RS Copulas consist of j regimes and j Copulas, which vary in shape and intensity. However, the Copulas and their parameter sets remain constant, only their probabilities of representing the dependence varies over time. Consequently, the shapes of RS Copulas change over time, because different portions of the time series are expressed through different Copulas. In order to avoid excessive parameterization, I limit the model to two regimes. Hence, I am closest to Garcia and Tsafak (2007) and Chollete et al. (2009) who are the only other authors I know that use a multidimensional Regime-Switch Copula. This work extents the possible Copula choices within the regimes to multivariate Mixture Copulas, adding additional flexibility to comprise asymmetric dependencies. In the remainder of this section I explain the Regime-Switch Copula that allows different dependence structures and intensities for different subsamples of the data.

Figure 3.2 – Contour Plot of a Multidimensional Mixture Copula

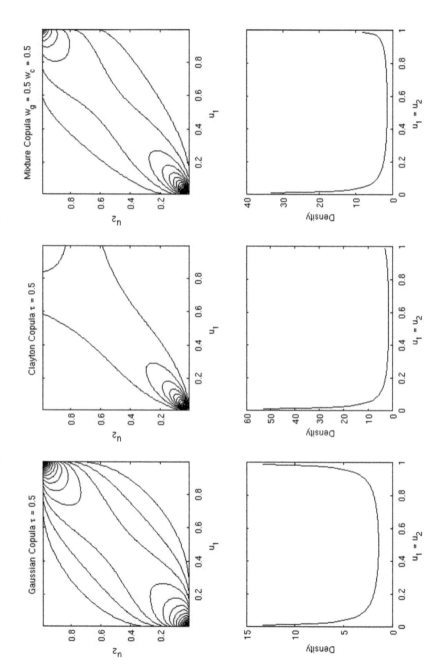

I follow Hamilton (1989) who switches between different density functions to describe the data. In contrast to his univariate framework, I consider the joint density of multiple time series based on the Copula function. Due to the fact that Copula functions only vary with respect to their dependence characteristics, the regimes only affect the dependence structure. Consequently, I describe different portions of the joint data density with different Copula functions. The data density conditional on being in regime j is

$$f(\mathbf{X}_t|\mathbf{X}_{t-1}, s_t = j) = c^{(j)}(F_1(x_{1,t}), ..., F_d(x_{d,t}); \theta_c^{(j)}) \prod_{i=1}^{d} f_i(x_{i,t}; \theta_{m,i}), \qquad (3.9)$$

where $\mathbf{X}_t = (x_{1,t}, ..., x_{d,t})$, s_t is the state variable for the regime, $c^{(j)}(.)$ is the Copula density function in regime j with its parameter set $\theta_c^{(j)}$, F_i is the distribution and f_i the corresponding density function of the marginal x_i, with parameters $\theta_{m,i}$. The latent state variable is assumed to be governed by the transition probability matrix,

$$\mathbf{P} = \Pr(s_t = i|s_{t-1} = j) = p_{i,j}, \text{ for } i,j = 1,2. \qquad (3.10)$$

Due to the non-observeability of the Markov chain s_t, I stick to Hamilton's (1989) filter. Within this filter, the transition probability drives the regime probabilities which in return define the density function of the complete dataset. More specifically, the filtered process obeys

$$\zeta_{t|t} = \frac{\zeta_{t|t-1} \odot \delta_t}{1'(\zeta_{t|t-1} \odot \delta_t)'} \qquad (3.11)$$

$$\zeta_{t+1|t} = \mathbf{P}'\zeta_{t|t} \qquad (3.12)$$

$$\delta_t = \begin{pmatrix} c^{(1)}\left(F_1(x_{1,t}|x_1^{t-1}), ..., F_d(x_{d,t}|x_d^{t-1}); \theta_c^{(1)}\right) \\ c^{(2)}\left(F_1(x_{1,t}|x_1^{t-1}), ..., F_d(x_{d,t}|x_d^{t-1}); \theta_c^{(2)}\right) \end{pmatrix} \qquad (3.13)$$

where $\zeta_{t|t}$ is a (2 x 1) vector containing the regime probabilities at time t, conditional on the observations up to time t; 1 is a (2 x 1) vector of 1s; and $\odot$ denotes the Hadamard product. The transition probability matrix $\mathbf{P}$ depicts the regime probabilities $\zeta_{t+1|t}$ at time $t+1$, conditional on observations up to time t. As this procedure is recursive, the n-step ahead forecast for the regime probabilities ($\zeta_{t+n|t}$) is simple. The vector δ_t contains the Copula densities at time t, conditional on being in each one of the two regimes. The filtered system requires a starting value for the regime probabilities, $\zeta_{1|0}$.

3.4 Multivariate Dynamic Copulas

3.4.1 Dynamic Archimedian Copulas

Engle and Sheppard (2001) set the basis for dynamic dependence models with the introduction of dynamic correlation coefficients (DCC). Patton (2006) adapted their idea to bivariate Archimedian Copulas by modeling the parameters via an ARMA(1,1)-like process. He first calculates a transformed Copula parameter as a Kendall's rank correlation (ρ) at time t:

$$\rho_t = \Lambda \left(k^{(ac)} + a^{(ac)} \theta_{t-1} + b^{(ac)} \frac{1}{10} \sum_{j=1}^{10} |u_{1,t-j} - u_{2,t-j}| \right), \qquad (3.14)$$

where $(u_{1,t}, u_{2,t})$ are two observations at time t and $\Lambda(y) = \frac{1}{1+e^{-y}}$ is a logistic transformation to keep $\rho \in [0,1]$. This is in line with the Archimedian Copulas' limitation to model positive dependence. In case of the Clayton Copula, its parameter (θ_t) at time t is calculated via $\theta = \frac{2\rho}{(1-\rho)}$ and in case of the Gumbel Copula via $\theta = \frac{1}{(1-\rho)}$. In contrast to an ARMA process, $k^{(ac)}$, $a^{(ac)}$ and $b^{(ac)}$ are unrestricted. They are collected in the dynamic process parameter vector $\theta_c^{(dp)} = (k^{(ac)}, a^{(ac)}, b^{(ac)})$, where ac indicates the Dynamic Archimedian Copula skeleton.

However, this thesis focuses on flexible multivariate Copulas. Therefore, I propose an extension of Patton's concept to higher dimensions and slightly modify the ARMA(1,1)-like process to allow simple multistep forecasts. Equation 3.14 is limited to the bivariate case through the absolute distance measure $|u_{1,t-j} - u_{2,t-j}|$. An alternative to measure the absolute distance in a multidimensional framework as a scalar is contained in the K-Means clustering algorithm. In general, K-Means clustering is a method of cluster analysis to partition T observations into K clusters in which each observation belongs to the cluster with the nearest median. There exist various distance measures, but to stick closest to equation 3.14, I apply the absolute distance methodology. Given a set of observations $\mathbf{U}^{T \times d}$, the K-Means clustering aims to partition the T observations into K sets ($K < T$), $S = S_1, ..., S_K$ so as to minimize the within-cluster sum of absolute values. However, I do not aim at clustering the observations, but to calculate their absolute distance at time t. Therefore, I define only one cluster ($K = 1$) and calculate the absolute difference (AD) between the observations $(u_{1,t}, ..., u_{d,t})$ and their median (m_t) at time t as: $AD_t = \sum_{j=1}^{K} \sum_{i=1}^{d} |u_{i,t} - m_{j,t}| = \sum_{i=1}^{d} |u_{i,t} - m_t|$. Replacing the bivariate absolute distance measure in equation 3.14 with the K-Means algorithm results a dynamic process for the multivariate transformed Copula parameter. However, multistep forecasts based on this process are still complicated. Hafner and Manner (2009) propose a solution to this problem. They assume the unobserved Copula parameter follows a well defined Gaussian AR(1) process. In this manner, I follow their idea and slightly modify the ARMA(1,1) process:

$$\iota_t = k^{(ac)} + a^{(ac)} \iota_{t-1} + b^{(ac)} L^{-1} \sum_{j=1}^{L} \sum_{i=1}^{d} |u_{i,t-j} - m_{t-j}|. \tag{3.15}$$

The according parameter transformations are $\theta = exp(\iota)$ for the Clayton and $\theta = exp(\iota) + 1$ for the Gumbel Copula which account for the Archimedian Copula parameter constraints (Table 3.1). In contrast to equation 3.14, I limit $|a^{(ac)}| < 1$ and $|b^{(ac)}| < 1$ to account for stationarity and invertibility, whereas $k^{(ac)}$ remains unrestricted. Thus, equation 3.15 is a well defined ARMA(1,1) process because ι relies on its own, non-transformed history. L indicates the lags of the multivariate absolute distance calculation. In allusion to Patton (2006), I choose $L = 10$ although this choice is arbitrary. Overall, the slight modifications of Patton's (2006) setup allow to model the parameter of a multidimensional Archimedian Copula via a dynamic process.

3.4.2 Dynamic Elliptical Copulas

The previous section proposes an extension of bivariate Dynamic Archimedian Copulas to the multivariate case. Next to Archimedian Copulas, this thesis considers multivariate Elliptical Copulas. In cooperation with Martin Grziska, I implement a dynamic process into the Elliptical Copula. Due to the fact that both Elliptical Copulas (Gaussian and Student's-t) contain a correlation matrix, Engle and Sheppard's (2001) dynamic correlation coefficients (DCC) model sets a well defined basis. In 2006, Cappiello et al. implement an additional factor into the DCC framework which accounts for asymmetric response of the correlation to good and bad news. The correlation matrix ($\mathbf{R}$) in the asymmetric dynamic correlation coefficient (ADCC) model follows a stochastic process:

$$\mathbf{Q}_t = (\bar{\mathbf{R}} - z\bar{\mathbf{R}} - v\bar{\mathbf{R}} - g\bar{\mathbf{N}}) + z\eta_{t-1}\eta_{t-1}' + g\eta_{t-1}^{-}\eta_{t-1}^{-'} + v\mathbf{Q}_{t-1} \tag{3.16}$$

$$\mathbf{R}_t = \mathbf{Q}_t^{*-1}\mathbf{Q}_t\mathbf{Q}_t^{*-1}, \tag{3.17}$$

where η are standardized residuals and $\bar{\mathbf{R}} = E[\eta_t\eta_t']$ and $\mathbf{Q}_t^* = [q_{ii,t}^*] = [\sqrt{q_{ii,t}}]$ is a diagonal matrix with the square root of the ith diagonal element of $\mathbf{Q}_t$ on its ith diagonal position. $\eta_t^{-} = I[\eta_t < 0] \odot \eta_t$ ($I[\cdot]$ is an indicator function which takes on value 1 if the argument is true and 0 otherwise, while $\odot$ indicates the Hadamard product) and $\bar{\mathbf{N}} = E[\eta^- \eta^{-'}]$. Hence, η_t^- indicates the asymmetry parameter which represents the different impacts of positive and negative news on the correlation structure. $\mathbf{Q}_t$ needs to be positive definite to guarantee that $\mathbf{R}_t$ is a correlation matrix. Therefore, the scalars z, v and g are constrained to $0 \leq z, v, g$ and to $z + v + \Pi g < 1$, where $\Pi = \max\{eigenvalue[\bar{\mathbf{R}}^{-1/2} \bar{\mathbf{N}} \bar{\mathbf{R}}^{-1/2}]\}$. The dynamic process parameters are collected via $\theta_c^{(dp)} = (z, v, g)$.

Inside the Elliptical Copula skeleton, we replace the static correlation matrix with the ADCC setup and receive a Dynamic Elliptical Copula whose correlation matrix follows a stochastic process. The only other work in progress concerned with the integration of the ADCC framework into Elliptical Copulas is Jin (2009). In case of the Gaussian Copula the dynamic extension results

$$C(u_1, ..., u_d; \mathbf{R}_t) = \Phi_{\mathbf{R}_t}\left(\Phi^{-1}(u_1), ..., \Phi^{-1}(u_d)\right) \tag{3.18}$$

and the dynamic formulation of the Student's-t Copula is

$$C(u_1, ..., u_d; v, \mathbf{R}_t) = t_{v, \mathbf{R}_t}\left(t_v^{-1}(u_1), ..., t_v^{-1}(u_d)\right). \tag{3.19}$$

In order to avoid excessive estimation, we keep v of the Dynamic Student's-t Copula constant. However, it could simply follow a separate, well defined dynamic process.

3.4.3 Dynamic Mixture Copulas

In this section I combine several multivariate Dynamic Copulas into a Dynamic Mixture Copula. The choice of the individual Dynamic Copulas inside the Mixture skeleton is arbitrary. In addition, I model the weights of the Mixture construct with a dynamic process. This introduces additional flexibility and enhances the dependence representation. The only other work which proposes dynamic weights for a Mixture Copula is Ng (2008). He adopts Patton's (2006) dynamic process and simply replaces the historical Copula parameter with historical weights. This results an ARMA(1,1)-like process for the weights (w), which lacks stationary and invertibility. Therefore, Ng (2008) has to stick to the exponential transformation to keep the weights limited to $w \in [0, 1]$:

$$w_{i,t} = \left[1 + exp\left(-\left(k_i^{(dw)} + a_i^{(dw)} w_{i,t-1} + b_i^{(dw)} L^{-1} \sum_{l=1}^{L} |x_{1,t-l} - x_{2,t-l}|\right)\right)\right]^{-1}, \tag{3.20}$$

for $i = [1, ..., n]$. The scalars $k^{(dw)}$, $a^{(dw)}$ and $b^{(dw)}$ are the unconstrained parameters of the ARMA-like weights process, L indicates the lags for the absolute distance calculation and dw indicates the dynamic weight process parameters. Although the Mixture weights are dynamic, he keeps the parameters of the individual Copulas constant. Additionally, his model is limited to the bivariate case.

In contrast, I follow Patton's (2007) appeal to extent flexible Copulas to multiple dimensions and propose a multidimensional Dynamic Mixture Copula. Its weights follow a well defined ARMA(1,1) process and its individual Copulas' parameters follow dynamic processes, as well. Those features introduce additional flexibility to the Mixture structure and allow a more precise adaptation to the data, resulting a more accurate representation of the dependence structure. In contrast to Ng (2008), I base the dynamic weights process on its own history and on the historic Copula densities:

$$w_{i,t} = \left(k_i^{(dw)} + a_i^{(dw)} w_{i,t-1} + b_i^{(dw)} L^{-1} \sum_{l=1}^{L} \left[\frac{c_i \left(u_1, ..., u_d; \theta_{i,t-l} \right)}{\sum_{j=1}^{n} c_j \left(u_1, ..., u_d; \theta_{j,t-l} \right)} \right] \right), \qquad (3.21)$$

for $i = [1, ..., n-1]$ and the weights have to satisfy $\sum_{i=1}^{n} w_i = 1$. θ_t is the Copula parameter set at time t. The scalars $k^{(dw)}$, $a^{(dw)}$ and $b^{(dw)}$ are the parameters of the ARMA process for the dynamic weights. In order to allow simple multistep forecasts, I account for stationary ($|a^{(dw)}| < 1$) and invertibility ($|b^{(dw)}| < 1$). Those constraints satisfy the general ARMA process. However, from an economic perspective the weight forecasts have to stay within the range $w \in [0, 1]$. In order to generate reasonable multistep weight forecasts without transformations, this requires the implementation of additional constraints on the ARMA process. By definition, $0 \leq w_{i,t-1} \leq 1$ and $0 \leq L^{-1} \sum_{l=1}^{L} \left[\frac{c_i(u_1, ..., u_d; \theta_{i,t-l})}{\sum_{j=1}^{n} c_j(u_1, ..., u_d; \theta_{j,t-l})} \right] \leq 1$. To ensure that equation 3.21 always results $0 \leq w_{i,t} \leq 1$, I implement three constraints: $k^{(dw)} \geq |a^{(dw)}| + |b^{(dw)}|$; $k^{(dw)} + a^{(dw)} + b^{(dw)} \leq 1$; $0 \leq k^{(dw)} \leq 1$. Due to $w_{i,t+m} \rightarrow k^{(dw)} (1 - a^{(dw)})^{-1}$ for $m \rightarrow \infty$, I constrain $k^{(dw)} + a^{(dw)} < 1$ to ensure $w_{i,t+m} \in [0, 1]$. Enders (2003) and Tsay (2005) give deeper insights into multistep ARMA forecasts and the related constraints. L indicates the lags of the proportional Copula density. In allusion to Patton (2006), I choose $L = 10$ although this choice is arbitrary.

Comparing equations 3.20 and 3.21 depicts the major differences between both approaches. First, I implement several constraints on the dynamic weight process to avoid the necessity of a transformation. This is a great advantage for multistep forecasts. Second, Ng (2008) bases his dynamic process on the absolute differences between two return series. This limits him to the bivariate case. In contrast, I define the weight of the Copula within the Mixture construct via its density relative to the sum of all Copula densities. The advantage lies in Copulas' different density structures. Copulas which model left tail dependence only, reveal the greatest density in the left tail and vice versa (Figure 3.2). Therefore, each Copula's weight is directly linked to its ability to represent the current dependence structure. Changes in the dependence structure directly result shifts in the dynamic weights. Third, the multidimensional Copulas in equation 3.21 avoid any dimensional limitations.

Implementing dynamic weights and individual Dynamic Copulas into the skeleton of the Static Mixture Copula results the Dynamic Mixture Copula:

$$C(u_1, ..., u_d; w_{1,t}, ..., w_{n,t}, \theta_{1,t}, ..., \theta_{n,t}) = \sum_{j=1}^{n} \left[w_{j,t} C_j \left(u_1, ..., u_d; \theta_{j,t} \right) \right], \qquad (3.22)$$

where $\theta_{j,t}$ are the path dependent parameter sets of the individual Dynamic Copulas in the Mixture model at time t. The vector $\theta_c^{(dp)} = (\theta_{c,1}^{(dp)}, ..., \theta_{c,n}^{(dp)}, k^{(dw)}, a^{(dw)}, b^{(dw)})$ collects the dynamic process parameters of a Dynamic Mixture Copula, consisting of n Dynamic Copulas. The greatest advantage of the Dynamic Mixture Copula is its tremendous flexibility. An increase of one Dynamic Copula's relative density indicates its increasing adaptability to this data portion. Hence, its weight in the Mixture structure and its influence on the Mixture Copula density increases. Consequently, the parameter estimation procedure focuses to adapt each Copula's dynamic parameters most accurately to those portions of the data which naturally match the Copula characteristics. In return, the estimation procedure neglects those portions where the Copula's relative weight decreases. The intuition is simple: Decreasing weight results less influence on the Mixture density, reducing the negative impact of inaccurate parameter fitting. In contrast, increasing weight increases the influence on the Mixture density and amplifies well fitted parameters. Overall, each individual Dynamic Copula matches only a certain portion of the dataset, but their consolidation in the Dynamic Mixture Copula via the dynamic weights results the most flexible and accurate dependence representation.

3.5 Two-Step Estimation

Regardless of the Copula model, I separate the estimation of the ARMA-GARCH process and the Copula. This results two great advantages. First, the marginal models are only estimated once, regardless of the Copula function. This reduces the amount of parameters to be estimated in each step. Second, the residuals, which set the basis for any Copula estimations, are filtered by exactly the same marginal models. Hence, all Copulas are calibrated on the exact same data basis what allows a direct comparison of the Copulas. In contrast to one-step estimations, the Copulas are not biased by differences in the marginals. Nevertheless, the total loglikelihood (LL) depends on all the data ($\mathbf{X}^{T \times d}$) and is given by:

$$LL\left(\mathbf{X}; \theta_m, \theta_c\right) = \sum_{t=1}^{T} log \, f\left(\mathbf{X}_t | \mathbf{X}^{t-1}; \theta_m, \theta_c\right) \tag{3.23}$$

where $\mathbf{X}^{t-1} = (\mathbf{X}_1, ..., \mathbf{X}_t)$ represents the history of the full process, θ_m are the parameters of the marginal models and θ_c are the Copula parameters. Consequently, I can decompose the loglikelihood into one part for the marginals (LL_m) and one part for the Copula (LL_c):

$$LL(\mathbf{X}; \theta_m, \theta_c) = LL_m(\mathbf{X}; \theta_m) + LL_c(\mathbf{X}; \theta_m, \theta_c) \tag{3.24}$$

$$LL_m(\mathbf{X}; \theta_m) = \sum_{t=1}^{T} \sum_{i=1}^{d} log \, f_i(x_{i,t} | x_i^{t-1}; \theta_{m,i}) \tag{3.25}$$

$$LL_c(\mathbf{X}; \theta_m, \theta_c) = \sum_{t=1}^{T} log \, c(F_1(x_{1,t} | x_1^{t-1}; \theta_{m,1}), ..., F_d(x_{d,t} | x_d^{t-1}; \theta_{m,d}); \theta_c), \tag{3.26}$$

where $x_i^{t-1} = (x_{i,1}, ..., x_{i,t})$ denotes the full history of variable i. The likelihood of the marginals (LL_m) is defined through the marginal parameter $\theta_m = (\theta_{m,1}, ..., \theta_{m,d})$, which collects the parameters for each of the d density functions f_i.

If a Static Copula model is implemented, the vector θ_c collects the Copula parameters. If a RS Copula is applied, the vector $\theta_c = (\theta_c^{(1)}, \theta_c^{(2)}, \mathbf{P}, \zeta_{1|0})$ collects the Copula parameters over both regimes, the transitions probability matrix and the initial probabilities. In case of a Dynamic Copula, the vector $\theta_c = \theta_c^{(dp)}$ collects the dynamic process parameters. Regardless of the Copula framework, θ_c indirectly also depends on the parameters of the marginal densities, through the distribution function F_i, because F_i transforms the observations into uniform [0,1] variables that are the input for the Copula.

Fortunately, Newey and McFadden (1994) proofed that one- and two-step estimations are similarly efficient. At first, I assume the marginals depend only on their own history, but are independent from each other. Consequently, I can estimate each series properties separately:

$$\hat{\theta}_{m,i} = \underset{\theta_{m,i}}{\text{argmax}} \sum_{t=1}^{T} log \ f_i(x_{i,t}|x_i^{t-1}, \theta_{m,i}) \qquad (3.27)$$

and collect the coefficients in a vector: $\hat{\theta}_m = (\hat{\theta}_{m,1}, ..., \hat{\theta}_{m,d})$. With this procedure I only have to estimate between 5 to 8 parameters at once for each marginal model. In a second step I bundle the marginal parameters as given and reuse them to estimate the Copula parameters:

$$\hat{\theta}_c = \underset{\theta_c}{\text{argmax}} \ LL_c(\mathbf{X}; \hat{\theta}_m, \theta_c). \qquad (3.28)$$

In regards to the RS Copula, there are two reasons why I limit myself to only two regimes. First, the economic interpretation of intense and weak dependence is reasonable, whereas semi weak/strong dependence seems unreasonable. Second, estimating more than two regimes requires to estimate more than two Copulas, as well. Hence, the estimation procedure would turn inefficient as Copulas imply nonlinearities in the parameter optimization.

In order to amplify the advantage of separate estimations of the marginal and the Copula models, I consider two one-step estimation examples. First, a RS Copula which comprehends a Gaussian and a Student's-t Copula. In case of 7 return series, I have to estimate 21 correlation coefficients for each Copula and one degree of freedom (v) for the Student's-t Copula. The RS Copula also requires to estimate the transition probability matrix, adding another two parameters. In addition, each marginal model requires at least 5 parameters. Overall, a one-step procedure needs to estimate a minimum of 80 parameters under conditions of nonlinearity for a RS Copula with only two regimes. The second example is a Dynamic Mixture Copula which comprehends one Gaussian and one Clayton Copulas. In case of 7 return series, the Dynamic Gaussian Copula requires 3, the Dynamic Clayton Copula 3 and the dynamic weight process 3 dynamic process parameters. In addition, each marginal model requires at least 5 parameters. Overall, a one-step procedure would have to estimate at least 35 parameters for the marginal models and 9 parameters under conditions of nonlinearity for the dynamic processes. In contrast, applying the two-step estimation to both examples, requires 7 independent marginal model and two separate Copula estimations. This reduces the amount of parameters to be estimated during each procedure, tremendously. Note, the two-step procedure reuses the same univariate model estimates for both Copula calibrations.

3.6 Standard Errors for Copulas

The two-step estimation procedure is also known as method of *inference functions for margins* or IFM method (Joe and Xu (1996)). To calculate the Copula standard errors, the IFM estimator ($\hat{\theta}_{IFM}$) collects the parameters of the marginal and the Copula models as a vector, $\hat{\theta}_{IFM} = [\hat{\theta}_{m,1}, ..., \hat{\theta}_{m,d}, \hat{\theta}_c]$. I stick to the approach of Durrleman et al. (2000), who propose to calculate the Copula standard errors on basis of the Godambe information ratio. They show that the IFM estimator verifies the property of asymptotic normality resulting:

$$\sqrt{T}\left(\hat{\theta}_{IFM} - \theta_0\right) \to N\left(0, \mathbf{G}^{-1}\left(\theta_0\right)\right), \tag{3.29}$$

with $\mathbf{G}(\theta_0)$ the information matrix of Godambe. Further they define a score function, $sc(\theta) = \left(\partial_{\theta_{m,1}} LL_{m,1}, ..., \partial_{\theta_{m,d}} LL_{m,d}, \partial_{\theta_c} LL_c\right)$. The Godambe information matrix takes the form (Joe (1997)):

$$\mathbf{G}(\theta_0) = \mathbf{D}^{-1}\mathbf{M}\left(\mathbf{D}^{-1}\right)', \tag{3.30}$$

where $\mathbf{D} = E\left[\frac{\partial sc(\theta)'}{\partial \theta}\right]$ and $\mathbf{M} = E\left[sc(\theta)'sc(\theta)\right]$. The estimation of the covariance matrix requires to calculate many derivatives. Joe and Xu (1996) suggest the Jacknife method for an efficient estimation.

Chapter 4

Data and Parameter Estimation

4.1 Data Descriptives

This section gives a short overview on the three datasets I examine in this thesis. Any data are collected via Thomson Reuters Datastream. I utilize one pure Bond yield, one pure Stocks and one Multi Asset Classes (MAC) datasets to demonstrate the adaptabilities of the GARCH and Copula models to various types of data. The three datasets cover different time-frames to demonstrate that the proposed Dynamic Copulas forecast accurate portfolio risk levels, regardless of the chosen calibration time period (Chapter 6). The G7 Bond yields are calculated from the according 10 year government Bonds and behave oppositely to Bond prices but are non-investable. Why then use Bond yields instead of Bond prices? The risk of Bond prices are depreciations, whereas the risk of Bond yields are appreciations. The economic interpretation of a Bond price drop is equal to a Bond yield increase. Hence, joint appreciations of Bond yields cause severe monetary losses. This feature requires a framework which captures right tail dependence to model an accurate joint distribution and to predict the upper Bond yield portfolio quantiles, precisely. I utilize this dataset to demonstrate each Copula's ability to model right tail dependencies.

In contrast, Stock price depreciations destroy financial wealth. Left tail dependent Stocks amplify portfolio depreciations because they generate negatively skewed joint distributions. Negatively skewed distributions reveal a longer left tail which increases the probabilities of severe losses. Copulas which capture left tail dependence model precise joint distributions which match the empirical patterns. In return, calculating the quantiles of those Copula based joint distributions results accurate portfolio risk estimates. Therefore, I utilize a Stocks only

33

dataset, which contains the G7 countries, to investigate each Copula's ability to quantify left tail dependence. The accuracies of the portfolio risk forecasts set the basis to identify the "best-fit" Copula.

Table 4.1 – Descriptives. The G7 Bond yield descriptives (reference maturity 10 years) cover the time 06.Mar.1991 to 03.Feb.2010. The G7 Stocks descriptives cover the time 31.Dec.1997 to 20.Jan.2010. The Multi Asset Classes descriptives cover the time 02.Jan.1989 to 01.Feb.2010. The table reports the annualized mean returns (Mean) and the annualized standard deviations (Std.Dev.). The rest of the descriptives is based on weekly data. The skewness (Skew), Kurtosis and quantiles (Q_{SL}) for the 0.1, 0.05 and 0.01 significance levels (SL) are presented. Maxima (Max.) and Minima (Min.) are disclosed. The Bond yield dataset is labeled (B) and the Stocks dataset is labeled (S). The abbreviation of the countries are: Germany (GER), Italy (I), Canada (C), United Kingdom (UK), France (F), Japan (J), United States of America (USA). The Multi Asset Classes indices are abbreviated: REX10Y (REX), USD/EUR (U/E).

	Mean	Std.	Skew	Kurtosis	Quantiles			Min.	Max.
					$Q_{0.1}$	$Q_{0.9}$			
GER(B)	0.052	0.106	0.640	2.398	0.035	0.075		0.029	0.087
I(B)	0.069	0.245	0.938	2.284	0.040	0.128		0.032	0.153
C(B)	0.059	0.134	0.595	2.223	0.039	0.089		0.028	0.103
UK(B)	0.060	0.132	0.706	2.165	0.042	0.087		0.031	0.104
F(B)	0.054	0.119	0.822	2.552	0.036	0.082		0.031	0.093
J(B)	0.024	0.105	1.335	3.800	0.013	0.047		0.004	0.069
USA(B)	0.054	0.094	0.172	2.295	0.038	0.072		0.022	0.084
					$Q_{0.1}$	$Q_{0.05}$	$Q_{0.01}$		
GER(S)	0.029	0.269	-0.541	5.098	-0.043	-0.064	-0.119	-0.177	0.152
I(S)	0.019	0.253	-0.065	10.698	-0.037	-0.053	-0.112	-0.211	0.256
C(S)	0.086	0.253	-0.465	7.663	-0.040	-0.058	-0.100	-0.213	0.211
UK(S)	0.005	0.214	-0.273	8.605	-0.034	-0.049	-0.091	-0.158	0.198
F(S)	0.050	0.245	-0.218	7.074	-0.039	-0.054	-0.109	-0.164	0.207
J(S)	0.008	0.234	0.007	4.425	-0.040	-0.050	-0.081	-0.153	0.114
USA(S)	0.014	0.194	-0.545	7.211	-0.031	-0.043	-0.071	-0.162	0.126
					$Q_{0.1}$	$Q_{0.05}$	$Q_{0.01}$		
REX	0.076	0.125	-0.123	3.639	-0.021	-0.027	-0.044	-0.064	0.063
DAX	0.079	0.250	-0.465	6.056	-0.038	-0.058	-0.106	-0.176	0.173
GOLD	0.041	0.152	0.198	5.237	-0.024	-0.032	-0.056	-0.083	0.105
U/E	-0.006	0.105	0.305	4.445	-0.018	-0.022	-0.035	-0.056	0.068

The third dataset contains multiple asset classes. The risk of portfolios comprising multiple asset classes is characterized by joint price drops of the securities. Thus, left tail dependence is a severe danger to financial wealth and requires a Copula which is able to capture this feature. I utilize the MAC dataset in my analyses because empirical portfolios are often diversified among several asset classes. In more detail, I examine a dataset containing one Stock market, one Bond price, one commodities and one exchange rate indices (Table 4.1). The investigation of the MAC dataset aims at four important questions. First, which dependence framework is flexible enough to model an accurate joint distribution for different security types? Second, does the interaction of different asset classes change dramatically over time? Third, are different asset classes tail dependent? Fourth, is diversification via multiple asset classes more efficient than global diversification within one asset class? Of course, those issues have a major impact on portfolio risk computations and on portfolio selection procedures.

Table 4.2 – Unconditional Linear Correlation Matrices for the Complete Bond yields, Stocks and Multi Asset Classes datasets. The G7 Bond yields cover the time 06.Mar.1991 to 03.Feb.2010. The G7 Stocks cover the time 31.Dec.1997 to 20.Jan.2010. The Multi Asset Classes cover the time 02.Jan.1989 to 01.Feb.2010. The abbreviation of the countries are: Germany (GER), Italy (I), Canada (C), United Kingdom (UK), France (F), Japan (J), United States of America (USA). The Multi Asset Classes indices are abbreviated: REX10Y (REX), USD/EUR (U/E).

	I	C	UK	F	J	USA
			Bonds			
GER	0.768	0.534	0.714	0.907	0.277	0.643
I		0.434	0.576	0.797	0.206	0.491
C			0.528	0.519	0.170	0.695
UK				0.670	0.218	0.569
F					0.229	0.603
J						0.212
			Stocks			
GER	0.845	0.641	0.808	0.904	0.551	0.719
I		0.601	0.799	0.874	0.530	0.656
C			0.657	0.643	0.487	0.707
UK				0.875	0.522	0.718
F					0.542	0.710
J						0.453

	DAX	GOLD	U/E
	Multi Asset Classes		
REX	-0.043	-0.070	-0.084
DAX		0.005	0.067
GOLD			0.314

Throughout this thesis, I assume a currency hedged USD investor to focus on the assets' interactions and to eliminate exchange rate effects. This allows to incorporate currencies as an individual asset class into the analysis. The descriptives of the three datasets are presented in table 4.1 and their unconditional correlations are given in table 4.2.

4.2 GARCH Models

This section presents the estimation results for the marginal models. At first, I analyze the parameters adjusted to the Bond yields dataset (Table 4.3). The first line of the table indicates the marginal model with the most significant BIC values. In most cases, the asymmetric

EGARCH model represents the data characteristics more precisely than the symmetric GARCH setup (Section 2.2). The only exceptions are the French, Japanese and the USA time series. The GARCH model with an asymmetric Student's-t distribution adapts best to these yield data. As expected, the skewness parameters of the distribution functions are positive. This indicates that severe positive yield changes occur rather seldom, but they are more amplified than their negative counterparts. This is in line with the Bond yield characteristics which I described earlier. Surprisingly, the leverage parameters (γ) of the EGARCH models reveal negative signs for the Bond yields. This indicates that negative shocks (Bond yield drops) drive the volatility of the Bond yields.

The marginal models play a tremendous role for dependence modeling. They filter the univariate time series from autocorrelation and GARCH effects and generate the input data for the Copula models. Hence, improperly specified marginal models dilute the Copula estimations. In combination, misspecified GARCH and Copula models result improper portfolio risk forecasts. To avoid this issue, I apply several goodness-of-fit (GoF) tests to the univariate models. The results of the Kolmogorov-Smirnov (KS) tests indicate how well the assumed univariate distributions adapt to the empirical data. According to those statistics, the chosen GARCH models adapt very well to the Bond yield dataset except for the UK time series. The Ljung-Box statistics check the null hypothesis of no autocorrelation for the squared standardized residuals with the lags 1, 2, 3, 5 and 10. This null hypothesis is not rejected at very significant levels, indicating no autocorrelation in the residuals. Hence, the marginal models have strong explanatory power for the Bond yields.

Table 4.4 presents the estimated parameters for the univariate Stocks models. Again, the BIC favors the EGARCH model in most cases. The symmetric GARCH model with a skewed-t distribution is preferred only in case of the Canadian and UK Stock indices. The skewness parameters of the skewed-t distributions are negative indicating longer left than right tails. This result amplifies the importance to account for asymmetric return distributions. If the magnitude of the left tail is underestimated, the according quantiles are inefficient, resulting in imprecise risk forecasts. The EGARCH models reveal negative leverage factors what is in line with the economic interpretation: Negative shocks have a more significant impact on volatility than positive shocks (Figure 2.1). The Kolmogorov-Smirnov tests indicate good fits of the assumed distribution functions. Again, applying a distribution function that matches the data characteristics is highly important to predict the according quantiles, accurately. Finally, the Ljung-Box statistics indicate no autocorrelation in the squared standardized residuals. The conducted GoF analyses indicate well fitted marginal models which have strong explanatory power.

Table 4.3 – Univariate Models G7 Bond yields: The first line indicates the univariate GARCH model which has been selected via the BIC statistic (Model). The second line presents the distribution of the residuals (Dist). Lines 3 to 9 present the ARMA process parameters for the univariate models. The AR and MA terms are limited to a maximum of 3 Lags. Lines 10 to 15 show the GARCH(1,1) process parameters. The standard errors of the parameters are given in brackets. Lines 16 to 18 present the p-values for the following tests: The Kolmogorov-Smirnov (KS) test examines the alternative hypothesis that the population cdf is not from a Uniform [0,1]. KS+, tests the alternative hypothesis that the population cdf is larger than a Uniform [0,1], while KS-, tests the alternative hypothesis that the population cdf is smaller than a Uniform [0,1]. Lines 19 to 23 present the p-values for the Ljung-Box (LB_{Lag}) test. The post-estimate LB analysis uses squared standardized innovations based on the estimated model. The estimation is based on the complete data sample (06.Mar.1991 to 03.Feb.2010).

	Germany	Italy	Canada	UK	France	Japan	USA
Model	EGARCH	EGARCH	EGARCH	EGARCH	GARCH	GARCH	GARCH
Dist	gaussian	gaussian	gaussian	gaussian	skew-t	skew-t	skew-t
ω	-0.002	-0.002	-0.001	-0.002	-0.001	-0.002	-0.001
	(0.000)	(0.001)	(0.002)	(0.000)	(0.000)	(0.001)	(0.001)
$\lambda_{1,1}$		-0.138	0.220		0.610	0.944	-0.188
		(0.528)	(1.4534)		(0.885)	(0.147)	(0.289)
$\lambda_{1,2}$			0.032		-0.307	-0.732	0.189
			(0.059)		(0.763)	(0.144)	(0.170)
$\lambda_{1,3}$					0.083	-0.028	0.099
					(0.058)	(0.062)	(0.041)
$\lambda_{2,1}$		0.203	-0.259		-0.624	-0.937	0.182
		(0.524)	(1.453)		(0.893)	(0.155)	(0.290)
$\lambda_{2,2}$					0.301	0.793	-0.169
					(0.799)	(0.114)	(0.165)
$\lambda_{2,3}$							
κ	-0.109	-0.308	-0.374	-0.270	0.000	0.000	0.000
	(0.082)	(0.152)	(0.228)	(0.196)	(0.000)	(0.000)	(0.000)
α	0.199	0.215	0.159	0.138	0.056	0.101	0.038
	(0.044)	(0.055)	(0.048)	(0.047)	(0.023)	(0.037)	(0.019)
γ	-0.082	-0.015	-0.050	-0.039			
	(0.025)	(0.027)	(0.030)	(0.028)			
β	0.986	0.961	0.951	0.965	0.923	0.893	0.950
	(0.010)	(0.019)	(0.029)	(0.025)	(0.031)	(0.033)	(0.024)
ν					9.029	4.540	14.049
					(2.642)	(0.667)	(6.130)
ϖ					0.174	0.148	0.053
					(0.052)	(0.043)	(0.061)
KS	0.962	0.931	0.715	0.124	0.842	0.763	0.879
KS+	0.635	0.556	0.378	0.112	0.629	0.478	0.573
KS-	0.603	0.599	0.575	0.062	0.468	0.409	0.500
LB_1	0.787	0.620	0.575	0.078	0.277	0.162	0.675
LB_2	0.913	0.834	0.763	0.164	0.429	0.286	0.196
LB_3	0.590	0.464	0.887	0.189	0.595	0.461	0.093
LB_5	0.788	0.591	0.964	0.290	0.615	0.482	0.142
LB_{10}	0.901	0.810	0.999	0.385	0.591	0.393	0.435
LB_{15}	0.697	0.687	1.000	0.699	0.645	0.328	0.364

The parameters of the univariate models for the MAC dataset are presented in table 4.5. According to the BIC, EGARCH is the preferred volatility model for all securities. Comparing the REX10Y and the DAX parameters to the estimates in tables 4.3 and 4.4 shows slight differences. In case of the Bond index they are caused by two factors. First, Table 4.3 reports the parameters for the Bond yields whereas the REX10Y is the according Bond price. Bond prices behave contrary to yields causing the mean to flip its sign, but the parameter magnitudes remain similar. Second, the MAC dataset covers the timeframe 1989 to 2010 whereas the Bond yield data covers the time 1991 to 2010 (Section 4.1). Of course, two years of additional information cause differences in the parameter estimates. The variations of the parameters in case of the DAX are also caused by the different time frames. Nevertheless, the absolute parameter differences remain small for both indices. A comparison of the parameters of the univariate models in table 4.5 reveals more interesting features. The leverage factors of the DAX and USD/EUR EGARCH processes are negative, a clear sign that negative returns impact the volatility more significantly than positive shocks. In contrast, γ is positive for the REX10Y and GOLD return series. The opposite behavior indicates possible diversification potential. Again, I apply the Kolmogorov-Smirnov test to analyze the goodness-of-fit of the models to the empirical data. According to those tests, the assumption of normally distributed returns in the EGARCH models is in line with the empirical data. In addition, the Ljung-Box statistics allude that the marginal models filter the autocorrelations of the return series. The GoF statistics indicate well fitted EGARCH models which capture the features of the univariate time series precisely and consequently generate accurate volatility forecasts.

Although the univariate models are not the center of attention in this thesis, their accuracies directly impact the Copula parameters during the two-step estimation (Section 3.5). They filter the univariate return series from GARCH effects and from autocorrelation, resulting accurate residuals which set the basis for the Copula calibrations. I allow a maximum of three lags in the ARMA processes to filter the univariate time series from autocorrelation. The Ljung-Box tests indicate no autocorrelation in the squared standardized residuals. This result holds true for any examined time series and supports the conclusion of well fitted ARMA-GARCH models. The Kolmogorov-Smirnov tests show that the GARCH model distributions fit the empirical data very well. Well calibrated marginal models ensure accurate univariate volatility forecasts which play a key role for the portfolio risk predictions. This justifies the large amount of GoF tests for the marginal models. The filtered volatilities are presented in the appendices A.1, A.2, A.3.

Table 4.4 – Univariate Models G7 Stocks: The first line indicates the univariate GARCH model which has been selected via the BIC statistic (Model). The second line presents the distribution of the residuals (Dist). Lines 3 to 9 present the ARMA process parameters for the univariate models. The AR and MA terms are limited to a maximum of 3 Lags. Lines 10 to 15 show the GARCH(1,1) process parameters. The standard errors of the parameters are given in brackets. Lines 16 to 18 present the p-values for the following tests: The Kolmogorov-Smirnov (KS) test examines the alternative hypothesis that the population cdf is not from a Uniform [0,1]. KS+, tests the alternative hypothesis that the population cdf is larger than a Uniform [0,1], while KS-, tests the alternative hypothesis that the population cdf is smaller than a Uniform [0,1]. Lines 19 to 23 present the p-values for the Ljung-Box (LB_{Lag}) test. The post-estimate LB analysis uses squared standardized innovations based on the estimated model. The estimation is based on the complete data sample (31.Dec.1997 to 20.Jan.2010).

	Germany	Italy	Canada	UK	France	Japan	USA
Model	EGARCH	EGARCH	GARCH	GARCH	EGARCH	EGARCH	EGARCH
Dist	gaussian	gaussian	skew-t	skew-t	gaussian	gaussian	gaussian
ω	0.002	0.006	0.003	0.001	0.002	0.000	-0.004
	(0.002)	(0.002)	(0.001)	(0.001)	(0.001)	(0.000)	(0.002)
$\lambda_{1,1}$	-0.077	-0.031				0.250	-0.715
	(0.052)	(0.052)				(0.176)	(0.051)
$\lambda_{1,2}$		-0.823				0.631	-0.251
		(0.059)				(0.193)	(0.091)
$\lambda_{1,3}$		0.093				0.061	0.034
		(0.070)				(0.062)	(0.050)
$\lambda_{2,1}$		0.000				-0.191	0.717
		(0.027)				(0.169)	(0.011)
$\lambda_{2,2}$		0.918				-0.718	0.218
		(0.039)				(0.166)	(0.011)
$\lambda_{2,3}$		-0.083					
		(0.046)					
κ	-0.186	-0.088	0.000	0.000	-0.321	-1.135	-0.273
	(0.111)	(0.073)	(0.000)	(0.000)	(0.139)	(0.550)	(0.122)
α	0.183	0.174	0.104	0.201	0.259	0.212	0.122
	(0.060)	(0.053)	(0.036)	(0.036)	(0.068)	(0.099)	(0.058)
γ	-0.078	-0.037			-0.101	-0.162	-0.168
	(0.028)	(0.030)			(0.032)	(0.064)	(0.033)
β	0.974	0.989	0.878	0.772	0.956	0.840	0.964
	(0.016)	(0.010)	(0.041)	(0.041)	(0.019)	(0.078)	(0.016)
v			18.369	14.876			
			(13.244)	(13.244)			
ϖ			-0.165	-0.230			
			(0.073)	(0.073)			
KS	0.686	0.852	0.975	0.749	0.940	0.804	0.908
KS+	0.359	0.476	0.631	0.400	0.568	0.438	0.530
KS-	0.592	0.594	0.635	0.603	0.644	0.578	0.618
LB_1	0.754	0.150	0.088	0.602	0.612	0.874	0.463
LB_2	0.508	0.265	0.223	0.530	0.132	0.987	0.764
LB_3	0.716	0.353	0.391	0.728	0.243	0.635	0.806
LB_5	0.897	0.440	0.362	0.831	0.248	0.793	0.772
LB_{10}	0.992	0.542	0.239	0.800	0.368	0.940	0.861

Table 4.5 – Univariate Models Multi Asset Classes: The first line indicates the univariate GARCH model which has been selected via the BIC statistic (Model). The second line presents the distribution of the residuals (Dist). Lines 3 to 9 present the ARMA process parameters for the univariate models. The AR and MA terms are limited to a maximum of 3 Lags. Lines 10 to 15 show the GARCH(1,1) process parameters. The standard errors of the parameters are given in brackets. Lines 16 to 18 present the p-values for the following tests: The Kolmogorov-Smirnov (KS) test examines the alternative hypothesis that the population cdf is not from a Uniform [0,1]. KS+, tests the alternative hypothesis that the population cdf is larger than a Uniform [0,1], while KS-, tests the alternative hypothesis that the population cdf is smaller than a Uniform [0,1]. Lines 19 to 23 present the p-values for the Ljung-Box (LB_{Lag}) test. The post-estimate LB analysis uses squared standardized innovations based on the estimated model. The estimation is based on the complete data sample (02.Jan.1989 to 01.Feb.2010).

	REX10Y	DAX	GOLD	USD/EUR
Model	EGARCH	EGARCH	EGARCH	EGARCH
Dist	gaussian	gaussian	gaussian	gaussian
ω	0.002	0.003	0.000	0.000
	(0.000)	(0.008)	(0.000)	(0.000)
$\lambda_{1,1}$		-0.059		
		(0.035)		
$\lambda_{1,2}$		-0.032		
		(0.035)		
$\lambda_{1,3}$		0.069		
		(0.034)		
$\lambda_{2,1}$				
$\lambda_{2,2}$				
$\lambda_{2,3}$				
κ	-0.471	-0.209	-0.508	-0.253
	(0.211)	(0.087)	(0.225)	(0.157)
α	0.201	0.222	0.187	0.106
	(0.045)	(0.044)	(0.050)	(0.039)
γ	0.022	-0.060	0.046	-0.012
	(0.025)	(0.026)	(0.029)	(0.016)
β	0.952	0.972	0.936	0.970
	(0.022)	(0.012)	(0.029)	(0.018)
ν				
ϖ				
KS	0.942	0.812	0.855	0.879
KS+	0.571	0.445	0.577	0.500
KS-	0.684	0.619	0.479	0.586
LB_1	0.754	0.587	0.984	0.180
LB_2	0.928	0.861	0.660	0.388
LB_3	0.290	0.952	0.690	0.108
LB_5	0.386	0.953	0.895	0.227
LB_{10}	0.450	0.991	0.175	0.576

4.3 Static Copulas

This section discusses the parameter estimates of the Static Copulas. According to the two-step estimation procedure, the same filtered residuals from the ARMA-GARCH processes are reused for any Copula estimations (Section 3.5). Table 4.6 presents the Copula parameters for the Bond yield dataset. I analyze the dependence structures of the Bond yield dataset in three steps. At first, I focus on the interactions of the European Union countries. The Static Copulas indicate strict comovements of the Euro countries Bond yields (Germany, Italy and France). This result is supported by any Copula function. The strict dependence of the Bond yields in the Euro zone is due to their joint central bank, their extremely interlaced economies and the Schengen contract (Bernoth et al. (2004)). Second, I analyze the dependence structure of the USA and Canadian Bond yields. Although they are not united in a political union, their economies are linked through several trade agreements and their geographical neighborhood, resulting in strong interactions of their financial markets. The parameters of any Copula model reflect the strong linkage between those two countries. The American and the European Bond yields reveal weaker comovements. Transforming the Copula parameters into linear correlations yields coefficients of about 0.6. This outcome holds true for any Copula function and for any transatlantic interaction. Third, I examine the comovements of the Japanese Bond yields with the European and the American Bond yields. Surprisingly, the dependencies of the European-Japanese and American-Japanese Bond yields are similarly low. Again, any Static Copula supports this conclusion and the appendant linear correlation coefficients range from about 0.24 to 0.31. Overall, the parameter estimations reveal diversification potential among global Bond markets which diminishes with increasing political and geographical propinquity.

A comparison of the individual Copulas indicates tail dependence of the Bond yields. The Student's-t Copula reveals a v of 8 by itself and in the Mixture construct a v of 10. In addition, the shares of the Gumbel Copulas in both Mixtures are about 11%, indicating right tail dependence. This result is in line with the Bond yield characteristics and is supported by the loglikelihood values. The difference between the Gaussian and Student's-t Copula is more distinct than between the two Mixtures. The greater magnitude of the discrepancy between both Elliptical Copulas is due to the Gaussian Copula's inability and the Student's-t Copula's ability to model tail dependence. In contrast, both Mixtures capture tail dependence what demagnifies the disparity of the loglikelihood values.

41

Table 4.6 – G7 Bond yields Static Copula Parameters. The marginal models are the same for all Copulas. The pair-Copulas within the Canonical-Vine Copula are located inside the table. The first Mixture Copula (Mix1) combines one Gaussian, one Clayton and one Gumbel Copulas. The second Mixture Copula (Mix2) combines one Student's-t, one Clayton and one Gumbel Copulas. Inside the table, the Copula families are abbreviated: F (Frank); GU (Gumbel); CL (Clayton); GA (Gaussian); St (Student's-t). LL denotes the Loglikelihood value. AIC denotes the Akaike Criterion. BIC denotes the Bayesian Information Criterion.

	Frank Coeff	Frank t-stat	Gumbel Coeff	Gumbel t-stat	Clayton Coeff	Clayton t-stat	Gaussian Coeff	Gaussian t-stat	Student's-t Coeff	Student's-t t-stat	Canonical-Vine	Canonical-Vine Coeff	Canonical-Vine t-stat	Mix1 Coeff	Mix1 t-stat	Mix2 Coeff	Mix2 t-stat
GER:IT							0.781	(1.10)	0.826	(0.47)	CL	1.707	(10.10)	0.908	(0.12)	0.903	(0.46)
GER:CAN							0.558	(0.98)	0.564	(0.81)	CL	0.690	(10.00)	0.633	(0.80)	0.604	(0.28)
GER:UK							0.701	(1.13)	0.726	(1.84)	CL	1.153	(12.11)	0.794	(0.38)	0.783	(0.53)
GER:FRA							0.883	(2.53)	0.899	(1.41)	CL	2.529	(12.18)	0.947	(0.13)	0.939	(0.48)
GER:JAP							0.317	(1.13)	0.303	(2.00)	CL	0.342	(6.73)	0.295	(0.22)	0.287	(0.79)
GER:USA							0.633	(3.29)	0.629	(0.75)	CL	0.894	(12.28)	0.679	(0.26)	0.659	(0.20)
IT:CAN							0.487	(1.13)	0.508	(0.79)	CL	0.211	(5.30)	0.593	(0.66)	0.566	(0.30)
IT:UK							0.627	(1.05)	0.657	(1.73)	CL	0.293	(7.28)	0.735	(0.33)	0.727	(0.52)
IT:FRA							0.794	(2.59)	0.834	(1.39)	GA	0.484	(11.18)	0.912	(0.13)	0.904	(0.49)
IT:JAP							0.225	(-0.69)	0.228	(-1.07)	GA	0.022	(0.64)	0.243	(-0.22)	0.235	(-0.84)
IT:USA							0.530	(2.00)	0.551	(0.73)	GA	0.189	(4.70)	0.636	(0.26)	0.614	(0.21)
CAN;UK							0.551	(1.10)	0.569	(1.79)	GA	0.332	(9.55)	0.650	(0.38)	0.624	(0.54)
CAN;FRA							0.539	(1.91)	0.549	(1.19)	GA	0.166	(4.80)	0.629	(0.13)	0.596	(0.46)
CAN;JAP							0.244	(1.08)	0.249	(2.01)	GA	0.128	(3.70)	0.246	(0.22)	0.240	(0.72)
CAN;USA							0.713	(3.20)	0.733	(0.75)	GA	0.592	(20.11)	0.800	(0.26)	0.781	(0.20)
UK;FRA							0.671	(1.62)	0.702	(1.23)	GA	0.116	(2.93)	0.779	(0.13)	0.766	(0.53)
UK;JAP							0.284	(1.17)	0.278	(1.43)	GA	0.112	(3.38)	0.277	(0.23)	0.271	(0.73)
UK;USA							0.554	(1.65)	0.560	(0.53)	GA	0.093	(2.81)	0.624	(-0.23)	0.604	(-0.21)
FRA;JAP							0.265	(-0.81)	0.265	(-0.52)	GA	-0.002	(-0.30)	0.259	(-0.21)	0.258	(-0.49)
FRA;USA							0.601	(1.68)	0.603	(0.72)	GA	0.090	(2.11)	0.662	(-0.08)	0.640	(0.12)
JAP;USA							0.278	(1.73)	0.258	(0.78)	GA	0.086	(2.59)	0.230	(-0.61)	0.234	(0.15)
ν									8.052	(13.93)						10.386	(8.08)
θ_{cl}					0.578	(16.52)								0.046	(1.27)	0.021	(0.62)
θ_{gu}			1.437	(60.21)										1.672	(12.47)	1.616	(15.50)
θ_{f}	3.201	(25.17)															
w_{el}														0.775	(18.82)	0.816	(21.76)
w_{cl}														0.108	(5.52)	0.076	(4.41)
w_{gu}														0.117	(3.78)	0.106	(4.22)
LL	1256		1212		1047		2254		2439			1942		2481		2526	
AIC	-2510		-2422		-2092		-4467		-4833			-3841		-4910		-4999	
BIC	-2503		-2415		-2085		-4323		-4683			-3697		-4732		-4814	

42

Table 4.7 – G7 Stocks Static Copula Parameters. The marginal models are the same for all Copulas. The pair-Copulas within the Canonical-Vine Copula are located inside the table. The first Mixture Copula (Mix1) combines one Gaussian, one Clayton and one Gumbel Copulas. The second Mixture Copula (Mix2) combines one Student's-t, one Clayton and one Gumbel Copulas. Inside the table, the Copula families are abbreviated: F (Frank); GU (Gumbel); CL (Clayton); GA (Gaussian); St (Student's-t). LL denotes the Loglikelihood value. AIC denotes the Akaike Criterion. BIC denotes the Bayesian Information Criterion.

	Frank Coeff	Frank t-stat	Gumbel Coeff	Gumbel t-stat	Clayton Coeff	Clayton t-stat	Gaussian Coeff	Gaussian t-stat	Student's-t Coeff	Student's-t t-stat	Canonical-Vine Coeff	Canonical-Vine t-stat	Fam	Mix1 Coeff	Mix1 t-stat	Mix2 Coeff	Mix2 t-stat
GER;IT							0.831	(0.57)	0.841	(6.28)	2.316	(11.86)	CL	0.867	(0.72)	0.862	(2.09)
GER;CAN							0.638	(1.02)	0.639	(4.74)	1.049	(7.23)	CL	0.655	(1.09)	0.643	(3.20)
GER;UK							0.768	(1.23)	0.779	(4.90)	1.673	(11.32)	CL	0.811	(4.50)	0.801	(2.54)
GER;FRA							0.889	(3.03)	0.898	(2.79)	3.059	(10.62)	CL	0.924	(2.11)	0.917	(2.10)
GER;JAP							0.562	(0.80)	0.569	(4.74)	0.910	(8.03)	CL	0.570	(2.79)	0.572	(2.40)
GER;USA							0.693	(3.37)	0.702	(8.63)	1.206	(8.36)	CL	0.739	(1.92)	0.715	(1.57)
IT;CAN							0.579	(1.01)	0.583	(5.27)	0.169	(2.40)	GA	0.587	(1.14)	0.586	(2.76)
IT;UK							0.768	(1.24)	0.777	(4.80)	0.405	(6.51)	GA	0.808	(4.45)	0.797	(2.57)
IT;FRA							0.863	(3.03)	0.870	(2.81)	0.521	(10.79)	GA	0.897	(2.10)	0.890	(2.09)
IT;JAP							0.500	(0.82)	0.515	(5.40)	0.094	(0.77)	GA	0.510	(2.86)	0.519	(2.03)
IT;USA							0.618	(3.01)	0.626	(6.23)	0.182	(2.23)	GA	0.652	(1.82)	0.637	(0.37)
CAN;UK							0.650	(1.23)	0.655	(4.87)	0.337	(5.75)	GA	0.680	(4.48)	0.666	(2.54)
CAN;FRA							0.650	(3.04)	0.653	(2.81)	0.258	(4.02)	GA	0.665	(2.13)	0.657	(2.10)
CAN;JAP							0.504	(0.81)	0.493	(4.75)	0.241	(4.39)	GA	0.499	(2.76)	0.491	(2.41)
CAN;USA							0.682	(3.35)	0.678	(8.65)	0.459	(11.07)	GA	0.692	(1.92)	0.680	(1.57)
UK;FRA							0.845	(3.02)	0.851	(2.79)	0.423	(7.43)	GA	0.877	(2.11)	0.868	(2.09)
UK;JAP							0.528	(0.80)	0.531	(4.71)	0.124	(3.24)	GA	0.532	(2.73)	0.531	(2.40)
UK;USA							0.667	(3.35)	0.665	(8.86)	0.192	(3.28)	GA	0.696	(1.93)	0.679	(1.57)
FRA;JAP							0.563	(0.80)	0.571	(4.02)	0.083	(0.89)	GA	0.561	(1.04)	0.568	(2.12)
FRA;USA							0.688	(1.69)	0.698	(3.80)	0.051	(-0.10)	GA	0.725	(1.51)	0.711	(1.54)
JAP;USA							0.453	(3.02)	0.451	(3.68)	0.012	(0.13)	GA	0.446	(1.90)	0.445	(1.57)
ν									13.896	(4.55)						16.169	(4.13)
θ_{cl}					0.998	(14.86)								1.564	(2.25)	1.309	(9.11)
θ_{gu}			1.659	(39.86)										1.078	(5.20)		
θ_f	4.582	(22.90)															
w_{cl}														0.861	(16.79)	0.904	(16.64)
w_{cl}														0.116	(2.60)	0.095	(2.56)
w_{gu}														0.023	(0.07)	0.001	(0.19)
LL	1289		1182		1242		1871		1914		1760			1917		1934	
AIC	-2573		-2362		-2483		-3699		-3784		-3478			-3782		-3814	
BIC	-2567		-2355		-2477		-3565		-3644		-3344			-3616		-3641	

Table 4.8 – Multi Asset Classes Static Copula Parameters. The marginal models are the same for all Copulas. The pair-Copulas within the Canonical-Vine Copula are located inside the table. The first Mixture Copula (Mix1) combines one Gaussian, one Clayton and one Gumbel Copulas. The second Mixture Copula (Mix2) combines one Student's-t, one Clayton and one Gumbel Copulas. Inside the table, the Copula families are abbreviated: F (Frank); GU (Gumbel); CL (Clayton); GA (Gaussian); St (Student's-t). The time series are abbreviated: REX (REX10Y), U/E (USD/EUR). LL denotes the Loglikelihood value. AIC denotes the Akaike Criterion. BIC denotes the Bayesian Information Criterion.

	Frank Coeff	Frank t-stat	Gumbel Coeff	Gumbel t-stat	Clayton Coeff	Clayton t-stat	Gaussian Coeff	Gaussian t-stat	Student's-t Coeff	Student's-t t-stat	Canonical-Vine Coeff	Canonical-Vine t-stat		Mix1 Coeff	Mix1 t-stat	Mix2 Coeff	Mix2 t-stat
REX:DAX							0.009	(1.01)	0.014	(5.69)	0.048	(2.11)	CL	0.103	(0.07)	0.067	(4.48)
REX:GOLD							-0.074	(0.59)	-0.064	(1.51)	0.000	(0.00)	CL	-0.182	(0.13)	-0.088	(1.49)
REX:U/E							-0.125	(1.99)	-0.146	(2.33)	0.000	(0.00)	CL	-0.319	(0.12)	-0.209	(3.27)
DAX:GOLD							0.070	(0.56)	0.075	(0.90)	0.073	(0.06)	GA	0.133	(0.13)	0.117	(4.96)
DAX:U/E							0.142	(1.76)	0.141	(3.47)	0.147	(0.25)	GA	0.204	(0.12)	0.194	(4.86)
GOLD:U/E							0.342	(1.91)	0.357	(2.96)	0.336	(0.22)	GA	0.755	(0.12)	0.556	(5.32)
ν									7.091	(6.05)						5.204	(4.84)
θ_{cl}																0.001	(0.90)
θ_{gu}			1.047	(77.84)										1.147	(1.66)	1.237	(24.11)
θ_f	0.375	(5.82)			0.084	(5.17)								1.020	(31.80)		
w_{el}														0.449	(10.00)	0.652	(11.23)
w_{cl}														0.008	(1.18)	0.347	(2.13)
w_{gu}														0.543	(6.17)	0.001	(3.58)
LL	13		22		16		82		132		75			125		142	
AIC	-24		-43		-29		-153		-250		-137			-229		-259	
BIC	-18		-36		-23		-114		-206		-99			-159		-182	

Next, I analyze the parameter estimates of the Static Copulas for the G7 Stocks dataset (Table 4.7). Again, I analyze the interactions in three steps, first the European, second the American and European and third the Asian, American and European countries. Any Copula model reveals strict dependence of the European Stock markets. On average, the transformed Copula parameters result a linear correlation coefficient of about 0.8. I find slightly weaker dependence between the Euro countries and the UK. Hence, the interaction of the European Stock markets and Bond yields are similarly intense. Overall, the strict interdependence of the European Stock and Bond markets reflects the distinct linkage between the European economies which is a result of their geographic propinquity, the political union and the Euro currency. The Canadian and USA Stock markets exhibit similar dependence magnitudes as their Bond yields, which translate into an average linear correlation coefficient of about 0.7. Nevertheless, compared to the European countries their linkage is less intense. Interestingly, the amplitudes of the transatlantic and the American Stock market dependencies are almost identically pronounced, except for Italy. This finding is supported by any Copula function and clearly indicates missing diversification potential. Finally, I examine the comovement intensities of the Japanese and the European Stock markets and the Japanese and the American Stock markets. They are almost twice as dependent as the according Bond markets. Expressed as linear correlation coefficients, the Stock market linkages range from 0.45 to 0.55. However, the Japanese and the American Stock markets are less dependent than the Japanese and the European Stock markets. The same holds true for the Bond markets. Overall, the parameter estimates reveal highly dependent Stock markets which hardly offer any diversification potential. Additionally, a more detailed examination of the Copula parameters indicates left tail dependent Stock markets. The first adumbrations of tail dependency are the dominant loglikelihood and BIC values of the Student's-t over the Gaussian Copula. Both Mixture Copulas allot about 10% of their shares to the Clayton Copula but almost none to the Gumbel Copula. This clearly indicates left tail dependence. In regards to diversification and portfolio loss avoidance, this feature is hazardous, especially if it remains undetected. To capture asymmetric dependencies in the G7 Stocks data, it is advantageous to rely on Copula functions which account for tail dependencies.

The Static Copula parameters for the Multi Asset Classes dataset are given in table 4.8. In contrast to the G7 Bond yields and the G7 Stocks, the different asset classes are rather independent among each other. On average, the transformed Copula parameters yield linear correlation coefficients between -0.15 and 0.15. Only Gold and the USD/EUR exchange rate are significantly correlated by 0.35. At first glance, those results indicate diversification potential but the fairly small v of the Student's-t Copula insinuates tail dependence. Although the dominant loglikelihood and BIC values of the Gumbel over the Clayton Copula suggests right tail dependence, both Copula parameters indicate independence. This supports the theory of symmetric tail dependence. An examination of the Mixture construct, containing one Student's-t, one Clayton and one Gumbel Copulas, also reveals symmetric tail dependence. At first glance, this interpretation is counterintuitive because the Gumbel and Clayton weights inside the Mixture structure are about 0% and 35%, a natural indication of left tail dependence. However, the Clayton parameter in the Mixture is almost 0 what translates to independence. In contrast, the Student's-t Copula reveals a v of 5 inside the Mixture structure, denoting intense symmetric tail dependence. Therefore, the Mixture suggests individual return distributions whose middle parts are independent but whose tails are strictly dependent. This increases the probabilities of joint positive or negative extremes. Hence, in general the individual securities move independently but they comove during extreme situations. Nevertheless, according to the Static Copula parameters the MAC returns are less dependent than the G7 Bond yields or the G7 Stock markets.

I conclude from the Static Copula parameter estimates, that regional diversification within one asset class is rather inefficient. Global diversification across various continents reduces the dependence within one asset class, but not to a neglectable level. The calibrations of Copulas which account for tail dependence reveal the existence of this feature. More advanced Copula structures reveal right tail dependence in the Bond yields and left tail dependence in the Stocks datasets. Those features indicate shifts in the dependence structures over time. The Student's-t Copula also indicates tail dependence in the Multi Asset Classes dataset. However, its parameters denote only weakly dependent middle parts of the univariate return distributions. This feature insinuates diversification potential across different asset classes.

4.4   Regime-Switch Copulas

This section discusses the parameter estimates of the Regime-Switch (RS) Copulas. Any Copula model is estimated on basis of the same residuals, filtered from the univariate models (Section 4.2). Table 4.9 presents the RS Copula parameters for the G7 Bond yield dataset. A transformation of the Copula parameters suggests linear correlation coefficients around 0.8 for the UK Euro countries interaction and above 0.95 for the three Euro countries (Germany, France,

Italy) during the high dependence regime. During the low dependence regime, the according Bond yield correlations range from 0.5 to 0.8. Those parameters reveal severe changes of the dependence structure in the European Bond markets over time. Next, I analyze the dependence structures between the European and the American countries. During the high dependence regime, the transformed Copula parameters insinuate linear correlations between the European countries and Canada of about 0.65. The linkages between the USA and the European countries are slightly more intense at levels around 0.7 while the US and Canadian Bond yields reveal the strongest correlation of about 0.8. During the low dependence regime, the European and American Bond yields reveal linear correlations in the range from 0.35 to 0.55. In contrast, the estimated Copula parameters indicate a strong linkage of 0.65 between the USA and Canada during this phase. Hence, the transatlantic dependence structures vary significantly across the regimes, but the American interaction remains fairly tight. Finally, I examine the interaction of the Japanese with the European and American Bond yields. The Copula parameters reveal almost identical magnitudes of dependence during both regimes, Italy being the only exception. The average correlation of the Japanese Bond yields with the rest of the G7 Bond yields is about 0.25 for both regimes. This is a very interesting information in regards to diversification potential and portfolio selection. Changes in the dependence intensities are especially important for accurate portfolio risk calculations and for efficient portfolio selection procedures. Additionally, RS Copulas containing at least one regime that accounts for tail dependence increase the loglikelihood values. The RS Student's-t|Student's-t Copula results the most pronounced loglikelihood value and both degrees of freedom are relatively small. This clearly detects tail dependence in both regimes. An additional indicator for well fitted RS models are the stable regime switch probabilities (Table 4.9). Based on the parameter estimates, I conclude that flexible Copulas which account for tail dependence provide advantageous information to risk management. Hence, they should improve the accuracy of Bond portfolio risk forecasts.

Overall, any RS Copulas ascribe the same time frames to the high and low dependence regimes and reveal similar amplitudes of interaction (Figure 4.1). Regardless of the RS Copula choices, the dataset is divided into three phases. The low dependence regime is dominant before 1999, the year of the Euro introduction. In 1999, a regime shift occurs and the G7 Bond yields jump into the high dependence regime. This reveals that the Euro introduction fundamentally tightens the dependencies of the Bond yields and diminishes diversification potential. However, the intensities of the dependence changes vary significantly. The observed increase is most distinct among the Euro members. Their average correlation jumps from 0.68 during the low dependence regime to 0.96 during the high dependence regime. This regime shift also increases the average transatlantic Bond correlation from 0.42 to 0.7. Only the Japanese Bond yield interactions with any other G7 Bond yields remain at equal levels before and after the Euro introduction. Any RS Copulas denote a shift into the low dependence regime in 2009. The linkages between the Bond yields diminish due to rising debt levels of several European countries and increasing probabilities of country defaults. Especially, the UK and Italian Bond yields increase significantly and behave contrary to the German and French Bonds, causing the regime shift. Overall, measuring the interactions of the G7 Bond yields with a RS Copula skeleton identifies shifts in their dependence structure.

Next, I fit the RS Copulas to the G7 Stocks dataset (Table 4.10). During the high dependence regime the Euro countries reveal Copula parameters which translate to linear correlation coefficients around 0.9. Their interactions with the UK Stock market are slightly weaker. The same picture holds true for the low dependence regime, but the transformed Copula parameters of the Euro countries result linear correlations between 0.7 and 0.8. Figure 4.2 shows the time paths of the high dependence regimes. In contrast to the Bond markets, the introduction of the Euro in 1999 did not cause a regime shift in the Stock markets. The major regime shift was caused by the terror attacks in 2001. Thereafter, any RS Copula suggests the Stock markets remain almost constantly in the high dependence regime. This finding is also supported by the Copula parameters representing the dependence between the European and the American Stock markets. Transforming the Copula parameters of the low dependence regime reveals linear correlation coefficients of 0.5, on average. This result holds true for all transatlantic linkages, whereas the USA and Canadian Stock markets are slightly more interconnected during this regime. A shift to the high dependence regime causes the transformed Copula parameters to jump to levels of 0.7 to 0.8. During this regime, the linkages between the USA and European Stock markets are slightly more pronounced than between the Canadian and the European markets. The dependence between the USA and the Canadian Stocks is similarly pronounced in both regimes. Finally, I examine the Copula parameters describing the dependence between the Japanese and the European / American Stock markets. During the low dependence regime the Japanese Stock market is modestly interrelated with the European and the American Stock markets by about 0.4. In contrast, during the high dependence regime the average correlation of the Japanese and the other G7 Stock markets rises to 0.6 and some of the individual correlation coefficients more than double.

Overall, the RS Copula estimates provide evidence for changes in the dependence structure of international Stock markets. The regime probabilities in figure 4.2 identify a fundamental change in the dependence structure in 2001, the year of the terror attacks. Ever since, the interdependence of the international Stock markets has remained at higher levels. This reduces the diversification effects among Stocks, tremendously. Although all RS models insinuate similar regime time-paths, they differ in regards to their individual features. The second battery of RS Copulas models at least one regime via the Student's-t framework which accounts for tail dependency. However, the large degrees-of-freedom indicate no superior adaptation of those models to the G7 Stocks dataset.

The RS Copulas suggest diversification potential across various asset classes but very strong linkages within each individual asset class. Hence, global diversification within one asset class offers less risk reduction potential than diversification among different security types.

Table 4.11 presents the results of the RS Copula estimations based on the Multi Asset Classes dataset. Any estimated RS models indicate stronger dependencies at the beginning of the observations and a fundamental shift into the low dependence regime after the 2001 terror attacks. Ever since, the RS models suggest almost independent asset classes, even during the economic crisis in 2008/2009. A more detailed examination of the dependence parameters reveals interesting features about the changes in the dependence structures. The interaction of the REX10Y and the USD/EUR are similar in both regimes and translate to a linear correlation of about -0.1. The same holds true for the DAX and GOLD indices, which are almost independent from each other during both regimes (linear correlations of about 0.05 and 0.07). In contrast, the REX10Y and DAX indices comove significantly during the high dependence regime (linear correlation of 0.44), but turn significantly counter related during the low dependence regime (linear correlation of -0.36). I find a similar dependence pattern for the GOLD and USD/EUR indices, but they turn independent during the low dependence regime. The correlation of the DAX and the USD/EUR indices jumps from 0.2 during the high dependence regime to 0.1 during the high dependence regime. Those results indicate severe changes in the dependence structure among Multiple Asset Classes which significantly impact the diversification potential. Therefore, it is very important to account for shifts in their interactions to calculate accurate portfolio risks.

Figure 4.1 – G7 Bond yields High Dependence Regime Probabilities.

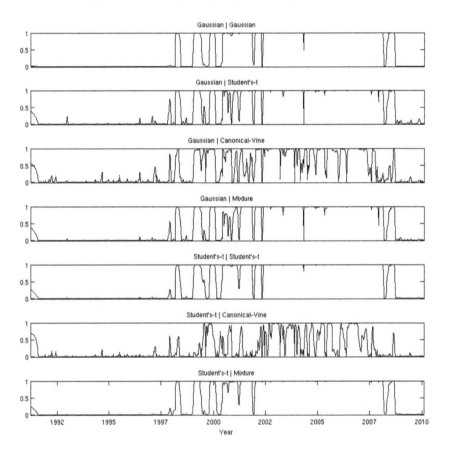

Figure 4.2 – G7 Stocks High Dependence Regime Probabilities.

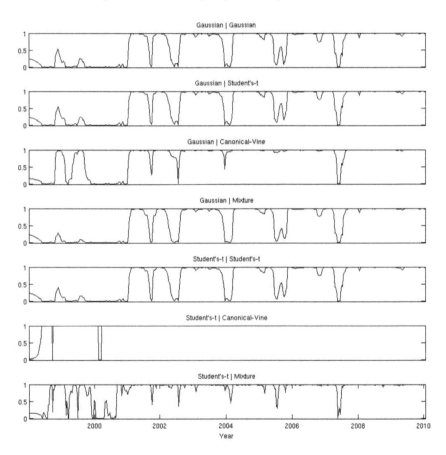

Table 4.9 – G7 Bond yields Regime-Switch Copula Parameters. The marginal models are the same for all Copulas. The RS Copulas always consist of two Copulas and are abbreviated as: GA|GA is a Gaussian|Gaussian RS Copula. GA|St is a Gaussian|Student's-t RS Copula. GA|CV is a Gaussian|Canonical-Vine RS Copula. GA|M is a Gaussian|Mixture RS Copula. St|St is a Student's-t|Student's-t RS Copula. St|CV is a Student's-t|Canonical-Vine RS Copula. St|M is a Student's-t|Mixture RS Copula. The pair-Copulas of the Canonical-Vine Copula are given inside the table. Inside the Canonical-Vine Copula the Gaussian Copula is abbreviated GA and the Clayton Copula is Cl. The Mixture Copula consists of one Gaussian, one Clayton and one Gumbel Copulas. AIC denotes the Akaike Criterion. BIC denotes the Bayesian Information Criterion. The estimation is based on the complete data sample (06.Mar.1991 to 03.Feb.2010).

	GA|GA Coeff	t-stat	GA|St Coeff	t-stat	GA|CV Coeff	t-stat	GA|M Coeff	t-stat	St|St Coeff	t-stat	St|CV Coeff	t-stat	St|M Coeff	t-stat
							Regime 1							
GER:IT	0.609	(0.61)	0.608	(0.12)	0.658	(0.28)	0.973	(3.84)	0.617	(0.65)	0.753	(3.49)	0.624	(2.04)
GER;CAN	0.449	(1.50)	0.449	(1.65)	0.464	(0.24)	0.677	(8.87)	0.462	(0.84)	0.512	(7.36)	0.458	(2.35)
GER:UK	0.601	(1.29)	0.588	(0.12)	0.628	(2.86)	0.830	(7.98)	0.623	(0.77)	0.684	(4.37)	0.627	(3.56)
GER:FRA	0.806	(2.55)	0.806	(4.26)	0.837	(0.56)	0.974	(5.84)	0.811	(0.47)	0.879	(1.19)	0.816	(1.68)
GER:JAP	0.343	(0.78)	0.336	(3.11)	0.376	(0.36)	0.294	(1.23)	0.331	(0.45)	0.321	(6.91)	0.330	(3.88)
GER:USA	0.531	(1.52)	0.528	(2.27)	0.559	(0.70)	0.746	(3.30)	0.530	(0.95)	0.593	(0.17)	0.531	(3.78)
IT:CAN	0.331	(1.36)	0.334	(1.00)	0.364	(0.24)	0.660	(0.88)	0.343	(0.24)	0.436	(0.66)	0.342	(0.75)
IT:UK	0.483	(1.28)	0.470	(0.12)	0.524	(2.45)	0.811	(0.59)	0.490	(0.55)	0.590	(0.20)	0.496	(0.82)
IT:FRA	0.651	(2.33)	0.650	(3.40)	0.700	(0.55)	0.963	(1.87)	0.662	(0.47)	0.781	(0.20)	0.669	(6.13)
IT:JAP	0.169	(0.60)	0.167	(1.16)	0.224	(0.36)	0.280	(1.41)	0.157	(0.35)	0.212	(0.48)	0.159	(0.93)
IT:USA	0.342	(0.24)	0.343	(0.05)	0.400	(0.36)	0.736	(5.86)	0.343	(0.74)	0.477	(0.90)	0.348	(1.59)
CAN:UK	0.446	(1.20)	0.439	(0.12)	0.478	(2.39)	0.683	(6.42)	0.470	(0.77)	0.541	(0.18)	0.477	(4.80)
CAN:FRA	0.421	(1.54)	0.417	(1.72)	0.445	(0.54)	0.671	(1.02)	0.436	(0.35)	0.493	(0.24)	0.435	(1.02)
CAN:JAP	0.234	(0.79)	0.239	(1.58)	0.273	(0.38)	0.243	(5.82)	0.264	(0.40)	0.270	(4.26)	0.254	(1.23)
CAN:USA	0.644	(1.48)	0.646	(2.29)	0.633	(0.69)	0.788	(1.66)	0.680	(0.96)	0.688	(0.24)	0.684	(1.47)
UK:FRA	0.545	(0.78)	0.532	(0.83)	0.584	(0.46)	0.824	(3.65)	0.575	(0.46)	0.654	(0.32)	0.591	(1.93)
UK:JAP	0.290	(0.73)	0.283	(1.66)	0.315	(0.36)	0.282	(3.18)	0.294	(0.37)	0.285	(0.22)	0.287	(0.89)
UK:USA	0.463	(1.03)	0.448	(1.48)	0.484	(0.65)	0.674	(8.86)	0.474	(0.81)	0.531	(0.18)	0.477	(1.84)
FRA:JAP	0.247	(0.69)	0.244	(1.06)	0.285	(0.35)	0.280	(1.13)	0.243	(0.42)	0.263	(0.02)	0.247	(1.15)
FRA:USA	0.475	(0.82)	0.469	(0.86)	0.514	(0.66)	0.736	(0.87)	0.478	(0.48)	0.557	(0.06)	0.485	(0.96)
JAP;USA	0.300	(1.09)	0.303	(1.75)	0.347	(0.66)	0.246	(1.82)	0.298	(0.53)	0.287	(11.36)	0.292	(1.34)
v_1									13.102	(3.88)	10.018		13.177	(8.63)

– continued on next page –

Table 4.9 – continued –

	Coeff	t-stat	Coeff	t-stat		Coeff	t-stat	Coeff (Reg. 2)	t-stat	Coeff	t-stat		Coeff	t-stat	Coeff	t-stat
GER:IT	0.969	(1.02)	0.972	(2.10)	CL	9.461	(14.26)	0.677	(5.46)	0.972	(0.88)	CL	13.463	(9.53)	0.974	(1.61)
GER:CAN	0.675	(0.64)	0.679	(19.85)	CL	1.361	(14.56)	0.515	(1.94)	0.668	(0.86)	CL	1.569	(2.92)	0.692	(1.13)
GER:UK	0.811	(0.73)	0.829	(20.20)	CL	2.434	(13.89)	0.658	(8.15)	0.815	(1.88)	CL	2.894	(6.34)	0.828	(2.29)
GER:FRA	0.970	(1.10)	0.973	(8.29)	CL	6.351	(17.41)	0.856	(2.10)	0.970	(2.47)	CL	6.327	(32.02)	0.975	(4.43)
GER:JAP	0.286	(0.93)	0.292	(3.47)	CL	0.242	(23.38)	0.330	(4.83)	0.294	(0.67)	CL	0.317	(3.88)	0.286	(6.25)
GER:USA	0.739	(1.68)	0.744	(5.10)	CL	1.517	(19.87)	0.561	(8.03)	0.730	(0.65)	CL	1.691	(4.35)	0.745	(15.39)
IT:CAN	0.664	(0.33)	0.664	(0.24)	GA	0.113	(0.40)	0.401	(0.88)	0.655	(0.81)	GA	0.030	(1.59)	0.671	(1.83)
IT:UK	0.791	(0.71)	0.812	(0.69)	GA	0.081	(0.47)	0.515	(3.23)	0.795	(1.70)	GA	-0.023	(4.24)	0.805	(3.29)
IT:FRA	0.959	(1.11)	0.962	(4.49)	GA	0.303	(7.03)	0.733	(1.64)	0.959	(2.33)	GA	0.265	(6.86)	0.964	(6.61)
IT:JAP	0.272	(0.24)	0.277	(0.26)	GA	-0.053	(0.20)	0.144	(6.95)	0.280	(0.65)	GA	-0.095	(1.01)	0.277	(2.67)
IT:USA	0.733	(0.88)	0.736	(0.85)	GA	0.166	(0.43)	0.375	(1.44)	0.724	(0.24)	GA	0.142	(0.15)	0.736	(1.37)
CAN:UK	0.669	(0.76)	0.683	(4.36)	GA	0.283	(3.47)	0.506	(2.02)	0.665	(1.80)	GA	0.135	(4.98)	0.687	(4.95)
CAN:FRA	0.666	(0.68)	0.673	(0.51)	GA	0.120	(0.20)	0.493	(0.96)	0.658	(1.63)	GA	0.162	(1.55)	0.682	(2.09)
CAN:JAP	0.244	(0.31)	0.242	(0.73)	GA	0.055	(1.02)	0.261	(6.43)	0.246	(0.62)	GA	0.011	(2.19)	0.252	(2.83)
CAN:USA	0.792	(1.65)	0.793	(4.61)	GA	0.694	(13.13)	0.753	(9.34)	0.790	(0.65)	GA	0.722	(8.27)	0.800	(2.08)
UK:FRA	0.805	(1.02)	0.824	(1.58)	GA	0.146	(1.76)	0.625	(1.23)	0.806	(1.27)	GA	0.132	(1.29)	0.820	(1.89)
UK:JAP	0.273	(0.33)	0.281	(0.72)	GA	0.104	(0.54)	0.273	(1.03)	0.281	(0.64)	GA	0.111	(1.50)	0.287	(0.96)
UK:USA	0.653	(1.20)	0.673	(1.34)	GA	0.057	(1.62)	0.482	(3.82)	0.652	(0.63)	GA	0.044	(1.88)	0.670	(1.26)
FRA:JAP	0.273	(0.92)	0.278	(0.84)	GA	0.029	(0.94)	0.248	(0.82)	0.285	(0.60)	GA	0.056	(1.15)	0.275	(1.21)
FRA:USA	0.725	(0.39)	0.734	(0.54)	GA	0.023	(0.88)	0.521	(6.42)	0.717	(0.58)	GA	0.036	(1.18)	0.734	(2.32)
JAP:USA	0.246	(0.54)	0.242	(0.51)	GA	-0.040	(0.57)	0.272	(2.94)	0.237	(0.65)	GA	0.013	(2.14)	0.244	(1.69)
ν_2			155.570	(3.79)				0.021	(4.05)	12.793	(6.03)					
θ_{cl}								2.215	(3.09)							
θ_{gu}								0.100	(4.90)							
w_{cl}								0.068	(1.03)							
w_{gu}								0.832	(3.17)							
w_{el}																
								Regime Probabilities								
$p_{1,1}$	0.992	(6.82)	0.969	(11.65)		0.943	(11.77)	0.967	(65.01)	0.982	(12.56)		0.952	(10.03)	0.984	(20.47)
$p_{2,2}$	0.999	(5.59)	0.966	(11.76)		0.916	(11.40)	0.972	(32.13)	0.981	(13.78)		0.856	(9.46)	0.983	(35.45)
LL	2714		2741			2453		2777		2795			2520		2785	
AIC	-5345		-5396			-4821		-5461		-5503			-4954		-5474	
BIC	-5057		-5102			-4534		-5139		-5202			-4659		-5145	

Table 4.10 – G7 Stocks Regime-Switch Copula Parameters. The marginal models are the same for all Copulas. The RS Copulas always consist of two Copulas and are abbreviated as: GA|GA is a Gaussian|Gaussian RS Copula. GA|St is a Gaussian|Student's-t RS Copula. GA|CV is a Gaussian|Canonical-Vine RS Copula. GA|M is a Gaussian|Mixture RS Copula. St|St is a Student's-t|Student's-t RS Copula. St|CV is a Student's-t|Canonical-Vine RS Copula. St|M is a Student's-t|Mixture RS Copula. The pair-Copulas of the Canonical-Vine Copula are given inside the table. Inside the Canonical-Vine Copula the Gaussian Copula is abbreviated GA and the Clayton Copula is CL. The Mixture Copula consists of one Gaussian, one Clayton and one Gumbel Copulas. AIC denotes the Akaike Criterion. BIC denotes the Bayesian Information Criterion. The estimation is based on the complete data sample (31.Dec.1997 to 20.Jan.2010).

	GA|GA		GA|St		GA|CV		GA|M		St|St		St|CV		St|M	
	Coeff	t-stat	Coeff	t-stat	Coeff	t-stat	Coeff	t-stat	Coeff	t-stat	Coeff	t-stat	Coeff	t-stat
							Regime 1							
GER:IT	0.731	(0.85)	0.729	(0.17)	0.885	(0.25)	0.893	(6.98)	0.894	(5.05)	0.567	(9.48)	0.875	(2.07)
GER:CAN	0.535	(0.82)	0.538	(0.29)	0.676	(0.15)	0.688	(7.10)	0.688	(1.25)	-0.590	(1.55)	0.661	(0.05)
GER:UK	0.647	(1.90)	0.645	(0.24)	0.823	(0.15)	0.838	(4.75)	0.840	(2.24)	0.220	(1.06)	0.827	(1.06)
GER:FRA	0.807	(1.14)	0.805	(4.38)	0.935	(0.11)	0.940	(3.57)	0.940	(0.51)	0.470	(0.17)	0.929	(13.22)
GER:JAP	0.448	(2.70)	0.448	(0.29)	0.617	(0.16)	0.644	(2.57)	0.642	(0.89)	0.350	(0.17)	0.599	(3.95)
GER:USA	0.516	(0.82)	0.517	(3.67)	0.756	(0.39)	0.784	(5.10)	0.781	(9.09)	-0.763	(1.22)	0.750	(4.29)
IT:CAN	0.419	(0.04)	0.419	(0.16)	0.651	(0.15)	0.680	(1.96)	0.678	(1.81)	-0.244	(2.16)	0.617	(0.05)
IT:UK	0.642	(1.50)	0.639	(0.25)	0.834	(0.15)	0.855	(4.08)	0.854	(0.91)	0.035	(0.61)	0.823	(5.18)
IT:FRA	0.794	(1.19)	0.792	(2.88)	0.906	(0.11)	0.913	(3.21)	0.913	(4.03)	0.249	(3.15)	0.901	(6.09)
IT:JAP	0.310	(0.01)	0.308	(0.12)	0.590	(0.17)	0.634	(0.97)	0.632	(0.05)	0.243	(0.13)	0.547	(0.73)
IT:USA	0.430	(0.76)	0.430	(1.04)	0.684	(0.47)	0.729	(0.97)	0.723	(0.13)	-0.647	(0.18)	0.679	(0.93)
CAN:UK	0.491	(1.59)	0.491	(0.24)	0.714	(0.15)	0.742	(3.82)	0.739	(9.90)	-0.715	(8.75)	0.702	(4.30)
CAN:FRA	0.504	(0.88)	0.505	(1.25)	0.704	(0.11)	0.729	(2.67)	0.726	(8.61)	-0.551	(1.72)	0.685	(1.83)
CAN:JAP	0.406	(2.20)	0.407	(0.29)	0.538	(0.15)	0.567	(2.31)	0.564	(1.97)	-0.486	(6.85)	0.534	(1.92)
CAN:USA	0.603	(0.85)	0.602	(2.72)	0.717	(0.39)	0.718	(4.70)	0.718	(2.06)	0.710	(2.51)	0.704	(3.28)
UK:FRA	0.746	(1.10)	0.744	(2.42)	0.882	(0.11)	0.901	(3.18)	0.901	(1.53)	0.715	(7.77)	0.885	(5.72)
UK:JAP	0.444	(1.81)	0.443	(0.29)	0.573	(0.16)	0.591	(1.59)	0.591	(2.89)	0.678	(1.38)	0.556	(1.49)
UK:USA	0.513	(0.84)	0.516	(1.60)	0.705	(0.16)	0.760	(0.80)	0.755	(0.77)	-0.240	(0.60)	0.711	(0.30)
FRA:JAP	0.438	(0.72)	0.438	(0.25)	0.625	(0.14)	0.658	(1.11)	0.656	(0.09)	0.757	(0.15)	0.594	(0.37)
FRA:USA	0.495	(0.81)	0.495	(1.14)	0.762	(0.44)	0.799	(1.71)	0.794	(0.26)	-0.169	(0.37)	0.748	(1.26)
JAP:USA	0.315	(0.78)	0.318	(1.32)	0.496	(0.38)	0.553	(1.46)	0.548	(0.71)	-0.026	(0.25)	0.486	(1.08)
v_1									188.305	(192.52)	198.846	(100.27)	189.733	(140.33)

– continued on next page –

54

Table 4.10 – continued –

	Coeff	t-stat	Coeff	t-stat	Cop	Coeff	t-stat	Coeff (Reg. 2)	t-stat	Coeff	t-stat	Cop	Coeff	t-stat	Coeff	t-stat
GER;IT	0.894	(1.94)	0.894	(0.28)	GA	1.428	(5.66)	0.791	(3.92)	0.736	(1.30)	CL	2.388	(3.14)	0.888	(4.46)
GER;CAN	0.688	(0.15)	0.686	(3.74)	CL	0.823	(2.80)	0.570	(2.55)	0.542	(4.61)	CL	1.058	(1.17)	0.587	(1.70)
GER;UK	0.839	(3.33)	0.839	(0.48)	CL	1.314	(2.25)	0.710	(4.81)	0.654	(4.05)	CL	1.735	(4.46)	0.461	(1.85)
GER;FRA	0.939	(0.63)	0.939	(0.61)	GA	1.721	(5.85)	0.854	(4.22)	0.810	(2.01)	CL	3.214	(1.43)	0.752	(9.09)
GER;JAP	0.639	(3.68)	0.639	(0.69)	CL	0.551	(2.55)	0.468	(3.01)	0.449	(1.67)	CL	0.930	(2.93)	0.626	(0.85)
GER;USA	0.781	(4.54)	0.778	(0.90)	CL	0.698	(1.77)	0.547	(3.85)	0.525	(0.64)	CL	1.236	(9.34)	-0.104	(2.95)
IT;CAN	0.677	(0.16)	0.675	(1.80)	GA	0.043	(0.31)	0.407	(1.36)	0.425	(2.27)	GA	0.184	(1.19)	0.446	(0.91)
IT;UK	0.854	(3.08)	0.854	(0.48)	GA	0.312	(2.01)	0.681	(1.95)	0.648	(0.62)	GA	0.439	(2.74)	0.659	(1.44)
IT;FRA	0.913	(0.61)	0.913	(0.61)	GA	0.509	(3.77)	0.838	(3.09)	0.798	(0.48)	GA	0.567	(6.88)	0.822	(2.85)
IT;JAP	0.630	(0.65)	0.629	(0.57)	GA	0.010	(0.07)	0.301	(0.79)	0.314	(0.14)	GA	0.110	(2.00)	0.795	(0.31)
IT;USA	0.723	(0.75)	0.721	(0.69)	GA	0.158	(1.77)	0.427	(1.40)	0.437	(0.00)	GA	0.173	(3.62)	-0.288	(0.69)
CAN;UK	0.740	(3.04)	0.738	(0.48)	GA	0.147	(0.55)	0.515	(2.02)	0.498	(0.87)	GA	0.350	(1.88)	0.226	(1.44)
CAN;FRA	0.727	(0.60)	0.724	(0.60)	GA	0.135	(0.58)	0.513	(1.48)	0.510	(0.20)	GA	0.261	(1.36)	0.430	(0.80)
CAN;JAP	0.564	(1.72)	0.562	(0.68)	GA	0.254	(2.44)	0.384	(2.75)	0.407	(1.35)	GA	0.246	(9.13)	0.182	(1.85)
CAN;USA	0.719	(4.11)	0.718	(0.90)	GA	0.379	(1.93)	0.606	(2.63)	0.608	(0.10)	GA	0.433	(9.22)	0.223	(3.89)
UK;FRA	0.900	(0.62)	0.900	(0.61)	GA	0.387	(3.14)	0.782	(2.10)	0.751	(0.90)	GA	0.381	(3.80)	0.508	(2.11)
UK;JAP	0.588	(1.63)	0.589	(0.59)	GA	0.201	(1.39)	0.450	(1.49)	0.445	(0.24)	GA	0.096	(4.36)	0.479	(0.69)
UK;USA	0.755	(0.45)	0.752	(0.43)	GA	0.316	(3.51)	0.532	(2.34)	0.516	(0.00)	GA	0.197	(1.17)	0.001	(0.85)
FRA;JAP	0.652	(0.37)	0.653	(0.52)	GA	0.108	(0.60)	0.419	(0.69)	0.439	(0.47)	GA	0.078	(8.14)	0.650	(0.29)
FRA;USA	0.794	(1.62)	0.791	(0.75)	GA	-0.109	(1.71)	0.511	(1.82)	0.502	(0.01)	GA	0.061	(5.82)	-0.089	(0.81)
JAP;USA	0.545	(1.48)	0.543	(0.78)	GA	0.101	(1.43)	0.266	(1.30)	0.312	(0.01)	GA	0.022	(5.39)	-0.073	(0.81)
ν_2			196.547	(229.70)						183.200	(54.02)					
θ_{cl}								1.107	(24.36)							
w_{cl}								1.288	(89.16)							
w_{gu}								0.852	(2.57)							
w_{el}						0.000	(11.55)	0.148	(0.71)							
							Regime Probabilities									
$p_{1,1}$	0.950	(3.17)	0.951	(2.98)		0.986	(3.44)	0.981	(15.14)	0.980	(2.22)		0.655	(8.55)	0.974	(3.34)
$p_{2,2}$	0.980	(8.27)	0.979	(7.81)		0.938	(9.85)	0.960	(13.43)	0.955	(6.53)		0.995	(2.42)	0.808	(11.19)
LL	1969		1970			1967		1977		1972			1818		1953	
AIC	-3855		-3855			-3851		-3860		-3856			-3549		-3810	
BIC	-3586		-3580			-3582		-3560		-3574			-3275		-3503	

Table 4.11 – Multi Asset Classes Regime-Switch Copula Parameters. The marginal models are the same for all Copulas. The RS Copulas always consist of two Copulas and are abbreviated as: GA|GA is a Gaussian|Gaussian RS Copula. GA|St is a Gaussian|Student's-t RS Copula. GA|CV is a Gaussian|Canonical-Vine RS Copula. GA|M is a Gaussian|Mixture RS Copula. St|St is a Student's-t|Student's-t RS Copula. St|CV is a Student's-t|Canonical-Vine RS Copula. St|M is a Student's-t|Mixture RS Copula. The pair-Copulas of the Canonical-Vine Copula are given inside the table. Inside the Canonical-Vine Copula the Gaussian Copula is abbreviated GA and the Clayton Copula is CL. The Mixture Copula consists of one Gaussian, one Clayton and one Gumbel Copulas. AIC denotes the Akaike Criterion. BIC denotes the Bayesian Information Criterion. The estimation is based on the complete data sample (02.Jan.1989 to 01.Feb.2010).

	GA|GA Coeff	GA|GA t-stat	GA|St Coeff	GA|St t-stat	GA|CV Coeff	GA|CV t-stat	GA|M Coeff	GA|M t-stat	St|St Coeff	St|St t-stat	St|CV Coeff	St|CV t-stat	St|M Coeff	St|M t-stat
							Regime 1							
REX:DAX	0.438	(1.99)	-0.359	(3.98)	-0.359	(1.63)	0.429	(1.10)	0.439	(4.37)	-0.357	(1.21)	0.431	(4.52)
REX:GOLD	-0.113	(0.72)	-0.028	(0.99)	-0.029	(0.99)	-0.103	(0.46)	-0.113	(1.71)	-0.026	(0.93)	-0.104	(1.61)
REX:U/E	-0.123	(0.91)	-0.110	(4.52)	-0.113	(1.25)	-0.131	(1.17)	-0.123	(1.81)	-0.138	(2.22)	-0.132	(1.99)
DAX:GOLD	0.079	(0.46)	0.050	(0.59)	0.051	(0.51)	0.103	(0.49)	0.081	(2.48)	0.047	(0.94)	0.103	(2.49)
DAX:U/E	0.182	(0.83)	0.101	(4.05)	0.099	(1.43)	0.177	(1.07)	0.182	(3.73)	0.110	(2.22)	0.176	(4.51)
GOLD:U/E	0.693	(0.76)	-0.020	(1.06)	-0.023	(1.98)	0.715	(1.13)	0.694	(10.62)	-0.003	(2.21)	0.716	(18.24)
ν_1									182.625	(11.12)	15.449	(22.45)	196.675	(41.31)
							Regime 2							
REX:DAX	-0.362	(6.03)	0.438	(0.59)	0.677 CL	(6.30)	-0.486	(0.71)	-0.361	(3.96)	0.677 CL	(6.35)	-0.484	(4.53)
REX:GOLD	-0.027	(1.70)	-0.109	(1.68)	0.002 CL	(0.70)	-0.053	(1.27)	-0.026	(0.03)	0.002 CL	(0.56)	-0.053	(0.07)
REX:U/E	-0.108	(2.14)	-0.129	(2.11)	0.002 CL	(0.52)	-0.149	(1.09)	-0.111	(2.72)	0.002 CL	(2.17)	-0.148	(0.01)
DAX:GOLD	0.053	(2.08)	0.092	(2.71)	0.140 GA	(2.20)	0.029	(0.26)	0.052	(0.03)	0.144 GA	(2.17)	0.029	(0.05)
DAX:U/E	0.100	(3.28)	0.162	(3.97)	0.243 GA	(4.14)	0.115	(0.86)	0.098	(1.93)	0.240 GA	(4.11)	0.114	(0.01)
GOLD:U/E	-0.025	(6.07)	0.694	(5.48)	0.687 GA	(20.77)	-0.037	(1.05)	-0.022	(0.89)	0.692 GA	(19.81)	-0.036	(0.01)
ν_2			8.845	(4.71)					189.336	(97.92)				
θ_{cl}							0.090	(6.48)					0.089	(3.75)
θ_{gu}							1.006	(15.63)					1.000	(13.85)
w_{cl}							0.233	(2.91)					0.229	(4.68)
w_{gu}							0.000	(0.22)					0.000	(0.16)
w_{el}							0.766	(1.80)					0.771	(2.97)
							Regime Probabilities							
$p_{1,1}$	0.988	(6.33)	0.991	(5.38)	0.991	(9.23)	0.986	(14.95)	0.988	(17.76)	0.991	(10.21)	0.986	(15.02)
$p_{2,2}$	0.991	(9.15)	0.988	(7.48)	0.989	(12.47)	0.989	(15.93)	0.991	(15.93)	0.988	(13.45)	0.989	(16.13)
LL	243		261		229		246		246		234		248	
AIC	-463		-496		-434		-459		-465		-442		-460	
BIC	-386		-413		-357		-350		-375		-359		-345	

Figure 4.3 – Multi Asset Classes High Dependence Regime Probabilities.

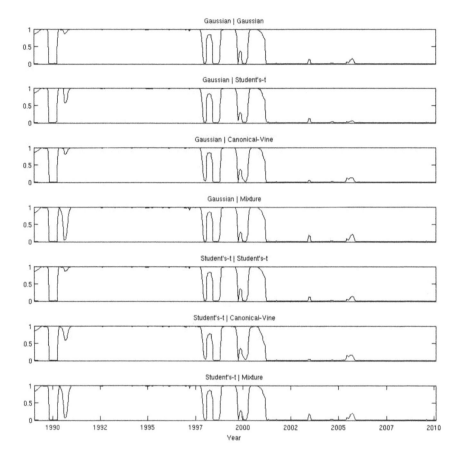

4.5 Dynamic Copulas

This section discusses the parameter estimates of the Dynamic Copulas. Any model is estimated on basis of the same residuals, filtered from the univariate models (Section 4.2). Table
4.12 presents the estimation results for the G7 Bond yield data. The superior loglikelihood
and BIC values of the Student's-t over the Gaussian Copula and its relatively low v indicate
the existence of tail dependence in this dataset. In addition, a comparison of the two Dynamic
Archimedian Copulas reveals a tendency towards right tail dependence due to the Gumbel Cop-

ula's stronger loglikelihood and BIC values. The parameters of the Dynamic Mixture Copulas support this result. They utilize the Gumbel Copula within their structure to represent phases of strict right tail dependence. Figures 4.5 and 4.4 illustrate this outcome graphically. At the beginning of the dependence observations, the majority of the Gaussian Copula correlation co-efficients indicate a drop in the dependence structure which is amplified by a Gumbel Copula parameter of almost 1 (independence) at that time (Figure 4.4, center). Simultaneously, the weight of the Gumbel Copula within the Mixture construct rises to about 25% (Figure 4.4, bottom). Thereafter, the Gaussian coefficients reveal tightening dependencies and the Gumbel parameter increases slightly but its weight reduces. This indicates a phase of tightening dependence which is captured by the Gaussian Copula. At the end of the observation period, the Bond yields turn significantly right tail dependent. This is reflected through the Gumbel parameter intensity increase and ascending Gumbel weights in the Mixture structure. This result is supported by the single Dynamic Gumbel Copula (Figure 4.4, top). The same process holds true for the Dynamic Mixture containing one Student's-t and one Gumbel Copulas. The Dynamic Mixtures comprising an Elliptical and a Gumbel Copulas generate similar loglikelihood values. This denotes the existence of severe right tail dependence among the Bond yields.

Figures 4.5 and 4.4 demonstrate severe shifts in the Bond markets' dependence structure over time. Those are mainly driven by three economic shocks. First, the introduction of the Euro significantly increases the dependence among the Euro countries. It also tightens the dependencies between the Euro Bond yields and the rest of the examined G7 Bond yields. Due to the geographical propinquity of the Euro members and the UK, the Euro introduction significantly tightens their Bond yield comovements although the UK has not joined the Euro currency. Second, the comovements of the Japanese with the other G7 Bond yields significantly reduce after the Euro introduction in 1999. Figure 4.5 shows that this holds true for the Japanese interrelation with any other region and that it remained at a low level for about three years. Third, figure 4.5 also identifies changes in the dependence structure during the 2008/2009 global recession. The developments of the linkages between the European countries are especially interesting during this time. The introduction of the Euro resulted strict comovements among the European Bond yields, but in 2009 rising concern about the Italian and UK debt quality significantly reduced those linkages. While the transatlantic and inner European linkages between the two large solid countries, Germany and France, remained stable, Italy's Bond yield comovements with the G7 countries decreased tremendously due to doubts on its solvency. The same holds true for the UK Bond market, but at a smaller magnitude. Those results lead to the conclusion that Bond markets are mainly driven by fundamentals, such as a country's GDP development, its debt level and its debt service ratio relative to the US and/or Germany (Bernoth et al. (2004)). I cannot find indications of unreasonable contagion effects among the G7 Bond yields.

Table 4.12 – G7 Bond yields Dynamic Copula Parameters. The marginal models are the same for all Copulas. The Dynamic Copulas are abbreviated: GU is a Dynamic Gumbel Copula. CL is a Dynamic Clayton Copula. GA is a Dynamic Gaussian Copula. St is a Dynamic Student's-t Copula. Mix is a Dynamic Mixture Copula. Mix1 combines a Dynamic Gaussian and a Dynamic Clayton Copula. Mix2 combines a Dynamic Student's-t and a Dynamic Clayton Copula. Mix3 combines a Dynamic Gaussian and Dynamic Gumbel Copula. Mix4 combines a Dynamic Student's-t and a Dynamic Gumbel Copula. The Loglikelihood values are abbreviated with LL. AIC denotes the Akaike Criterion. BIC denotes the Bayesian Information Criterion. The t-statistics are given in brackets. The estimation is based on the complete data sample (06.Mar.1991 to 03.Feb.2010).

	GU	CL	GA	St	Mix1	Mix2	Mix3	Mix4
z			0.017	0.016	0.014	0.015	0.015	0.015
			(4.12)	(3.85)	(0.45)	(0.67)	(1.53)	(2.15)
g			0.010	0.014	0.028	0.021	0.027	0.020
			(2.96)	(3.26)	(1.27)	(1.82)	(0.78)	(1.28)
ν			0.976	0.975	0.971	0.973	0.971	0.973
			(162.52)	(124.25)	(14.35)	(21.59)	(68.27)	(55.28)
v				11.470		14.904		14.435
				(8.39)		(1.38)		(2.64)
k^{ac}	0.298	0.496			-3.248	0.053	0.048	-1.144
	(16.51)	(1.43)			(9.27)	(0.00)	(0.03)	(0.46)
a^{ac}	0.288	0.265			-0.834	0.985	0.986	0.991
	(23.57)	(1.49)			(0.85)	(6.97)	(0.10)	(0.39)
b^{ac}	-1.000	-1.000			-1.000	-0.114	-0.092	1.000
	(3.48)	(2.40)			(1.91)	(0.00)	(1.33)	(0.34)
k^{dw}					0.481	0.490	0.668	0.490
					(1.47)	(3.66)	(0.76)	(0.79)
a^{dw}					0.192	0.271	-0.041	0.096
					(1.01)	(0.29)	(0.05)	(0.70)
b^{dw}					0.289	0.219	0.332	0.394
					(2.73)	(1.46)	(23.43)	(3.45)
LL	1249	1089	2626	2742	2733	2767	2739	2769
AIC	-2492	-2171	-5245	-5476	-5444	-5509	-5455	-5514
BIC	-2471	-2151	-5225	-5449	-5368	-5427	-5380	-5432

59

Figure 4.4 – G7 Bond yields Dynamic Gumbel and Dynamic Mixture Copula Parameters: Dynamic Gumbel Copula (top), Dynamic Mixture Gumbel Copula (center) and Dynamic Mixture Copula Weights (bottom). The dashed line in the bottom graph represents the weight of the Dynamic Gumbel Copula and the solid line the weight of the Dynamic Gaussian Copula in the Mixture construct.

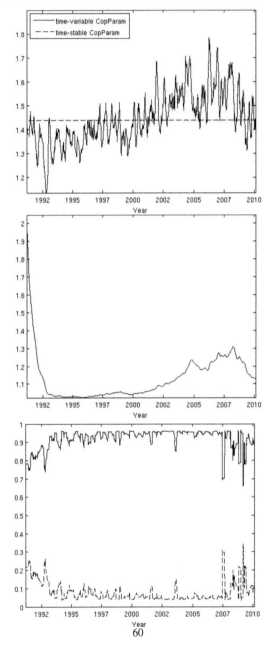

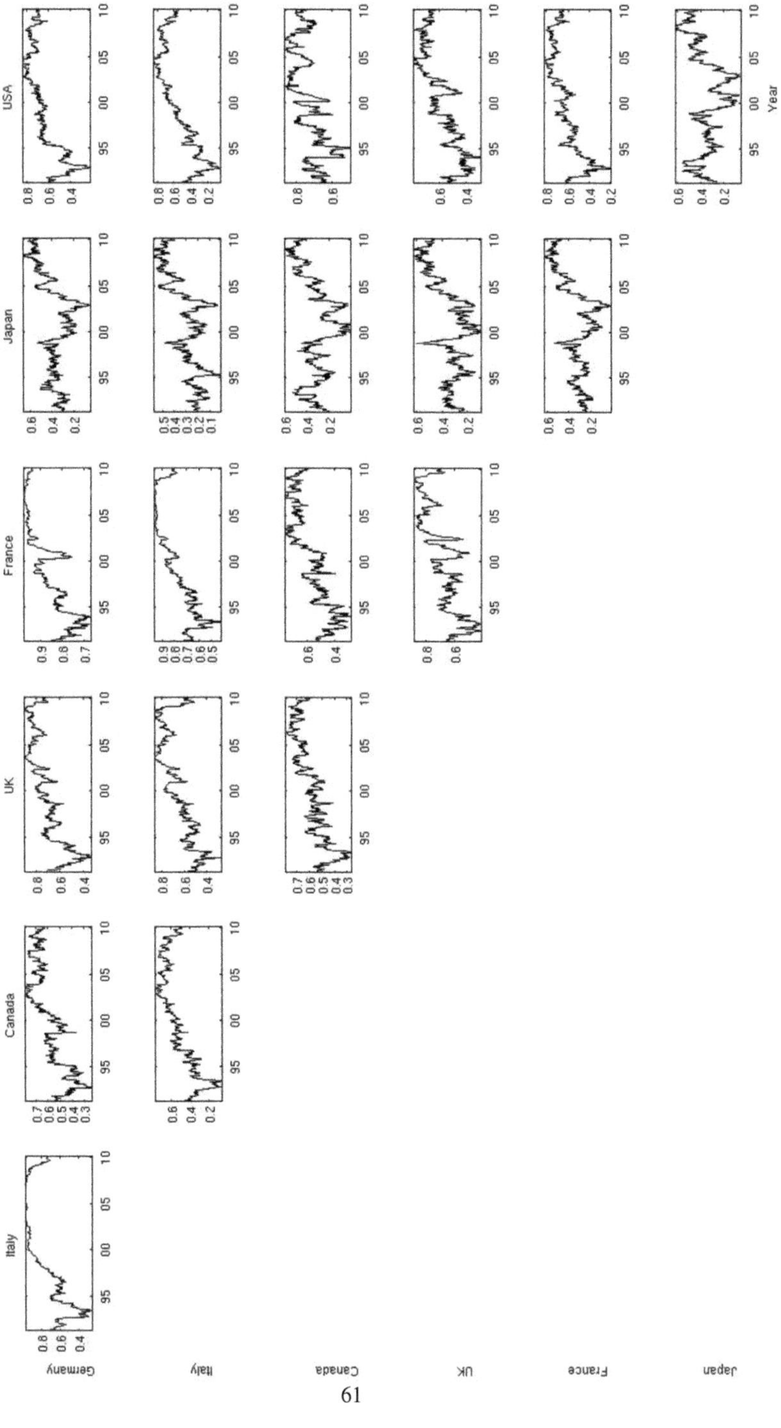

Figure 4.5 – G7 Bond yields Dynamic Mixture Copula Correlation Parameters: The Mixture Copula consists of one Dynamic Gaussian and one Dynamic Gumbel Copulas.

Next, I analyze the time paths of the G7 Stock markets dependencies. Again, a comparison of the Dynamic Student's-t and Gaussian Copulas indicates the existence of tail dependence in the data. However, in contrast to the Bond yield dataset the superior loglikelihood and BIC values of the Dynamic Clayton over the Dynamic Gumbel Copula suggest left tail dependence. This result is in line with various articles on this topic (Section 1.1). In addition, the hypothesis of left tail dependent Stock markets is supported by the Dynamic Mixture Copula estimates. The Mixtures combining one Dynamic Elliptical and one Dynamic Clayton Copulas generate the strongest loglikelihoods and BICs. The top and center graphs in figure 4.6 amplify the existence of left tail dependence. Although the weights of each Dynamic Copula within the Mixture skeleton remain fairly stable, greater portions are allocated towards the Clayton Copula whenever its parameter intensifies (Figure 4.6, bottom). Inside the Mixture structure the Clayton parameters insinuate much more significant left tail dependence than a single Dynamic Clayton Copula (Figure 4.6, center). This comparison suggests phases of very intense left tail dependence in the G7 Stock markets and demonstrates the advantages of the Dynamic Mixture concept. Inside its skeleton, the Dynamic Student's-t or Gaussian Copulas capture most of the dependence structure very precisely but the extremes are represented through intensely parameterized Dynamic Clayton Copulas. The Dynamic Weight process (Equation 5.3) provides additional flexibility to control the tail dependence magnitude. Hence, I conclude that Copulas which account for left tail dependence capture the linkages of Stocks most properly and should improve the accuracy of portfolio risk forecasts.

The time paths of the Copula parameter sets also allow to analyze the dependence structure of the G7 Stocks during the 2001 terror attacks and the 2008/2009 recession. At first, I analyze the changes of the Dynamic Clayton Copula parameter (Figure 4.6, top). It moves contrary to the Stock prices, indicating tightening dependence during downturn Stock markets. This conclusion is supported by the Clayton parameter of the Mixture construct. It follows almost the same path as the single Clayton but the parameter level is more intense (Figure 4.6, center). As explained earlier, this is due to its supportive function inside the Dynamic Mixture to model phases of extreme left tail dependence. Overall, the parameter paths of both Clayton Copulas clearly insinuate increasing left tail dependence during Stock market downturns (Figure 4.6). The Dynamic Student's-t inside the Mixture provides additional evidence of increasing dependencies during downturns. Its correlation coefficients indicate tighter comovements during the 2001 and 2008 Stock market drops (Figure 4.7). However, the magnitudes of the dependence changes are the least significant for the Euro countries. This is due to their joint central bank (ECB), their memberships in the European Union and their geographical propinquity. Those features preserve tight comovements of the EU countries' Stock markets. The time path of the Dynamic Weights increases the share of the Clayton Copula during Stock market downturns, denoting concentrated left tail dependence. Overall, I conclude from those findings that the linkages of the G7 Stock markets significantly increase during economic turmoil. Hence, the observed correlation meltdown significantly reduces the potential of loss protection through global diversification. This outcome is in line with findings reported by Karolyi and Stulz (1996), Longin and Solnik (2001), Ang and Bekaert (2002), Ang and Chen (2002), Guidolin and Timmerman (2002), Bae, Karolyi and Stulz (2003), Forbes and Rigobon (2003) and Das and Uppal (2004).

Table 4.13 – G7 Stocks Dynamic Copula Parameters. The marginal models are the same for all Copulas. The Dynamic Copulas are abbreviated: GU is a Dynamic Gumbel Copula. CL is a Dynamic Clayton Copula. GA is a Dynamic Gaussian Copula. St is a Dynamic Student's-t Copula. Mix is a Dynamic Mixture Copula. Mix1 combines a Dynamic Gaussian and a Dynamic Clayton Copula. Mix2 combines a Dynamic Student's-t and a Dynamic Clayton Copula. Mix3 combines a Dynamic Gaussian and Dynamic Gumbel Copula. Mix4 combines a Dynamic Student's-t and a Dynamic Gumbel Copula. The Loglikelihood values are abbreviated with LL. AIC denotes the Akaike Criterion. BIC denotes the Bayesian Information Criterion. The t-statistics are given in brackets. The estimation is based on the complete data sample (31.Dec.1997 to 20.Jan.2010).

	GU	CL	GA	St	Mix1	Mix2	Mix3	Mix4
z			0.010	0.012	0.017	0.017	0.013	0.014
			(0.67)	(0.73)	(1.66)	(1.71)	(0.24)	(0.73)
g			0.017	0.022	0.032	0.031	0.027	0.027
			(1.49)	(1.44)	(2.17)	(2.32)	(0.46)	(1.45)
v			0.972	0.958	0.935	0.933	0.958	0.946
			(25.35)	(19.33)	(42.15)	(34.02)	(8.35)	(9.28)
ν				19.044		24.737		21.014
				(3.57)		(2.73)		(3.52)
k^{ac}	0.386	0.143			0.442	0.357	-4.141	-8.344
	(0.12)	(15.32)			(1.11)	(1.15)	(0.13)	(1.35)
a^{ac}	0.604	0.909			0.874	0.898	-0.957	0.999
	(0.24)	(23.74)			(2.43)	(1.26)	(0.08)	(1.99)
b^{ac}	-0.703	-0.179			-0.452	-0.359	-0.114	0.736
	(0.43)	(3.14)			(0.71)	(0.76)	(0.87)	(0.65)
k^{dw}					0.535	0.528	0.612	0.980
					(1.01)	(0.66)	(0.12)	(1.24)
a^{dw}					0.465	0.472	0.359	0.019
					(0.03)	(0.87)	(0.70)	(0.98)
b^{dw}					-0.071	-0.056	0.017	-0.007
					(2.65)	(3.23)	(4.90)	(3.83)
LL	1220	1292	1926	1951	1961	1970	1943	1956
AIC	-2434	-2578	-3847	-3893	-3899	-3916	-3863	-3887
BIC	-2415	-2559	-3827	-3868	-3829	-3839	-3793	-3811

Figure 4.6 – G7 Stocks Dynamic Clayton and Dynamic Mixture Copula Parameters: Dynamic Clayton Copula (top), Dynamic Mixture Clayton Copula (center) and Dynamic Mixture Copula Weights (bottom). The dashed line in the bottom graph represents the weight of the Dynamic Clayton Copula and the solid line the weight of the Dynamic Student's-t Copula in the Mixture construct.

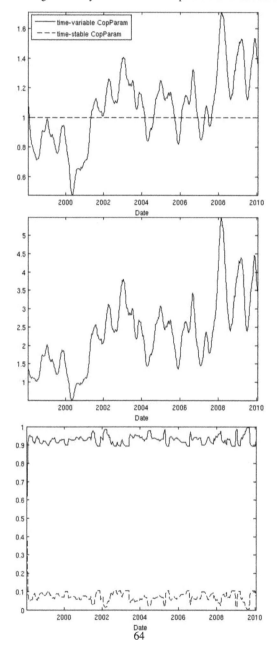

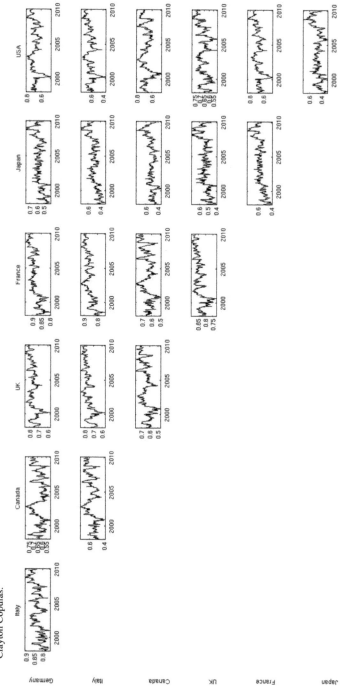

Figure 4.7 – G7 Stocks Dynamic Mixture Copula Correlation Parameters: The Mixture Copula consists of one Dynamic Student's-t and one Dynamic Clayton Copulas.

65

Finally, I examine the parameter estimates based on the Multi Asset Classes dataset. In contrast to the previous datasets, the focus of attention is not the regional diversification effect within one asset class, but the linkages between various security types. The Copula estimations allow to draw conclusions on the dataset's dependence characteristics. At first glance, the Dynamic Student's-t generates stronger loglikelihoods and BIC values than the Dynamic Gaussian Copula. This is a first indicator for tail dependence in the MAC dataset. A comparison of the single Gaussian Copula and the Mixtures containing a Gaussian and an Archimedian Copula supports the assumption of tail dependence. However, the loglikelihoods and BICs of the Student's-t based Mixtures and the single Student's-t reveal hardly any differences. In addition, both Archimedian Copulas result almost identical loglikelihoods and BICs and their parameters remain close to the independence level (Figure 4.9). This leads to the conclusion of symmetric tail dependence in this dataset.

The estimation results suggest the Dynamic Student's-t Copula represents the dependence structure of the MAC dataset most appropriately. Therefore, I examine its correlation coefficients' time paths in more detail. In contrast to the previously analyzed data, I find negative dependencies during some phases and the coefficients swing in a much wider range. A first very interesting result in regards to diversification potential is the time path of the REX10Y-DAX linkage. Figure 4.8 shows that the dependence between both securities declines dramatically to a negative amplitude during the 2001 and the 2008 Stock market downturns. Similarly, I find a recurring pattern for the GOLD-DAX linkage. It tightens during upturn phases and loosens during Stock market downturns, insinuating great diversification potential. In contrast, the time path of the USD/EUR-DAX coefficient reveals no direct relation to the underlying economic situations. The same holds true for the USD/EUR-GOLD dependence pattern. Nevertheless, the relation of the USD/EUR-REX10Y is very interesting. During the 2001 recession, those indices are negatively correlated, but during the credit crunch in 2009 their dependence coefficient jumps from -0.2 to 0.2. A possible explanation of this syndrome lies in the characteristics of both recessions. In 2001 only the Stock markets were in doubt which had no significant impact on the global exchange rates. At the end of 2009, some South European countries' solvencies were doubted, but the German and French ratings remained stable driving their Bond prices up. The doubt on the solvency of the South European countries caused severe EUR/USD drops. Therefore, the correlation of the REX10Y and the USD/EUR significantly increased at the end of 2009. Overall, the parameter estimations of this dataset reveal three interesting characteristics. First, I find significant diversification potential across the different security types. Second, I find no evidence for left or right tail dependence, but instead the linkages between the asset classes change individually. Hence, the application of a Dynamic Elliptical Copula is advantageous due to its parameter plurality. Third, the individual dependence coefficients swings are more pronounced for the Multi Asset Classes dataset than for the G7 Bond yield and the G7 Stocks datasets.

Table 4.14 – Multi Asset Classes Dynamic Copula Parameters. The marginal models are the same for all Copulas. The Dynamic Copulas are abbreviated: GU is a Dynamic Gumbel Copula. CL is a Dynamic Clayton Copula. GA is a Dynamic Gaussian Copula. St is a Dynamic Student's-t Copula. Mix is a Dynamic Mixture Copula. Mix1 combines a Dynamic Gaussian and a Dynamic Clayton Copula. Mix2 combines a Dynamic Student's-t and a Dynamic Clayton Copula. Mix3 combines a Dynamic Gaussian and Dynamic Gumbel Copula. Mix4 combines a Dynamic Student's-t and a Dynamic Gumbel Copula. The Loglikelihood values are abbreviated with LL. AIC denotes the Akaike Criterion. BIC denotes the Bayesian Information Criterion. The t-statistics are given in brackets. The estimation is based on the complete data sample (02.Jan.1989 to 01.Feb.2010).

	GU	CL	GA	St	Mix1	Mix2	Mix3	Mix4
z			0.031	0.033	0.038	0.037	0.039	0.037
			(4.16)	(4.68)	(1.06)	(0.04)	(0.90)	(0.11)
g			0.002	0.002	0.005	0.004	0.003	0.004
			(7.69)	(0.39)	(0.87)	(0.10)	(0.11)	(0.27)
v			0.961	0.958	0.959	0.957	0.959	0.957
			(62.60)	(65.90)	(11.09)	(3.52)	(11.93)	(9.05)
ν				10.318		10.311		10.273
				(5.95)		(5.39)		(5.10)
k^{ac}	0.212	0.225			-0.702	-5.115	0.171	0.106
	(0.18)	(2.51)			(0.86)	(0.69)	(0.31)	(0.17)
a^{ac}	0.869	0.933			1.000	1.000	0.951	0.970
	(1.44)	(22.98)			(0.56)	(0.44)	(2.09)	(0.37)
b^{ac}	-0.811	-0.523			-0.402	-0.287	-0.482	-0.325
	(0.73)	(2.52)			(0.72)	(0.12)	(0.74)	(0.19)
k^{dw}					0.887	0.825	0.597	0.487
					(0.90)	(0.59)	(1.49)	(0.13)
a^{dw}					-0.104	0.072	0.242	0.396
					(0.13)	(0.03)	(1.06)	(0.12)
b^{dw}					0.113	0.054	0.074	0.091
					(2.99)	(0.97)	(2.04)	(1.95)
LL	32	30	265	294	278	296	282	297
AIC	-58	-55	-523	-580	-534	-569	-541	-571
BIC	-39	-35	-504	-554	-464	-492	-471	-494

Overall, the dynamics of the comovements differ significantly in the three datasets. The G7 Bond yield dependencies are driven by fundamentals. This indicates that Bond investors distinguish the solvency of the individual countries based on fundamental economic data and their debt levels. Nevertheless, Bond yields are right tail dependent what causes joint Bond price drops. In contrast, the Copula estimates depict severely left tail dependent Stock markets. This is a very hazardous feature for investors who diversify their portfolios among Stock markets only. The reasoning is simple; While the dependence between the Stock markets is fairly low during upturn phases, it increases dramatically during downturns. Consequently, diversification effects disappear when they are needed the most. The third dataset contains multiple asset classes. I find strong support for my hypothesis that diversification among several security types reduces financial risks more effectively than global diversification within one asset class. In addition, the parameter time-paths clearly identify strongly shifting dependence patterns, what amplifies the advantage of applying Dynamic Copulas. The following chapter analyzes the interactions of the dependence structures, the univariate volatilities and the univariate returns, in more detail.

Figure 4.8 – Multi Asset Classes Dynamic Student's-t Copula Parameters.

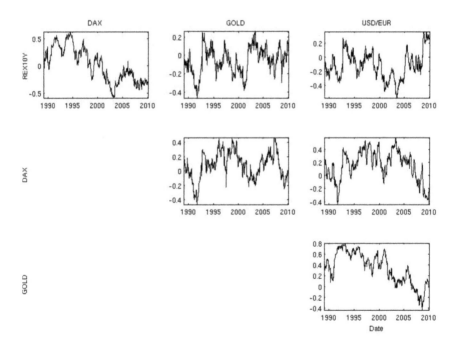

Figure 4.9 – Multi Asset Classes Dynamic Clayton (left) and Dynamic Gumbel (right) Copula Parameters.

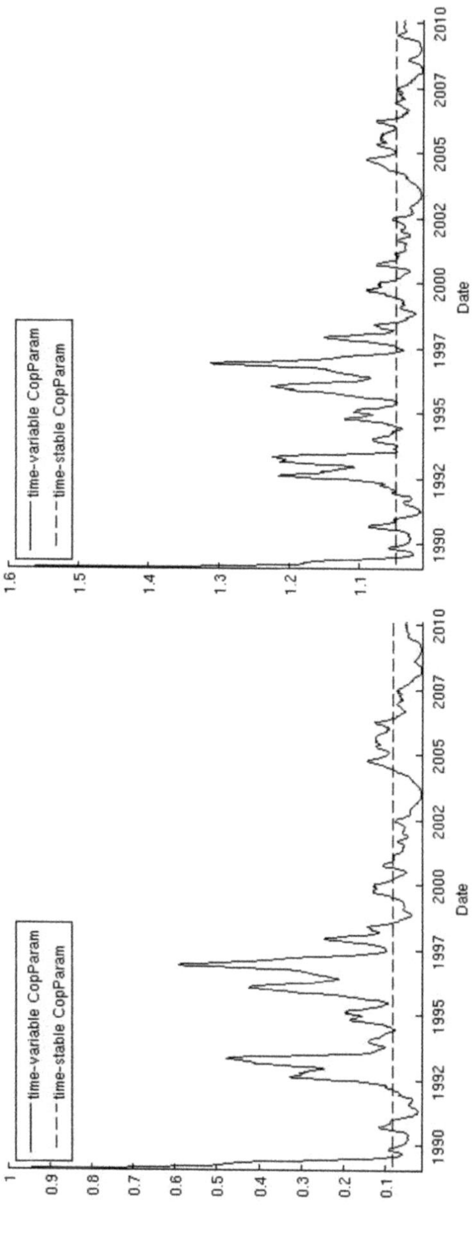

Chapter 5

Interaction of Dependence, Volatility and Returns

The previous chapter presents the Copula parameter estimates and draws conclusions on economic shocks that impact the dependence of financial assets. This chapter analyzes the interaction of dependence, volatility and returns in depth. I focus on the hypothesis that the linkages between financial markets tighten during market downturns and during volatile phases. The Static Copulas only indicate shifts in the dependence structure but cannot adapt to them. For example, the Clayton skeleton indicates tightening dependencies during market downturns but its parameter intensity remains constant. Therefore, I focus on the relations of the RS and Dynamic Copula parameters with the univariate volatilities and returns.

In case of the RS Copulas, I analyze the impact of the filtered univariate volatilities and the univariate returns on the high dependence regime probabilities. I measure their impacts via standard logistic regression techniques and therefore cluster the high dependence regime probabilities as:

$$\zeta_{t|t}^{cl} = \begin{cases} 0, & 0 \leq \zeta_{t|t} < 0.5, \\ 1, & 0.5 \leq \zeta_{t|t} \leq 1. \end{cases} \tag{5.1}$$

The intuition is simple; The RS Copulas combine two Copulas with individual shapes and parameterization. Nevertheless, their shapes and parameters remain constant within each regime. Hence $\zeta_{t|t}^{cl}$ simply indicates the occurrence of the high dependence regime as 1 and the low dependence regime as 0. I implement $\zeta_{t|t}^{cl}$ as the dependent variable and first examine the impacts of the filtered volatilities. In a second analysis, I replace the filtered volatilities with the univariate return series and measure their impacts on the high dependence regime.

Additionally, I explore the interactions of the Dynamic Copula parameters with the filtered univariate volatilities and the univariate return series. In contrast to the RS Copulas, the Dynamic Copula parameters do not jump between two regimes but they follow time paths. This feature introduces additional flexibility to adapt to shifts in the dependence structure but also requires different techniques to identify their interactions with the univariate time series. The most obvious and simplest choice to measure comovements is linear correlation. Therefore, I calculate the correlations ($\rho^{(PP)}$) between the equally weighted return series (PP) and the according Dynamic Copula parameter sets (θ) as:

$$\rho_i^{(PP)} = \frac{E\left[(PP_i - E[PP_i])\,(\theta_i - E\,[\theta_i])\right]}{\sqrt{E\left[(PP_i - E\,[PP_i])^2\right]\,E\left[(\theta_i - E\,[\theta_i])^2\right]}} \tag{5.2}$$

$$PP_t = PP_0\left[1 + \frac{1}{n}\sum_{i=1}^{t}\sum_{j=1}^{n}(x_{j,i})\right],$$

where x are logarithmic return vectors. In the same manner, I compute the correlation of the equally weighted volatility levels ($\bar{\sigma}$) and the according Dynamic Copula parameter sets:

$$\rho_i^{(\sigma)} = \frac{E\left[(\bar{\sigma}_i - E[\bar{\sigma}_i])\,(\theta_i - E\,[\theta_i])\right]}{\sqrt{E\left[(\bar{\sigma}_i - E\,[\bar{\sigma}_i])^2\right]\,E\left[(\theta_i - E\,[\theta_i])^2\right]}} \tag{5.3}$$

$$\bar{\sigma}_t = \frac{1}{n}\sum_{j=1}^{n}(\sigma_{j,t}),$$

where σ are the volatilities filtered from the GARCH processes. The number of indices contained in the equally weighted index is denoted by n and strictly depends on the Copula function. For example the Dynamic Archimedian Copulas capture the dependence structure of a d-dimensional dataset through one parameter, resulting $n = d$. In contrast, each of the correlation coefficients in the Dynamic Elliptical Copulas represents the dependence of two securities. Therefore, I calculate PP and $\bar{\sigma}$ for any possible combinations ($n = 2$). This procedure allows to compute the correlations between the time paths of the Copula parameters and the according price/volatility indices. Finally, I draw conclusions on the question if the Copula parameter intensities are related to price or volatility drifts. I analyze all three datasets in the same manner. This guarantees the comparability of the results.

5.1 Bond Yields

This section analyzes the impact of Bond yield changes and Bond yield volatilities on the G7 Bond yields dependence structure. At first, I examine the volatility impacts on the high dependence regimes filtered from the RS Copulas via standard logistic regression techniques. The McFadden pseudo R^2s indicate significant linkages between the individual Bond yield volatilities and the high dependence regimes (Table 5.1). In addition, the t-statistics reveal highly significant regression odds. This shows that the Bond yield volatilities impact the occurrence of the high dependence regime. However, the signs of the regression odds indicate no simple relation between the dependence regimes and the volatility levels. Regardless of the RS Copula, the German, French, Japanese and US odds signs are positive, whereas the Italian, Canadian and UK odds signs are negative. Although the odds do not represent the impact strength directly, their signs indicate positive or negative influences. Hence, the regression results insinuate that the German, French, Japanese and US Bond yield volatility levels positively impact the probabilities of the high dependence regime. The opposite holds true for the Italian, Canadian and UK Bond yield volatilities. This outcome contradicts the hypothesis that increasing Bond yield volatility generally causes shifts into the high dependence regime. This rejection is supported by figure A.1 and section 4.4. There is no graphical evidence that rising volatilities would cause a shift to the high dependence regime. The opposite is observed. As the Bond yield volatility levels explode in 2009 (except for Japan), the RS Copulas suggest low dependence regimes. This observation clearly contradicts the regression results. However, a comparison of the volatilities during the high and low dependence regimes sheds light on this diffusion. The volatilities of the German, French, Japanese and US Bond yields are slightly more distinct during the high than during the low dependence regimes. On average they differ by about 0.0025. The opposite holds true for the Italian, Canadian and UK Bond yields. Their volatility levels are slightly less distinct during the high dependence regimes (on average -0.0014). Although those discrepancies are neglectable, they define the odds signs of the logistic regression analyses. Therefore, I have to reject the hypothesis that increasing volatility would explain the occurrence of the high dependence regime among the Bond yields.

Next, I utilize standard logistic regression technique to examine the linkages between the Bond yield changes and the high dependence regime probabilities. In contrast to the previous analyses, the McFadden pseudo R^2s do not indicate significant linkages between the Bond yield changes and the high dependence regimes (Table 5.2). This outcome is supported by the insignificant t-statistics of the individual odds. Hence, the Bond yield changes cannot explain the RS Copula regime probabilities. Positive as well as negative yield changes occur during both dependence regimes. Therefore, I conclude that the occurrence of the high dependence regime is not directly linked to increasing or decreasing Bond yields. This phenomenon is well observed in the data. In 2009, the Italian and UK Bond yields increased dramatically, but simultaneously the RS Copulas indicate a shift to the low dependence regimes.

Table 5.1 – G7 Bond yields Volatility Impact on High Dependence Regimes. I examine the impact of the G7 Bond yield volatilities on the high dependence regimes, filtered from the RS Copulas, via logistic regression techniques. The table presents the logistic regression odds and the according t-statistics in brackets. Obs indicates the number of observations and McF-R^2 is McFadden's pseudo-R^2. GA|GA is a Gaussian|Gaussian RS Copula. GA|St is a Gaussian|Student's-t RS Copula. GA|CV is a Gaussian|Canonical-Vine RS Copula. GA|M is a Gaussian|Mixture RS Copula. St|St is a Students't-t|Student's-t RS Copula. St|CV is a Student's-t|Canonical-Vine RS Copula. St|M is a Student's-t|Mixture Copula. The multivariate Mixture Copula consists of one Gaussian, one Clayton and one Gumbel Copulas.

	GA|GA	GA|St	GA|CV	GA|M	St|St	St|CV	St|M
Constant	2.629	2.190	1.087	2.092	2.496	-0.252	2.531
	(5.43)	(4.98)	(2.79)	(4.75)	(5.39)	(0.60)	(5.57)
Germany	0.427	0.685	0.552	0.773	0.529	0.560	0.553
	(1.42)	(2.49)	(2.32)	(2.82)	(1.83)	(2.26)	(1.96)
Italy	-1.973	-1.556	-1.238	-1.399	-1.918	-0.627	-1.912
	(6.47)	(5.72)	(5.08)	(5.17)	(6.59)	(2.36)	(6.69)
Canada	-1.713	-1.501	-1.292	-1.480	-1.644	-0.941	-1.515
	(7.55)	(7.43)	(7.18)	(7.32)	(7.66)	(4.87)	(7.32)
UK	-2.065	-1.824	-1.682	-1.907	-2.037	-2.039	-1.910
	(8.60)	(8.39)	(8.44)	(8.67)	(8.82)	(8.94)	(8.53)
France	2.851	2.206	2.619	2.042	2.865	2.322	2.623
	(7.14)	(6.14)	(8.09)	(5.71)	(7.51)	(6.66)	(7.03)
Japan	0.413	0.350	0.304	0.347	0.397	0.235	0.349
	(8.60)	(8.20)	(8.48)	(8.29)	(8.62)	(6.76)	(8.01)
USA	0.535	0.397	-0.011	0.394	0.409	0.052	0.408
	(3.51)	(2.91)	(0.10)	(2.93)	(2.84)	(0.45)	(2.92)
Obs.	987	987	987	987	987	987	987
McF-R^2	0.401	0.372	0.249	0.365	0.397	0.237	0.394

Due to their ability to adjust their parameters to each data point, Dynamic Copulas are more flexible than RS Copulas and hence contain more information about the interactions of dependence structures and volatilities. I examine the linkages of the Dynamic Student's-t and Gumbel Copula parameters with the according volatility levels for two reasons. First, within their families both Copulas reveal the best fits. Second, both Copula structures differ significantly. The Dynamic Student's-t skeleton captures the dependencies of the G7 Bond yields via 21 dynamic correlation coefficients and one static degree of freedom. Therefore, I calculate the comovement intensities of the 21 Copula parameters and their according 21 Bond yield volatility levels

(Equation 5.3). Each of the 21 volatility indices contains two equally weighted volatility series whose dependence is captured via the appropriate Copula parameter. The first graph in figure 5.1 presents the correlation time-paths of the Dynamic Student's-t Copula parameters with their according volatility levels. In some cases, the equally weighted volatilities of two Bond yield indices increase dramatically but their according Copula parameter indicates no tightening dependence. Nevertheless, the Copula parameters are correlated to their according volatility levels by 0.22, on average. Thus, rising volatilities tighten the dependencies. In contrast, the Dynamic Gumbel Copula quantifies the dependencies of the G7 Bond yields via a single parameter. Therefore, I compute the comovement of this parameter and the 7 equally weighted Bond yield volatilities (Equation 5.3). Similarly to the Student's-t parameters, the Gumbel parameter and the equally weighted univariate volatilities are correlated by about 0.2. The bottom graph in figure 5.1 shows the time paths of the Dynamic Gumbel parameter and the joint volatility series. I conclude from the conducted examinations that volatility accession tightens the comovements of the G7 Bond yields and intensifies right tail dependence.

Table 5.2 – G7 Bond yields Impact on High Dependence Regimes. I examine the impact of the G7 Bond yield changes on the high dependence regimes, filtered from the RS Copulas, via logistic regression techniques. The table presents the logistic regression odds and the according t-statistics in brackets. Obs indicates the number of observations and McF-R^2 is McFadden's pseudo-R^2. GA|GA is a Gaussian|Gaussian RS Copula. GA|St is a Gaussian|Student's-t RS Copula. GA|CV is a Gaussian|Canonical-Vine RS Copula. GA|M is a Gaussian|Mixture RS Copula. St|St is a Students't-t|Student's-t RS Copula. St|CV is a Student's-t|Canonical-Vine RS Copula. St|M is a Student's-t|Mixture Copula. The multivariate Mixture Copula consists of one Gaussian, one Clayton and one Gumbel Copulas.

	GA|GA	GA|St	GA|CV	GA|M	St|St	St|CV	St|M
Constant	-0.110	-0.107	-0.376	-0.174	-0.085	-1.050	-0.106
	(1.73)	(1.74)	(6.53)	(2.83)	(1.37)	(17.31)	(1.71)
Germany	-1.926	-2.566	-0.091	-2.702	-1.406	-1.514	-2.168
	(0.25)	(0.34)	(0.01)	(0.36)	(0.18)	(0.20)	(0.28)
Italy	7.241	5.681	5.425	5.930	7.093	2.808	6.808
	(1.39)	(1.12)	(1.14)	(1.17)	(1.38)	(0.56)	(1.33)
Canada	-1.064	-0.879	3.587	-0.977	-1.252	3.871	-1.520
	(0.29)	(0.25)	(1.07)	(0.28)	(0.35)	(1.10)	(0.43)
UK	2.464	2.959	2.483	2.957	2.016	2.392	2.169
	(0.62)	(0.77)	(0.69)	(0.77)	(0.52)	(0.62)	(0.56)
France	-1.618	-0.480	0.348	-0.500	-1.081	-0.032	-1.036
	(0.21)	(0.06)	(0.05)	(0.07)	(0.14)	(0.00)	(0.14)
Japan	0.371	0.210	-0.031	0.094	0.314	-0.096	-0.013
	(0.28)	(0.16)	(0.03)	(0.07)	(0.24)	(0.08)	(0.01)
USA	-1.540	-1.562	-2.818	-1.374	-1.668	-2.284	-1.167
	(0.46)	(0.48)	(0.93)	(0.43)	(0.51)	(0.71)	(0.36)
Obs.	987	987	987	987	987	987	987
McF-R^2	0.138	0.144	0.219	0.158	0.136	0.352	0.141

Figure 5.1 – G7 Bond yields. The first graphic illustrates the correlations between the Dynamic Student's-t correlation coefficients and their according equally weighted Bond yield volatility levels (bars). The second graphic illustrates the correlations between the Dynamic Student's-t correlation coefficients and their according equally weighted Bond yields (bars). Each correlation coefficient captures the dependence of two assets. The 7 examined indices result 21 possible combinations and 21 correlation coefficients. The dashed line shows the median correlations. The third graph presents the equally weighted Bond yield changes containing all 7 Bond yield indices (dashed line), the according equally weighted volatility level (dotted line) and the time path of the according Dynamic Gumbel Copula Parameter (solid line). The equally weighted volatility level is rescaled by factor 20 for the graphical presentation.

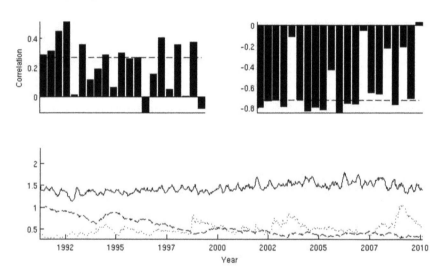

Further, I examine the interaction of the Dynamic Copula parameters with the Bond yields. Again, I focus on the Student's-t and Gumbel skeletons because they show the best adaptation to the data within their families. The Student's-t Copula contains a correlation matrix to capture the dependence structure of the data. Hence, there are 21 Copula coefficients to measure the G7 Bond yield interactions. I compute the associated 21 equally weighted and normed yields. Finally, I estimate the linear correlations of the equally weighted yields with their according Copula parameters (Equation 5.3). This procedure measures the comovement intensities between the yield drifts and the Copula parameters. The second graph of figure 5.1 presents the results graphically. The median correlation is about -0.73, indicating tightening correlations during negative yield drifts. This result contradicts previous findings which state right tail dependent Bond yields.

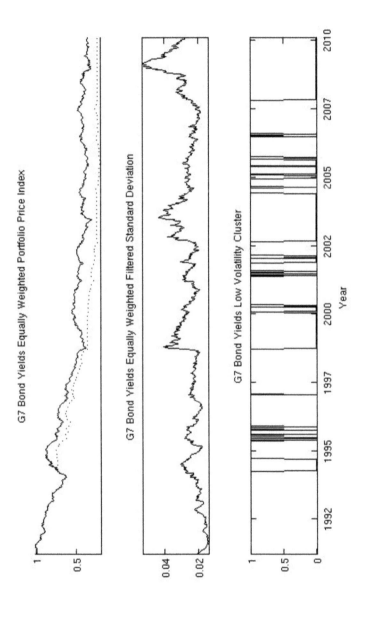

Figure 5.2 – G7 Bond yields. The top graph presents the index of the equally weighted yield changes (solid line) and the according index of yield changes during the low volatility cluster (dashed line). The second graph presents the equally weighted filtered standard deviation. In the third graph, 1 indicates the occurrence of the low volatility cluster and 0 indicates the occurrence of the high volatility cluster.

A more detailed examination of the Bond yields and their according Dynamic Student's-t Copula parameters identifies the cause for this phenomenon. The G7 Bond yields constantly decrease during the observation period and the Euro introduction severely tightens the dependencies. Hence, the G7 Bond yields are negatively correlated with their according Student's-t Copula parameters. Additionally, I analyze the interaction of the equally weighted and normed yields with the Dynamic Gumbel parameter (Equation 5.2). The bottom graph in figure 5.1 shows their time paths. The Gumbel Copula captures the dependence structure of all 7 Bond yields via a single parameter and therefore PP comprises all 7 Bond yield series. The Dynamic Gumbel parameter and the average yields are correlated by -0.57. Again, the negative correlation is due to permanently decreasing Bond yields whereas the Dynamic Gumbel parameter detects intensifying right tail dependence after the Euro introduction in 1999. The existence of right tail dependence is supported by the superior loglikelihood and BIC values of the Dynamic Gumbel over the Dynamic Clayton Copula. Nevertheless, section 4.5 shows that both Copulas' parameters insinuate decreasing dependencies during economic recessions among the G7 Bonds. This clearly contradicts the hypothesis of strict Bond yield comovements during economic turmoil. In contrast, those results suggest that fundamentals play a tremendous role for Bond valuations. A practical example are the turbulences at the European Bond markets in 2009. Within the G7 countries, the Italian and the UK Bond yields rose dramatically due to concerns on their liquidities and immense debt levels. Although Germany is part of the European Union, its Bond yield dropped at the same time. The individual behavior of the Bond yields and their reduced comovement intensities during 2009 demonstrate the significant influence of fundamentals.

Finally, I examine the interaction of the Bond yields and their according volatility levels. Empirical research provides evidence for the existence of volatility clusters (Chapter 2). Therefore, I utilize the K-Means algorithm to cluster the filtered Bond volatilities into one low and one high volatility categories. The mean yield change of the equally weighted time series is about 0.0012 during the high volatility cluster, -0.0025 in the low volatility cluster and -0.0011 for the complete sample. This outcome establishes a positive relation between volatility and Bond yields. Figure 5.2 supports this conclusion graphically. The third graph presents the low volatility cluster. The first graph shows the equally weighted Bond yields during the low volatility cluster (dotted line) and the equally weighted yield observations of the complete dataset (solid line). To confirm the results of the conducted analyses, I divide the univariate volatility levels into two clusters and investigate their means. Again, positive yield changes are observed during the high volatility cluster and negative yield changes during the low volatility cluster. The only exception is the Italian Bond yield series (Appendix B.1). Therefore, I conclude that dropping Bond prices are more likely during the high volatility cluster.

The conducted analyses on the interaction of dependence, volatilities and yields disclose three important features of the G7 Bond yield dataset. First, there is no direct linkage between the regimes of the RS Copulas and the univariate Bond yield volatility levels or the univariate yield drifts. Second, the Dynamic Copula parameters are positively correlated with the according Bond yield volatility levels and oppositely correlated with the respective yield series. This indicates tighter dependencies during volatile phases. Third, Bond yields increase during the high volatility cluster, on average. Hence, high volatility levels are an indicator of Bond market drops.

5.2 Stocks

This section analyzes the interaction of the G7 Stocks indices with the time-paths of the RS and the Dynamic Copula parameters. At first, I focus on the RS Copulas and apply standard logistic regression technique to identify linkages between the high dependence regime probabilities and the univariate filtered volatility levels. The results of this analysis are presented in table 5.3. In this table only the last two RS Copulas containing a Student's-t denote significant McFadden pseudo R^2s. This result is a first indicator that volatility cannot explain the time path of the high dependence regime. A more detailed examination of the regression odds supports this first impression. Although the table presents odds instead of transformed logits, their signs can be interpreted directly. If there was a simple and generally valid rule for the interaction of the univariate volatility levels and the dependence structure, all odds would reveal the same sign. This is not the case. Instead, the Italian, French and Canadian coefficients insinuate negative impacts while the Japanese, UK and USA coefficients suggest positive impacts. Therefore, I conclude that the univariate volatility levels are not the cause for the occurrence of the high dependence regime. This conclusion is supported by the observed volatility levels during the high and low dependence regimes. The average volatility during the high dependence regimes is about 0.028 and about 0.027 during the low dependence regimes.

Table 5.3 – G7 Stocks Volatility Impact on High Dependence Regimes. I examine the impact of the G7 Stock volatilities on the high dependence regimes, filtered from the RS Copulas, via logistic regression techniques. The table presents the logistic regression odds and the according t-statistics in brackets. Obs indicates the number of observations and McF-R^2 is McFadden's pseudo-R^2. GA|GA is a Gaussian|Gaussian RS Copula. GA|St is a Gaussian|Student's-t RS Copula. GA|CV is a Gaussian|Canonical-Vine RS Copula. GA|M is a Gaussian|Mixture RS Copula. St|St is a Students't-t|Student's-t RS Copula. St|CV is a Student's-t|Canonical-Vine RS Copula. St|M is a Student's-t|Mixture Copula. The multivariate Mixture Copula consists of one Gaussian, one Clayton and one Gumbel Copulas.

	GA|GA	GA|St	GA|CV	GA|M	St|St	St|CV	St|M
Constant	0.211	0.300	1.263	0.113	0.217	1.313	0.388
	(0.62)	(0.88)	(3.20)	(0.33)	(0.64)	(1.24)	(0.81)
Germany	-0.078	-0.090	0.891	-0.113	-0.098	1.048	0.887
	(0.32)	(0.37)	(3.04)	(0.46)	(0.40)	(1.49)	(2.75)
Italy	-0.494	-0.502	-0.622	-0.505	-0.502	-0.793	-0.869
	(3.30)	(3.35)	(3.90)	(3.33)	(3.33)	(2.55)	(5.15)
Canada	-0.210	-0.228	-0.618	-0.152	-0.204	-0.454	-0.319
	(1.36)	(1.48)	(3.61)	(0.98)	(1.32)	(1.20)	(1.69)
UK	0.689	0.697	1.327	0.677	0.670	0.969	1.392
	(3.65)	(3.68)	(5.67)	(3.61)	(3.56)	(1.64)	(5.01)
France	-0.074	-0.005	-1.200	-0.036	-0.015	-0.596	-0.859
	(0.09)	(0.02)	(3.57)	(0.13)	(0.05)	(0.72)	(2.26)
Japan	0.127	0.114	0.208	0.119	0.119	0.639	0.367
	(0.77)	(0.69)	(1.10)	(0.72)	(0.72)	(1.24)	(1.61)
USA	0.349	0.351	0.160	0.387	0.384	-0.052	0.084
	(1.83)	(1.84)	(0.73)	(2.02)	(2.01)	(0.10)	(0.34)
Obs.	629	629	629	629	629	629	629
McF-R^2	0.147	0.116	0.200	0.166	0.140	0.350	0.252

Further, I analyze the impacts of the univariate returns on the high dependence regime probabilities via logistic regression technique. Again, the McFadden pseudo-R^2s result almost no significant explanations except the RS Copulas containing a Student's-t and a Canonical-Vine or a Mixture. However, their McFadden R^2s are not meaningful because both RS Copulas remain almost constantly in the high dependence regime (Figure 4.1). A closer examination of the odds supports the conclusion of no explanatory power. The odds for Canada and France are negative while those for the UK, Japan and Germany are positive, regardless of the RS Copula model. Although returns can turn negative as well as positive, I would expect unique odd signs if the returns were the regime drivers. This is not the case and the McFadden pseudo-R^2s are insignificant. I conclude that negative as well as positive returns of any magnitude occur regardless of the dominant dependence regime. Nevertheless, the average annualized returns during the low dependence regimes are about 0.036 but -0.004 during the high dependence regimes.

Additionally, I analyze the interaction of the Dynamic Copula parameters with the univariate volatilities. Therefore, I calculate the correlations of the equally weighted volatility levels with their according Copula parameters (Equation 5.3). Figure 5.3 presents the results of this analysis for the Dynamic Student's-t and Clayton Copulas. I choose to present those two Copulas for two reasons. First, they show the best fits within their families (Section 4.5). Second, they differ significantly with respect to their structures. The Student's-t Copula contains a correlation matrix and each coefficient represents the dependence of two indices. Tail dependence in the dataset is captured via the Student's-t Copula's degree-of-freedom. In case of the G7 Stocks dataset, this results 21 correlation coefficients. Each of the according 21 volatility indices contains the appropriate 2 volatility series (Equation 5.3). The Dynamic Student's-t Copula parameters and their according volatility levels are positively correlated (first graph of Figure 5.3). The median correlation is about 0.4 indicating tightening Stock market dependencies as volatility increases. In contrast, the Dynamic Clayton Copula captures the dependence structure of all 7 indices via a single parameter. Therefore, I calculate the equally weighted volatility index, comprising the 7 univariate volatilities (Equation 5.3). Measuring the comovements of the Copula parameter with the volatility index insinuates strong comovements ($\rho^{(\sigma)} = 0.25$). The time paths of the joint volatilities and the Clayton parameter support this result graphically (Figure 5.3).

Table 5.4 – G7 Stocks Return Impact on High Dependence Regimes. I examine the impact of the G7 Stock returns on the high dependence regimes, filtered from the RS Copulas, via logistic regression techniques. The table presents the logistic regression odds and the according t-statistics in brackets. Obs indicates the number of observations and McF-R^2 is McFadden's pseudo-R^2. GA|GA is a Gaussian|Gaussian RS Copula. GA|St is a Gaussian|Student's-t RS Copula. GA|CV is a Gaussian|Canonical-Vine RS Copula. GA|M is a Gaussian|Mixture RS Copula. St|St is a Students't-t|Student's-t RS Copula. St|CV is a Student's-t|Canonical-Vine RS Copula. St|M is a Student's-t|Mixture Copula. The multivariate Mixture Copula consists of one Gaussian, one Clayton and one Gumbel Copulas.

	GA|GA	GA|St	GA|CV	GA|M	St|St	St|CV	St|M
Constant	0.661	0.686	1.269	0.565	0.634	3.482	1.799
	(0.21)	(0.30)	(1.26)	(0.11)	(0.22)	(1.31)	(17.60)
Germany	4.640	4.545	3.786	5.531	4.923	6.334	0.658
	(0.08)	(0.09)	(0.89)	(0.11)	(0.10)	(1.05)	(0.09)
Italy	0.189	0.068	-5.074	0.107	-0.133	-32.753	-11.887
	(0.49)	(0.50)	(0.62)	(0.50)	(0.50)	(0.79)	(1.79)
Canada	-0.539	-0.456	1.237	-0.827	-0.582	-12.530	-7.596
	(0.21)	(0.23)	(0.62)	(0.15)	(0.20)	(0.45)	(1.31)
UK	8.661	8.766	7.267	8.621	8.676	-9.602	14.234
	(0.69)	(0.70)	(1.33)	(0.68)	(0.67)	(0.97)	(1.71)
France	-12.660	-12.756	-7.795	-12.834	-12.695	17.594	-6.039
	(0.02)	(0.01)	(1.20)	(0.04)	(0.02)	(0.60)	(0.65)
Japan	0.022	0.105	3.041	-0.141	0.006	11.779	2.083
	(0.13)	(0.11)	(0.21)	(0.12)	(0.12)	(0.64)	(0.55)
USA	-0.055	0.039	-2.882	-0.192	0.085	8.981	2.924
	(0.35)	(0.35)	(0.16)	(0.39)	(0.38)	(0.05)	(0.43)
Obs.	629	629	629	629	629	629	629
McF-R^2	0.002	0.003	0.182	0.007	0.002	0.644	0.375

Figure 5.3 – G7 Stocks. The first graphic illustrates the correlations between the Dynamic Student's-t correlation coefficients and their according equally weighted volatility levels (bars). The second graphic illustrates the correlations between the Dynamic Student's-t correlation coefficients and their according equally weighted price indices (bars). Each correlation coefficient captures the dependence of two assets. The 7 examined indices result 21 possible combinations and 21 correlation coefficients. The dashed line shows the median correlations. The third graph presents the equally weighted Stocks price index containing all 7 Stock indices (dashed line), the equally weighted volatility level of all 7 Stock indices (dotted line) and the time path of the according Dynamic Clayton Copula Parameter (solid line). The equally weighted volatility level is rescaled by factor 20 for the graphical presentation.

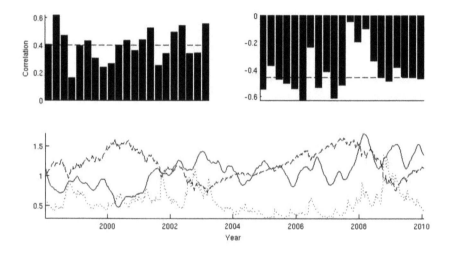

Next, I turn to the 21 correlation coefficients which represent the comovement intensities of the Copula coefficients and the respective return series. Due to the fact that the Copula parameters follow time paths, I transform the returns into standardized price indices via equation 5.2. The second graph of figure 5.3 presents the correlations of the Dynamic Student's-t Copula parameters and their according return series. The median correlation is about -0.45. This result proves the assumption of tightening Stock market dependencies during downturn phases. In contrast, the Dynamic Clayton captures the dependence structure of all 7 return series via a single parameter. Therefore, the correlation of the Copula parameter time path and the equally weighted return index, containing all 7 return series, is calculated. The third graph in figure 5.3 presents the time paths of the Dynamic Clayton parameter and the equally weighted returns. They are correlated by -0.42, denoting tightening dependence of Stock markets during downturn phases. The Clayton Copula's left tail dependence feature amplifies the probability of joint

82

market drops during downturn markets. In regards to risk avoidance, the conducted analyses assess the inefficiency of global diversification among Stock markets. In addition, the results emphasize the importance of a model that accounts for left tail dependence and distinct changes of the dependence intensities. The application of standard linear correlation matrices to capture Stock market dependencies neglects those features and definitely underestimates comovements during downturn phases. Therefore, its application is a tremendous hazard to financial wealth.

In the same manner, I examine the Dynamic Gaussian, Gumbel and Mixture Copulas. Similarly to the Student's-t Copula, the Gaussian Copula contains a correlation matrix which captures the dependencies of the return series. Therefore, the relations of both Copulas' parameters to the underlying return series and according volatility levels are almost identical. However, the features of the Archimedian Copulas differ significantly (Section 3.2.1). In contrast to the Clayton, the Gumbel Copula focuses on right tail dependence. This feature is not observed in the Stocks dataset and hence the correlation of its parameter and the equally weighted return index is only -0.32. Nevertheless, the negative relation indicates increasing dependence during downturn markets. The Mixture Copula parameters follow similar patterns as their individual components, but at higher intensities. Hence, their relations to the underlying return series and volatility levels are very similar and I abdicate the presentation of those results.

Finally, I analyze the interactions of the univariate returns and the univariate volatilities. Is there a simple relation between Stock market returns and their according volatility levels? I find a linear correlation coefficient of -0.42 between the equally weighted price indices and the equally weighted filtered volatility levels. Additionally, volatility clusters are an empirically observed and well documented feature (Section 2.1). Therefore, I utilize the K-Means clustering technique to divide the filtered volatilities into two clusters. The third graph in figure 5.4 presents the high and low volatility clusters filtered from the K-Means algorithm. The graph supports the theory of volatility clusters by fairly stable cluster dominances (low cluster switching probabilities). Finally, I calculate the mean returns of any equally weighted G7 Stocks portfolio during the low and the high volatility clusters. The low volatility cluster reveals an annualized mean return of 0.064. Computing a price index from those returns results the dashed line in the first graph of figure 5.4. In contrast, the annualized mean return during the high volatility cluster is about -0.052. In order to validate this finding, I conduct the same analysis for the single return series. However, there is no simple relation between the sign of the univariate returns and the univariate volatility levels (Appendix B.2).

83

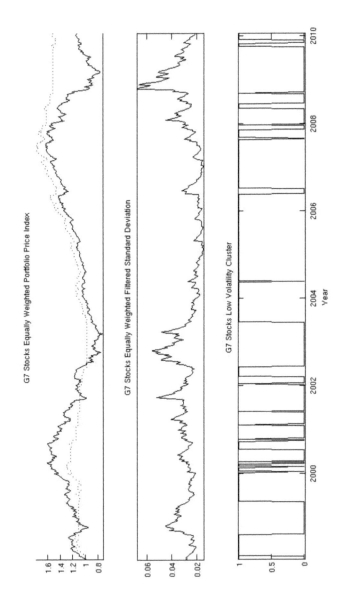

Figure 5.4 – G7 Stocks. The top graph presents the equally weighted returns index (solid line) and the according index of the equally weighted returns during the low volatility cluster (dashed line). The second graph presents the equally weighted filtered standard deviation. In the third graph, 1 indicates the occurrence of the low volatility cluster and 0 indicates the occurrence of the high volatility cluster.

The conducted analyses on the interaction of dependence, volatilities and returns disclose three important features of the G7 Stocks dataset. First, there is no direct linkage between the regimes of the RS Copulas and the univariate return trends or the univariate volatility levels. Second, the Dynamic Copula parameters are significantly oppositely correlated with the Stock prices. This indicates loosening dependencies during upturn and tightening dependencies during downturn Stock markets. I also find evidence that the Dynamic Copula parameters are positively correlated with the univariate volatility levels. This indicates tighter dependencies during volatile phases what diminishes diversification effects when they are needed the most. Third, I cannot identify a clear relation between the signs of the univariate Stock market returns and their volatility levels. Hence, high volatility levels are not an indicator of Stock market drops or vice versa.

5.3 Multi Asset Classes

This section analyzes the time paths of the dependencies in the Multi Asset Classes dataset. I utilize the same techniques as in the previous sections. Again, I first focus on the interaction of the dependence regimes, filtered from the RS Copulas, and the univariate volatility levels. Table 5.5 presents the results of the logistic regression analysis. The interpretation of the results follows the same logic as in the previous sections. If volatility had a significant impact on the regime probabilities, the signs of the odds would be identical. This theory is not supported by the regression outcome. Regardless of the RS Copula type, the odds of the Bond and exchange rate volatilities are positive whereas those of the Stocks and commodities are negative. Although the single odds are significant, there is no unique relation between the univariate volatility levels and the dependence regime. This conclusion is supported by the insignificant McFadden pseudo R^2s.

Further, I examine whether positive or negative returns significantly impact the occurrence of the high dependence regimes via logistic regressions (Table 5.6). The interpretation of the results is more complicated as the high dependence regime includes negative correlation coefficients (Table 4.11). Hence, the high dependence regime could be driven by positive returns of one index and negative returns of another index. Regardless of the RS Copula, the odds suggest this behavior and their signs are in line with the correlation coefficients of the high dependence regimes. However, the McFadden pseudo R^2s indicate no significant explanatory power.

Table 5.5 – Multi Asset Classes Volatility Impact on High Dependence Regimes. I examine the impact of the Multi Asset Classes volatilities on the high dependence regimes, filtered from the RS Copulas, via logistic regression techniques. The table presents the logistic regression odds and the according t-statistics in brackets. Obs indicates the number of observations and McF-R^2 is McFadden's pseudo-R^2. GA|GA is a Gaussian|Gaussian RS Copula. GA|St is a Gaussian|Student's-t RS Copula. GA|CV is a Gaussian|Canonical-Vine RS Copula. GA|M is a Gaussian|Mixture RS Copula. St|St is a Students't-t|Student's-t RS Copula. St|CV is a Student's-t|Canonical-Vine RS Copula. St|M is a Student's-t|Mixture Copula. The multivariate Mixture Copula consists of one Gaussian, one Clayton and one Gumbel Copulas.

	GA|GA	GA|St	GA|CV	GA|M	St|St	St|CV	St|M
Constant	0.101	0.089	0.110	0.202	0.103	0.132	0.201
	(0.24)	(0.21)	(0.27)	(0.49)	(0.25)	(0.32)	(0.49)
REX10Y	2.846	2.797	2.832	2.367	2.852	2.774	2.374
	(7.44)	(7.43)	(7.46)	(6.64)	(7.46)	(7.51)	(6.66)
DAX	-0.939	-0.964	-0.964	-0.999	-0.942	-1.000	-0.998
	(11.30)	(11.53)	(11.52)	(11.82)	(11.32)	(11.92)	(11.81)
GOLD	-1.060	-1.095	-1.041	-1.141	-1.061	-1.039	-1.141
	(6.66)	(6.90)	(6.57)	(7.21)	(6.67)	(6.66)	(7.20)
USD/EUR	1.834	1.956	1.853	2.228	1.834	1.916	2.223
	(6.38)	(6.82)	(6.46)	(7.74)	(6.39)	(6.77)	(7.72)
Obs.	1100	1100	1100	1100	1100	1100	1100
McF-R^2	0.127	0.131	0.125	0.098	0.126	0.121	0.099

I also examine the relation of the Dynamic Copula parameters and the univariate return series. I utilize equation 5.2 to analyze the interactions of the Dynamic Copula parameters with the univariate returns and equation 5.3 to analyze the interactions of the Dynamic Copula parameters with the univariate volatility levels. The Copula estimations show that the Archimedian family represents the dependence structure of the Multi Asset Classes data poorly (Section 4.5). A closer look at the univariate volatility levels reveals no stable comovements (Appendix A.3), what results significant swings in their dependence structures (Section 4.5). The Elliptical models even suggest negative dependencies for some assets. In contrast to the Archimedian skeletons, the Elliptical Copulas are able to capture negative dependencies and offer multiple parameters to quantify the dependence structure. Consequently, the Dynamic Student's-t Copula adapts most precisely to the data and I focus on the interaction of its parameters with the according univariate volatilities and returns.

In the following, I examine the interaction of the Dynamic Student's-t Copula parameters and their according univariate volatilities via equation 5.3. Interestingly, five out of the six computed correlations are negative, indicating a reduction of the dependence as the according joint volatility levels increase. A more accurate examination shows that only three combinations exhibit significant negative correlations of their joint volatility levels with their respective Copula parameters. This is the case for the REX10Y|DAX, the DAX|GOLD and the GOLD|USD/EUR combinations ($\rho_{R|D}^{(\sigma)} = -0.41$, $\rho_{D|G}^{(\sigma)} = -0.31$, $\rho_{G|EU}^{(\sigma)} = -0.16$). The REX10Y|GOLD and DAX|USD/EUR combinations disclose only weak correlations of their equally weighted volatilities with their appendant Copula parameters ($\rho_{R|G}^{(\sigma)} = -0.06$, $\rho_{D|EU}^{(\sigma)} = -0.11$). Only the REX10Y|USD/EUR combination features a positive relation between volatility and dependence ($\rho_{R|G}^{(\sigma)} = 0.17$). Figure 5.5 supports those findings graphically. Hence, diversification across multiple asset classes reduces the portfolio volatility.

Table 5.6 – Multi Asset Classes Return Impact on High Dependence Regimes. I examine the impact of the Multi Asset Classes returns on the high dependence regimes, filtered from the RS Copulas, via logistic regression techniques. The table presents the logistic regression odds and the according t-statistics in brackets. Obs indicates the number of observations and McF-R^2 is McFadden's pseudo-R^2. GA|GA is a Gaussian|Gaussian RS Copula. GA|St is a Gaussian|Student's-t RS Copula. GA|CV is a Gaussian|Canonical-Vine RS Copula. GA|M is a Gaussian|Mixture RS Copula. St|St is a Students't-t|Student's-t RS Copula. St|CV is a Student's-t|Canonical-Vine RS Copula. St|M is a Student's-t|Mixture Copula. The multivariate Mixture Copula consists of one Gaussian, one Clayton and one Gumbel Copulas.

	GA|GA	GA|St	GA|CV	GA|M	St|St	St|CV	St|M
Constant	-0.032	-0.050	-0.038	-0.082	-0.035	-0.068	-0.081
	(0.54)	(0.85)	(0.63)	(1.38)	(0.58)	(1.15)	(1.37)
REX10Y	10.284	10.132	10.685	11.225	10.255	10.878	11.227
	(1.43)	(1.41)	(1.49)	(1.57)	(1.43)	(1.53)	(1.57)
DAX	1.799	1.944	1.935	2.577	1.794	2.147	2.562
	(0.99)	(1.07)	(1.07)	(1.42)	(0.99)	(1.19)	(1.41)
GOLD	-6.793	-6.537	-6.725	-6.664	-6.780	-6.577	-6.681
	(2.28)	(2.20)	(2.26)	(2.25)	(2.27)	(2.24)	(2.25)
USD/EUR	10.776	10.560	10.708	11.650	10.768	11.150	11.629
	(2.49)	(2.45)	(2.48)	(2.71)	(2.49)	(2.61)	(2.70)
Obs.	1100	1100	1100	1100	1100	1100	1100
McF-R^2	0.126	0.130	0.127	0.138	0.126	0.136	0.138

Next, I calculate the correlations of the Dynamic Student's-t Copula parameters with their according price series via equation 5.2. This results correlations ranging from -0.73 to 0.28. More particularly, I find two return series combinations whose joint price indices are negatively correlated to their respective Copula parameters. This is the case for the REX10Y|DAX and the GOLD|USD/EUR combinations ($\rho_{R|D}^{(PP)} = -0.73$, $\rho_{G|EU}^{(PP)} = -0.65$). However, figure 5.5 shows that during the two drops of the REX10Y|DAX price index the according Copula parameter indicates decreasing dependence. This feature clearly contradicts $\rho_{R|D}^{(PP)}$ and offers great potential to reduce financial losses. In contrast, $\rho_{G|EU}^{(PP)}$ is supported by the graphical analysis. The equally weighted REX10Y|GOLD and DAX|GOLD indices and their according Copula parameters are positively correlated ($\rho_{R|G}^{(PP)} = 0.28$, $\rho_{D|G}^{(PP)} = 0.21$). Again, the graphical analysis supports this result. In case of the REX10Y|USD/EUR and DAX|USD/EUR, the Copula parameters and the according equally weighted return indices are almost independent according to equation 5.2. Figure 5.5 supports this result, too. Overall, the relations of the equally weighted return series and their according Copula parameters do not indicate tightening dependencies during market downturns, except for the GOLD|USD/EUR combination. Hence, diversification among different asset classes offers protection against financial losses.

Finally, I examine the relation of the univariate Multi Asset Classes returns and their according volatilities. Therefore, I cluster the filtered volatilities into two regimes via the K-Means algorithm. The high and the low volatility clusters are presented in the third graph of figure 5.6. The graphic shows that high and low volatility levels occur in clusters with fairly low cluster switching probabilities. This finding is in line with other empirical works concerned with volatility clustering. Hence, I compute the mean returns of the equally weighted return series for the complete sample and for the high and low volatility phases. The outcome is presented graphically in the first graph of figure 5.6. Obviously, volatility does not cause negative returns. This finding holds true for the equally weighted as well as for the individual return indices (Appendix B.3). However, a comparison of the Sharpe ratios and the annualized returns of the equally weighted return indices shows that the high volatility cluster features the least favorable characteristics. The Sharpe ratio of the equally weighted return indices for the complete sample is 0.078 at an annualized return of 0.045. The Sharpe ratio of the equally weighted return indices for the low volatility cluster is 0.074 at an annualized return of 0.026. The Sharpe ratio of the equally weighted return indices for the high volatility cluster is 0.04 at an annualized return of 0.019.

The interactions of dependence, volatilities and returns in the Multi Asset Classes data exhibit several important characteristics. There is no clear relation between the RS Copula regimes and the univariate volatilities or returns. In contrast, I find negative relations between the Dynamic Copula parameter intensities and the univariate volatility levels. This indicates that the RS Copula is not flexible enough to capture the dependence structure precisely. It also reveals great diversification potential among different asset classes to reduce portfolio volatility levels. In addition, the Dynamic Copula parameters do not suggest tightening dependencies during downturn phases. In regards to loss probabilities and severities, portfolio diversification among several asset classes is definitely superior to global diversification within the same asset class. Last but not least, the univariate volatilities and returns exhibit neither positive nor negative

88

interactions. However, the analyses show that the low volatility clusters feature more attractive risk/return characteristics than the high volatility clusters. This holds true for any examined dataset.

Figure 5.5 – Multi Asset Classes Returns and Copula Parameters. Each graph presents three features concerning the two indices named in the titles: the equally weighted return index (dashed line); the equally weighted filtered volatilities (dotted line). They are rescaled for graphical purposes; the according correlation coefficient from the Dynamic Student's-t Copula (solid line). The figure covers the complete data sample from 02.Jan.1989 to 01.Feb.2010.

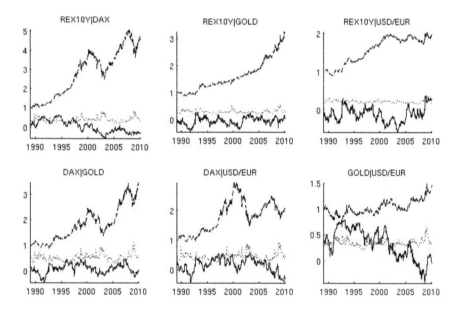

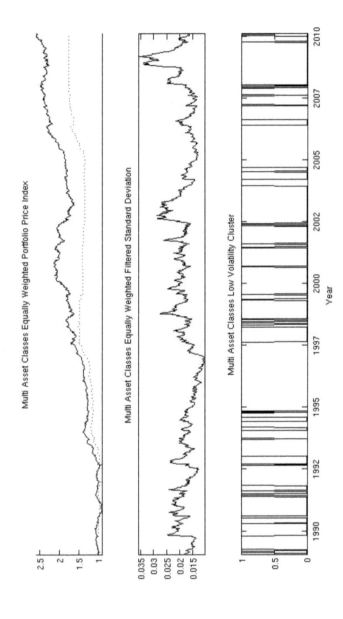

Figure 5.6 – Multi Asset Classes. The top graph presents the equally weighted returns index (solid line) and the according index of the returns during the low volatility cluster (dashed line). The second graph presents the equally weighted filtered standard deviation. In the third graph, 1 indicates the occurrence of the high volatility cluster and 0 indicates the occurrence of the low volatility cluster.

Chapter 6

Portfolio Risk Forecasting

Most investors hold a portfolio of multiple assets rather than a single security. Therefore, future portfolio risk plays a key role in finance. There are three common definitions of financial risks. Sharpe (1964) and Lintner (1965) utilize the covariance of the assets in their CAPM framework to define the portfolio risk. Hence, they assume normally distributed returns, an empirically rejected feature. An intuitively more appealing approach is to characterize risk as the shortfall probability beyond a threshold, Ξ. In more recent literature, this procedure is well known as Value-at-Risk (VaR). In regards to loss quantification, the VaR approach attained great popularity. Unfortunately, the VaR concept is incapable of handling losses that might occur beyond the indicated threshold amount. In contrast, the Conditional-Value-at-Risk (CVaR) explicitly accounts for losses beyond the threshold, Ξ, on the left distribution tail. The VaR_{SL} and $CVaR_{SL}$ values for a random vector A at any specified significance levels $SL \in [0, 1]$ with threshold Ξ are characterized as (Rockafellar and Uryasev (2002)):

$$VaR_{SL}(A) = max[\Xi \mid Pr\{A \leq \Xi\} \leq SL] \tag{6.1}$$

$$CVaR_{SL}(A) = E[A \mid A < VaR_{SL}(A)]. \tag{6.2}$$

Based on this risk definition, Roy (1952) enhances the Mean-Variance framework to a Mean-VaR framework. I adopt this risk definition and focus on forecasting joint distribution quantiles (VaR) and expected losses in case of VaR violations (CVaR), without the assumption of normally distributed returns. Consequently, three factors majorly impact the accuracy of the portfolio risk forecasts: the future dependence structure of the securities; the future univariate volatility forecasts; the univariate distribution shapes. The most common approximations of future dependencies are unconditional correlation matrices. Unfortunately, this procedure is very inaccurate because financial market interactions change over time. Therefore, I develop Copula skeletons which capture and forecast changes in the dependence structure (Sections 3.3, 3.4). In order to simultaneously account for shifts in the volatility and dependence structures, I combine the univariate GARCH and the multivariate Copula models. This enhances the accuracy of portfolio risk predictions.

According to the Sklar theorem (1959), Copulas are calibrated independently from the univariate models (Equation 3.1). In return, volatility is predicted by the univariate GARCH models for each time series, separately. This results univariate volatility forecasts which are unbiased by the Copula. Thereafter, the univariate volatility forecasts are nested via an arbitrarily chosen Copula function, resulting a multivariate distribution. Thus, nesting the same univariate forecasts via different Copulas results different multivariate distributions. The battery of GoF tests in section 4.2 depicts well calibrated univariate GARCH models what guarantees precise univariate volatility forecasts. Consequently, inaccuracies in the portfolio risk forecasts are solely caused by the utilized Copula functions. Therefore, the most accurate portfolio risk forecasts detect the Copula function which captures the multivariate dependence structure most precisely.

In order to detect the most precise Copula, I utilize this procedure for out-of-sample portfolio VaR and CVaR forecasts. I recalibrate the univariate models for each time period and the Copula models on a yearly basis during the backtest. Thereafter, the univariate volatilities $(\sigma_{t+1}, ..., \sigma_{t+n})$ and return drifts $(\mu_{t+1}, ..., \mu_{t+n})$ are forecasted for n periods. I simulate 50000 random variables from the selected Copula for each forecast period, $\mathbf{U}^{50000 \times d \times n} \sim U[0,1]$, which are transformed into standardized residuals, $\eta_{t+1}, ..., \eta_{t+n}$, via the univariate distribution functions (Sklar theorem (1959), Equation 3.1). Simulations from the RS and Dynamic Copulas vary in their dependence structure at each forecast period. Nesting the univariate volatility and return drift forecasts with the transformed Copula simulations at each forecast period results the return simulations $\mathbf{X}_{t+1}, ..., \mathbf{X}_{t+n}$ (Equation 2.7). Allocating the weighted return simulations along the second dimension generates 50000 possible portfolio return paths which define the n-step ahead portfolio distribution, F_{t+n}. The quantiles of F_{t+n} represent the n-step ahead portfolio VaR levels. This thesis is based on weekly data and I utilize the described method to calculate the one week ahead portfolio VaR and CVaR levels from F_{t+1}. A comparison of the realized portfolio returns and the predicted portfolio VaR and CVaR levels denotes the violation frequencies of the portfolio risk predictions (rel. Hit VaR, rel. Hit CVaR). The Kupiec test evaluates precise against imprecise VaR coverage (Kupiec (1995)). I also present the maximum predicted portfolio VaR level (Max. VaR), the minimum predicted portfolio VaR level (Min. VaR) and the maximum exceedance of the predicted portfolio VaRs and CVaRs (Max. VaR Excess, Max. CVaR Excess).

I apply the same risk forecasting procedure to three different datasets in order to examine the adaptability of the Copula skeletons to various asset classes. At first, I calculate quantile forecasts for the equally weighted G7 Bond yields portfolio. In contrast to investable assets, not a decrease but an increase of Bond yields is hazardous to investors. Therefore, the Copula models have to capture right tail dependencies accurately in order to model accurate joint distributions which define the portfolio risk forecasts. The economic interpretation of Bond yields is simple as they behave oppositely to Bond prices. The second portfolio contains the equally weighted G7 Stocks. Hence, the left tail of the joint distribution represents the portfolio risks and is the object of interest. The Copula models have to proof their abilities to capture left tail dependence. The third portfolio comprises equally weighted securities from multiple asset classes. This demonstrates the different Copulas' abilities to capture the dependence structures of realistic portfolios. Again, the left tail of the joint distribution represents the portfolio risks and hence the Copulas need to prove their abilities to quantify left tail dependencies, precisely. I construct equally weighted portfolios because this restricts the impact of all univariate models to the same magnitude. This amplifies the impact of the individual Copulas on the VaR and CVaR forecast accuracies.

6.1 Bond Yields Portfolio

Although Bond yield portfolios are not directly investable, their VaR and CVaR predictions are meaningful for two reasons. First, Bond yields behave oppositely to Bond prices. Second, the calculation of the quantiles at the 90%, 95% and 99% significance levels (SL) demonstrates each Copula's ability to capture right tail dependencies. In contrast, the VaR predictions of Stocks only and Multi Asset Classes portfolios require the Copulas to capture left tail dependencies. I utilize a four year timeframe (08.Feb.2006 to 03.Feb.2010) to examine the accuracies of the G7 Bond yield out-of-sample portfolio VaR and CVaR predictions.

Table 6.1 presents the backtest results based on the Static Copulas. The first line denotes the VaR hit ratios. According to this measure, the Gumbel, Gaussian, Student's-t and both Mixture Copulas perform similarly well. However, on the SL_{95} the Gumbel Copula is the best choice to measure the dependence of the Bond yield indices. This is due to its focus on right tail dependence which is a typical feature of Bond yields. The Kupiec tests suggest that most Static Copulas capture the dependencies accurately, resulting precise portfolio VaR forecasts, except for the Clayton and the Canonical-Vine Copulas. This does not surprise because both Copulas focus on left tail dependencies. However, the VaR hit ratios only exhibit the strike frequencies but do not provide information on the quantile violation depth. In regards to portfolio risk forecasting, the CVaR excess is one of the most significant measures as it represents realized losses beyond the expected loss. At the SL_{99}, the Gumbel, the Elliptical and the Mixture Copula CVaR predictions are not exceeded during the backtest. However, at the SL_{95} and the SL_{90} the Gumbel Copula based CVaR predictions are exceeded the least by 0.017 and 0.031, what illustrates the importance to account for right tail dependence among Bond yields. In case of VaR violations, the AAD CVaR reports the average absolute distance of the realized portfolio returns from the predicted portfolio CVaR levels. The AAD CVaRs for the Static Gumbel Copula are neglectable, what amplifies its ability to capture the dependence structure of Bond yields, accurately. Of course, the CVaR exceedances differ less at lower significance levels due to the decreasing importance of tail dependence. The Gumbel Copula focuses on right tail dependence and hence predicts the most distinct VaR and CVaR at the SL_{95} and the SL_{99}, followed by both Mixture Copulas which also explicitly account for right tail dependence. Considering the Copula models which are approved via the Kupiec tests, the variations of the maximum and minimum predicted VaR levels are neglectable at the SL_{95} and SL_{90}. Again, this is due to the decreasing importance of tail dependence for the portfolio VaR predictions at lower significance levels.

Next, I analyze the performance of the G7 Bond yield portfolio risk forecasts based on simulations from the RS Copulas. At the SL_{99}, the VaR hit ratios indicate precise portfolio quantile predictions (Table 6.2). This conclusion is supported by the according Kupiec test results. At the SL_{95} and SL_{90}, the VaR violation ratios are less precise, but they fulfill the Kupiec criteria. However, the Static and RS Copula based predictions reveal almost identical VaR violation ratios. This outcome rejects the assumption that the additional flexibility of the RS Copulas would improve the accuracy of the portfolio quantile forecasts.

Table 6.1 – Static Copula G7 Bond yields Equally Weighted Portfolio VaR and CVaR. I predict one-week VaR and CVaR at the 99%, 95% and 90% significance levels (*SL*). This table presents the relative violation frequencies for the VaR and CVaR predictions (rel. Hit VaR, rel. Hit CVaR) during the backtest. The Kupiec test evaluates the null hypothesis ($H_0 = 0$) of correct VaR coverage against imprecise VaR coverage ($H_0 = 1$) at the 95% significance level. The Max. VaR reports the maximum predicted VaR and the Min. VaR reports the minimum predicted VaR, for the backtest procedure. The Max. VaR (CVaR) Excess denotes the maximum exceedance of the VaR (CVaR) forecasts during the backtest. The average absolute distance of the realized returns from the predicted CVaR levels in case of VaR violations is denoted by AAD CVaR. F is a Frank Copula. GU is a Gumbel Copula. CL is a Clayton Copula. GA is a Gaussian Copula. St is a Student's-t Copula. Mix1 is a multivariate Mixture Copula which consists of one Gaussian, one Clayton and one Gumbel Copulas. CV is a Canonical-Vine Copula. Its pair-Copulas are presented in the parameter estimation section. Mix2 is a multivariate Mixture Copula which consists of one Student's-t, one Clayton and one Gumbel Copulas.

		F	GU	CL	GA	St	CV	Mix1	Mix2
rel. Hit VaR	SL_{99}	0.010	0.010	0.053	0.010	0.010	0.038	0.010	0.010
	SL_{95}	0.077	0.058	0.135	0.072	0.072	0.101	0.072	0.072
	SL_{90}	0.135	0.144	0.192	0.139	0.144	0.168	0.139	0.144
Kupiec Test	SL_{99}	0	0	1	0	0	1	0	0
	SL_{95}	0	0	1	0	0	1	0	0
	SL_{90}	0	0	1	0	0	1	0	0
Max. VaR	SL_{99}	0.095	0.128	0.076	0.111	0.113	0.089	0.115	0.115
	SL_{95}	0.073	0.077	0.057	0.074	0.074	0.063	0.073	0.073
	SL_{90}	0.057	0.055	0.046	0.057	0.056	0.051	0.056	0.055
Min. VaR	SL_{99}	0.030	0.041	0.024	0.033	0.034	0.026	0.034	0.035
	SL_{95}	0.021	0.023	0.016	0.021	0.021	0.018	0.021	0.021
	SL_{90}	0.016	0.015	0.013	0.015	0.015	0.014	0.015	0.015
Max. VaR Excess	SL_{99}	0.026	0.003	0.036	0.019	0.016	0.031	0.015	0.014
	SL_{95}	0.039	0.036	0.048	0.039	0.039	0.045	0.039	0.039
	SL_{90}	0.048	0.049	0.054	0.049	0.049	0.052	0.049	0.049
rel. Hit CVaR	SL_{99}	0.014	0.000	0.034	0.000	0.000	0.024	0.005	0.005
	SL_{95}	0.029	0.010	0.082	0.019	0.019	0.062	0.019	0.019
	SL_{90}	0.073	0.038	0.115	0.053	0.053	0.085	0.053	0.053
AAD CVaR	SL_{99}	0.000	0.000	0.000	0.000	0.000	0.000	0.000	0.000
	SL_{95}	0.001	0.001	0.001	0.001	0.001	0.001	0.001	0.001
	SL_{90}	0.001	0.001	0.002	0.001	0.001	0.002	0.001	0.001
Max. CVaR Excess	SL_{99}	0.024	0.000	0.031	0.000	0.000	0.027	0.002	0.002
	SL_{95}	0.032	0.017	0.042	0.024	0.024	0.038	0.025	0.025
	SL_{90}	0.042	0.031	0.047	0.035	0.035	0.045	0.035	0.035

Table 6.2 – Regime-Switch Copula G7 Bond yields Equally Weighted Portfolio VaR and CVaR. I predict one-week VaR and CVaR at the 99%, 95% and 90% significance levels (*SL*). This table presents the relative violation frequencies for the VaR and CVaR predictions (rel. Hit VaR, rel. Hit CVaR) during the backtest. The Kupiec test evaluates the null hypothesis ($H_0 = 0$) of correct VaR coverage against imprecise VaR coverage ($H_0 = 1$) at the 95% significance level. The Max. VaR reports the maximum predicted VaR and the Min. VaR reports the minimum predicted VaR, for the backtest procedure. The Max. VaR (CVaR) Excess denotes the maximum exceedance of the VaR (CVaR) forecasts during the backtest. The average absolute distance of the realized returns from the predicted CVaR levels in case of VaR violations is denoted by AAD CVaR. The RS Copulas are abbreviated: GA|GA is a Gaussian|Gaussian RS Copula. GA|St is a Gaussian|Student's-t RS Copula. GA|CV is a Gaussian|Canonical-Vine RS Copula. GA|M is a Gaussian|Mixture RS Copula. St|St is a Student's-t|Student's-t RS Copula. St|CV is a Student's-t|Canonical-Vine RS Copula. St|M is a Student's-t|Mixture RS Copula. The multivariate Mixture Copula consists of one Gaussian, one Clayton and one Gumbel Copulas.

		GA|GA	GA|St	GA|CV	GA|M	St|St	St|CV	St|M
rel. Hit VaR	SL_{99}	0.010	0.010	0.019	0.010	0.010	0.010	0.010
	SL_{95}	0.072	0.067	0.091	0.072	0.072	0.077	0.072
	SL_{90}	0.135	0.139	0.139	0.139	0.139	0.139	0.139
Kupiec Test	SL_{99}	0	0	0	0	0	0	0
	SL_{95}	0	0	1	0	0	0	0
	SL_{90}	0	0	0	0	0	0	0
Max. VaR	SL_{99}	0.102	0.106	0.098	0.106	0.104	0.111	0.105
	SL_{95}	0.068	0.070	0.064	0.070	0.069	0.073	0.070
	SL_{90}	0.053	0.053	0.048	0.053	0.053	0.055	0.053
Min. VaR	SL_{99}	0.034	0.034	0.027	0.035	0.036	0.028	0.036
	SL_{95}	0.022	0.022	0.019	0.022	0.022	0.020	0.022
	SL_{90}	0.016	0.016	0.014	0.016	0.016	0.015	0.016
Max. VaR Excess	SL_{99}	0.022	0.022	0.022	0.021	0.020	0.018	0.021
	SL_{95}	0.042	0.041	0.041	0.041	0.041	0.040	0.041
	SL_{90}	0.051	0.050	0.050	0.051	0.051	0.050	0.051
rel. Hit CVaR	SL_{99}	0.005	0.010	0.010	0.010	0.010	0.010	0.010
	SL_{95}	0.024	0.029	0.034	0.024	0.029	0.029	0.024
	SL_{90}	0.053	0.053	0.077	0.053	0.053	0.077	0.053
AAD CVaR	SL_{99}	0.000	0.000	0.000	0.000	0.000	0.000	0.000
	SL_{95}	0.001	0.001	0.001	0.001	0.001	0.001	0.001
	SL_{90}	0.001	0.001	0.001	0.001	0.001	0.001	0.001
Max. CVaR Excess	SL_{99}	0.011	0.011	0.013	0.010	0.011	0.010	0.010
	SL_{95}	0.030	0.030	0.030	0.029	0.030	0.030	0.029
	SL_{90}	0.038	0.038	0.039	0.038	0.038	0.039	0.038

Table 6.3 – Dynamic Copula G7 Bond yields Equally Weighted Portfolio VaR and CVaR. I predict one-week VaR and CVaR at the 99%, 95% and 90% significance levels (*SL*). This table presents the relative violation frequencies for the VaR and CVaR predictions (rel. Hit VaR, rel. Hit CVaR) during the backtest. The Kupiec test evaluates the null hypothesis ($H_0 = 0$) of correct VaR coverage against imprecise VaR coverage ($H_0 = 1$) at the 95% significance level. The Max. VaR reports the maximum predicted VaR and the Min. VaR reports the minimum predicted VaR, for the backtest procedure. The Max. VaR (CVaR) Excess denotes the maximum exceedance of the VaR (CVaR) forecasts during the backtest. The average absolute distance of the realized returns from the predicted CVaR levels in case of VaR violations is denoted by AAD CVaR. The Dynamic Copulas are abbreviated: GU is a Dynamic Gumbel Copula. CL is a Dynamic Clayton Copula. GA is a Dynamic Gaussian Copula. St is a Dynamic Student's-t Copula. Mix is a Dynamic Mixture Copula. Mix1 combines a dynamic Gaussian and a dynamic Clayton Copula. Mix2 combines a dynamic Student's-t and a dynamic Clayton Copula. Mix3 combines a dynamic Gaussian and dynamic Gumbel Copula. Mix4 combines a dynamic Student's-t and a dynamic Gumbel Copula.

		GU	CL	GA	St	Mix1	Mix2	Mix3	Mix4
rel. Hit VaR	SL_{99}	0.010	0.053	0.010	0.010	0.010	0.010	0.010	0.010
	SL_{95}	0.053	0.111	0.053	0.053	0.053	0.053	0.048	0.053
	SL_{90}	0.115	0.163	0.111	0.111	0.115	0.115	0.111	0.111
Kupiec Test	SL_{99}	0	1	0	0	0	0	0	0
	SL_{95}	0	1	0	0	0	0	0	0
	SL_{90}	0	1	0	0	0	0	0	0
Max. VaR	SL_{99}	0.130	0.079	0.125	0.125	0.124	0.125	0.123	0.125
	SL_{95}	0.078	0.059	0.081	0.082	0.080	0.080	0.082	0.082
	SL_{90}	0.056	0.048	0.062	0.062	0.061	0.061	0.062	0.062
Min. VaR	SL_{99}	0.043	0.024	0.038	0.038	0.038	0.038	0.039	0.039
	SL_{95}	0.025	0.017	0.024	0.024	0.024	0.023	0.024	0.024
	SL_{90}	0.017	0.013	0.017	0.017	0.017	0.017	0.018	0.017
Max. VaR Excess	SL_{99}	0.002	0.035	0.010	0.010	0.008	0.010	0.011	0.009
	SL_{95}	0.027	0.047	0.034	0.034	0.034	0.035	0.036	0.035
	SL_{90}	0.041	0.053	0.045	0.046	0.046	0.046	0.047	0.046
rel. Hit CVaR	SL_{99}	0.000	0.029	0.000	0.000	0.000	0.000	0.000	0.000
	SL_{95}	0.010	0.072	0.010	0.010	0.010	0.010	0.010	0.010
	SL_{90}	0.024	0.111	0.029	0.029	0.030	0.029	0.029	0.029
AAD CVaR	SL_{99}	0.000	0.000	0.000	0.000	0.000	0.000	0.000	0.000
	SL_{95}	0.001	0.001	0.001	0.001	0.001	0.001	0.001	0.001
	SL_{90}	0.001	0.002	0.001	0.001	0.001	0.001	0.001	0.001
Max. CVaR Excess	SL_{99}	0.000	0.029	0.000	0.000	0.000	0.000	0.000	0.000
	SL_{95}	0.015	0.040	0.018	0.018	0.018	0.019	0.019	0.019
	SL_{90}	0.028	0.045	0.031	0.030	0.030	0.030	0.030	0.029

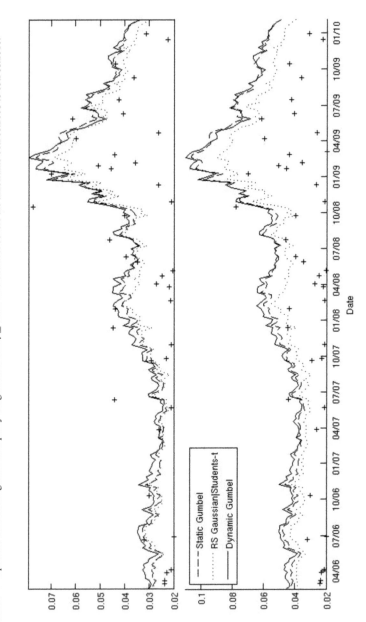

Figure 6.1 – G7 Bond yields Portfolio VaR and CVaR Forecasts. The top figure plots the 1-week VaR forecasts and the bottom figure plots the 1-week CVaR forecasts based on the Dynamic Gumbel, the RS Gaussian|Student's-t and the Static Gumbel Copulas at the SL_{95} for the equally weighted Bond yields portfolio. '+' represent the matching realized equally weighted returns $\bar{x}_t \geq 0.02$. The backtest covers the timeframe 08.Feb.2006 to 03.Feb.2010.

This rejection is supported by the maximum CVaR exceedances. At the SL_{99}, the maximum exceedances of the RS Copula based CVaR forecasts are about 0.011, on average. The comparable predictions of the adequate Static Copulas are not exceeded. Those results insinuate a disadvantageous dependence representation through the RS Copulas. Additionally, modeling the dependence structure via RS instead of Static Copulas reduces the maximum portfolio VaR forecasts by about 0.01, on average. A closer look at the RS Copula calibrations reveals a shift towards the low dependence regimes as the volatility levels of the Bond yields rise in 2009 (Figure 4.1). Consequently, the highly volatile Bond yields are modeled as fairly independent, reducing the portfolio VaR and CVaR predictions. Figure 6.1 illustrates the impact of the RS Copula's jump to the low dependence regime in 2009. Before the switch, the portfolio VaR and CVaR predictions of the Static, the RS and the Dynamic Copulas are quite similar, but after the regime switch the RS Copula risk predictions are significantly lower. A direct comparison of the portfolio VaR and CVaR forecasts is legitimate because they are all based on the same univariate models but different Copula setups. Consequently, the differences are caused solely by the Copulas.

Obviously, the Bond yields are more dependent than assumed by the RS Copulas, resulting less precise portfolio VaR and CVaR forecasts than the Static and the Dynamic Gumbel Copulas. A comparison of the VaR strike ratios suggests that the Dynamic Copulas capture the dependence structure most accurately (Table 6.3). Any Dynamic Copulas, except for the Dynamic Clayton, contribute to very exact portfolio VaR forecasts. The advantage of the Dynamic Copulas is most obvious in case of the VaR forecasts on the SL_{90}. On average, their application reduces the strike ratios by about 3 percentage points compared to the Static and RS Copulas. The Dynamic Gumbel Copula estimates the tightest right tail dependencies resulting the most distinct maximum VaR levels. In contrast, the Dynamic Clayton Copula underestimates right tail dependencies, but this is not surprising due to its left tail dependence character.

An examination of the maximum CVaR exceedances shows that the Dynamic Copulas capture changes in the dependence structure most accurately. The CVaR predictions of the Dynamic Copulas (except the Dynamic Clayton) are not exceeded at the SL_{99}. At the SL_{95} and the SL_{90}, the CVaR levels calculated via the Dynamic Gumbel Copula are exceeded the least by a maximum of 0.015 and 0.028. Compared to the CVaR levels from the Static Gumbel, those are reductions of 0.002 and 0.003. In contrast, the CVaR levels predicted via the RS Copulas are exceeded by a maximum of 0.03 and 0.039 at the SL_{95} and the SL_{90}. Figure 6.1 illustrates the superior portfolio VaR and CVaR forecasts of the Dynamic Gumbel Copula at the SL_{95} graphically. As the univariate volatility forecasts are the same for any risk predictions, the differences are solely caused by the chosen Copulas. It is obvious that the Dynamic Gumbel Copula predicts the tightest dependencies as the volatility levels explode. This results the most distinct portfolio VaR and CVaR forecasts, whose accuracies are supported by the backtest statistics.

6.2 Stocks Portfolio

This section is dedicated to out-of-sample VaR and CVaR forecasts of the G7 Stocks only portfolios. The left tail quantiles of the multivariate distribution define the portfolio risks. Ang and Chen (2002), Forbes and Rigobon (2003), Hong et al. (2007) and Statman and Scheid (2008) and many more present evidence of severe left tail dependence in Stock markets. Therefore, this analysis allows to examine which Copula framework captures asymmetric and time instable Stock market dependencies most accurately. The backtest procedure covers the time frame 25.Jan.2006 to 20.Jan.2010 and the portfolio VaR and CVaR levels are forecasted on basis of the Static, the RS and the Dynamic Copulas. Again, I construct equally weighted portfolios to amplify the impact of the individual Copulas on the VaR and CVaR forecasts.

Table 6.4 presents the results for the Static Copula models. The violation ratio of the predicted VaR levels is given in the first line. According to this measure, the Frank and the Gumbel Copulas model the dependence structure most inaccurately. This result does not surprise because the Frank Copula models symmetric dependence and the Gumbel Copula focuses on right tail dependence. Both Copulas belong to the Archimedian family which represents the dependence of several time series via a single parameter. In contrast, Stock markets feature left tail dependence what causes joint distributions with long left but rather short and fat right tails. Therefore, the application of the Frank and Gumbel Copulas to capture Stock market dependencies results imprecise portfolio VaR and CVaR forecasts. In contrast, the Clayton Copula focuses on left tail dependence, resulting in a very accurate portfolio VaR hit ratio at the 1% significance level (SL_1). This outcome is supported by the maximum predicted VaR level in the third block of table 6.4. According to the Kupiec test, the Clayton skeleton is the only Archimedian Copula that predicts the VaR for the G7 Stocks portfolio precisely. Due to its focus on left tail dependence, the VaR prediction qualities are less accurate at the 5% and 10% quantiles. At the SL_1, its CVaR predictions are exceeded by a maximum of 0.034 and at the SL_5 by a maximum of 0.069. Compared to the Elliptical Copulas, the Clayton Copula based CVaR levels reduce the exceedances by 0.008 and 0.003 at the SL_1 and the SL_5. This result identifies the necessity to account for left tail dependence among Stock markets. The Canonical-Vine Copula is closely related to the single Clayton Copula. Its hierarchical structure contains several bivariate Clayton Copulas with different parameter intensities (Table 4.7). Hence, it describes the asymmetric dependencies of the G7 Stocks via multiple parameters, what results in the most accurate VaR predictions among the Static Copulas. The additional flexibility to adapt to the data results the most extreme maximum VaR predictions and lowest CVaR exceedances at the SL_1 and SL_5 (0.03 and 0.066), where tail dependence matters the most.

Analyzing the relative violation of the VaR predictions of the Elliptical Copulas clearly identifies the Gaussian Copula's inability to capture tail dependence. Besides the Frank and the Gumbel Copulas, it is the only Static Copula which depicts an imprecise VaR violation ratio of 0.014 at the SL_1. In contrast, the Student's-t Copula exhibits a precise VaR hit ratio of 0.01 and its maximum VaR forecast exceeds the Gaussian by 0.004, at the SL_1. The differences are due to the Student's-t Copula's ability to capture tail dependence via its degree-of-freedom. At the 5% and 10% significance levels the importance of tail dependence decreases and hence both Copulas predict similar VaR levels. Nevertheless, the maximum CVaR exceedances of both Elliptical Copulas differ only insignificantly. A comparison with the Clayton and Canonical-Vine based exceedances shows that the Student's-t Copula is unable to capture extreme left tail dependence.

The Mixture Copulas combine the advantages of the Archimedian and the Elliptical families. Simply spoken, they consist of weighted Archimedian and Elliptical Copulas (Equation 3.8). According to their VaR violation ratios, they capture the dependence structure of the G7 Stocks more precisely than their single components alone. Regarding the VaR hit ratios, the Gaussian-Clayton-Gumbel Mixture Copula outperforms its single components by 0.005, 0.015 and 0.044 at the SL_5. The Student's-t-Clayton-Gumbel Copula outperforms its single components by 0.01, 0.015 and 0.044. Additionally, the Mixtures predict more distinct maximum VaR levels than the single Elliptical Copulas and they reduce the CVaR exceedances at the SL_1 and the SL_5 by 0.004 and by 0.003. Both results amplify the Mixtures' abilities to account for left tail dependence.

101

Table 6.4 – Static Copula G7 Stocks Equally Weighted Portfolio VaR and CVaR. I predict one-week VaR and CVaR at the 1%, 5% and 10% significance levels (SL). This table presents the relative violation frequencies for the VaR and CVaR predictions (rel. Hit VaR, rel. Hit CVaR) during the backtest. The Kupiec test evaluates the null hypothesis ($H_0 = 0$) of correct VaR coverage against imprecise VaR coverage ($H_0 = 1$) at the 95% significance level. The Max. VaR reports the maximum predicted VaR and the Min. VaR reports the minimum predicted VaR, for the backtest procedure. The Max. VaR (CVaR) Excess denotes the maximum exceedance of the VaR (CVaR) forecasts during the backtest. The average absolute distance of the realized returns from the predicted CVaR levels in case of VaR violations is denoted by AAD CVaR. F is a Frank Copula. GU is a Gumbel Copula. CL is a Clayton Copula. GA is a Gaussian Copula. St is a Student's-t Copula. Mix1 is a multivariate Mixture Copula which consists of one Gaussian, one Clayton and one Gumbel Copulas. CV is a Canonical-Vine Copula. Its pair-Copulas are presented in the parameter estimation section. Mix2 is a multivariate Mixture Copula which consists of one Student's-t, one Clayton and one Gumbel Copulas.

		F	GU	CL	GA	St	CV	Mix1	Mix2
rel. Hit VaR	SL_{99}	0.048	0.038	0.010	0.014	0.010	0.010	0.010	0.010
	SL_{95}	0.101	0.111	0.082	0.072	0.077	0.058	0.067	0.067
	SL_{90}	0.125	0.135	0.130	0.125	0.125	0.125	0.125	0.125
Kupiec Test	SL_{99}	1	1	0	0	0	0	0	0
	SL_{95}	1	1	0	0	0	0	0	0
	SL_{90}	0	0	0	0	0	0	0	0
Max. VaR	SL_{99}	-0.121	-0.125	-0.179	-0.160	-0.164	-0.184	-0.167	-0.166
	SL_{95}	-0.093	-0.089	-0.104	-0.104	-0.104	-0.110	-0.108	-0.107
	SL_{90}	-0.078	-0.071	-0.074	-0.078	-0.077	-0.078	-0.079	-0.079
Min. VaR	SL_{99}	-0.023	-0.024	-0.034	-0.031	-0.032	-0.036	-0.031	-0.032
	SL_{95}	-0.017	-0.017	-0.020	-0.020	-0.020	-0.021	-0.020	-0.020
	SL_{90}	-0.014	-0.013	-0.013	-0.015	-0.015	-0.014	-0.015	-0.015
Max. VaR Excess	SL_{99}	-0.085	-0.081	-0.057	-0.062	-0.060	-0.049	-0.059	-0.060
	SL_{95}	-0.100	-0.102	-0.093	-0.093	-0.093	-0.090	-0.091	-0.091
	SL_{90}	-0.108	-0.112	-0.111	-0.108	-0.107	-0.108	-0.107	-0.107
rel. Hit CVaR	SL_1	0.019	0.019	0.010	0.010	0.010	0.010	0.010	0.010
	SL_5	0.058	0.058	0.019	0.024	0.024	0.014	0.019	0.019
	SL_{10}	0.072	0.096	0.048	0.048	0.048	0.038	0.043	0.043
AAD CVaR	SL_1	0.000	0.001	0.000	0.000	0.000	0.000	0.000	0.000
	SL_5	0.001	0.001	0.001	0.001	0.001	0.001	0.001	0.001
	SL_{10}	0.002	0.002	0.001	0.001	0.001	0.001	0.001	0.001
Max. CVaR Excess	SL_1	-0.066	-0.070	-0.034	-0.042	-0.042	-0.030	-0.038	-0.038
	SL_5	-0.080	-0.088	-0.069	-0.072	-0.072	-0.066	-0.069	-0.069
	SL_{10}	-0.092	-0.098	-0.085	-0.086	-0.086	-0.083	-0.085	-0.085

Finally, the comparison of various Static Copulas shows that asymmetric features and parameter plurality enhance their abilities to comprise the dependence structure of the G7 Stocks. Modeling future dependencies via a Canonical-Vine Copula results superior portfolio risk forecasts. This is due to its ability to account for severe left tail dependencies. Thus, the conducted analyses support the hypothesis of left tail dependent Stock markets and identify the Canonical-Vine Copula as the most accurate framework to capture them.

Table 6.5 presents the results of the portfolio risk forecasts calculated on basis of the RS Copula simulations. The basic idea behind the RS Copulas is to split the dataset into one high and one low dependence regimes. The according Copulas reveal different characteristics and different parameter intensities. According to the Kupiec tests, any RS Copula represents the dependence features of the Stocks data accurately, resulting precise VaR forecasts. The accurate strike frequencies of the RS Copulas based VaR predictions support this result. The VaR strikes are the same for any RS Copulas, except the Gaussian|Gaussian and the Gaussian|Canonical-Vine RS Copulas. The Gaussian|Gaussian RS Copula is not able to capture tail dependence, resulting less accurate VaR violation ratios. However, a comparison of the maximum CVaR exceedances does not indicate superior performance of any RS Copula model. Regardless of the RS Copula, the maximum CVaR excess is about 0.04 at the SL_1, 0.07 at the SL_5 and 0.085 at the SL_{10} and occurs during the week of the Lehman Brothers Inc. bankruptcy (Figure 6.2). The impact of the RS Copulas on the portfolio VaR forecasts differs most significantly in regards to the maximum VaR predictions at the SL_1. The most pronounced VaR prediction is generated by the Gaussian|Mixture RS Copula (-0.176) whereas the Student's-t|Student's-t RS Copula exhibits the least extreme prediction (-0.168), at the SL_1. The Clayton Copula in the Mixture construct is responsible for the distinct left tail of the joint distribution.

Further, I compare the RS Copula based portfolio VaR forecasts with their Static Copula based counterparts. This comparison is meaningful because the univariate volatility forecasts are the same for any Copula model. Compared to the Static Gaussian Copula, the VaR predictions on basis of the Gaussian|Gaussian RS Copula are more precise in regards to their strike ratios and their maximum predicted levels at any examined quantile and the maximum CVaR exceedances reduce by 0.002 at the SL_5 and the SL_{10}. Consequently, the application of the RS Gaussian instead of the Static Gaussian Copula to quantify the dependence of Stocks enhances the portfolio risk measure. The Gaussian|Student's-t RS Copula results even greater advantages. Compared to its single Static Copulas (Gaussian and Student's-t), it enhances the VaR strike ra-

103

tios by 0.004 and 0.000 at the SL_1, 0.014 and 0.019 at the SL_5. In addition, the RS Copula reduces the maximum CVaR excesses at the 5% and 10% significance levels. This is due to the Student's-t Copula's ability to account for tail dependence during the high dependence regime. A comparison of the Gaussian|Canonical-Vine RS Copula and its single components reveals that the VaR forecasts based on the RS Copula outperform the Static Gaussian Copula regarding the VaR hit ratios, but the maximum CVaR excesses are identical for the Static and the RS Copula. However, risk predictions based on the Static Canonical-Vine Copula perform better than their RS Copula based counterparts. Its VaR violation ratios are exacter at the SL_5, but the greatest advantage exhibit the maximum VaR and maximum CVaR exceedances at the SL_1. The differences are due to the RS Copula setup, in which the Canonical-Vine represents the weak dependence regime while the Gaussian Copula represents the high dependence regime. Consequently, the Static Canonical-Vine Copula models more distinct left tail dependences, resulting superior portfolio VaR and CVaR predictions.

The Gaussian|Mixture RS Copula accounts for tail dependence in the Mixture regime, resulting more accurate VaR predictions than the Gaussian|Gaussian RS Copula. This clearly identifies asymmetries in the dependence structure during the low dependence regime. However, the high dependence regime is represented via the symmetric Gaussian Copula. Comparing the Gaussian|Mixture RS Copula and the Static Gaussian Copula based VaR forecasts shows the RS structure significantly improves the VaR violation ratios at the SL_1 and SL_5. In addition, the RS Copula predicts more distinct worst case VaRs at any tested significance level and results smaller maximum CVaR exceedances. The same holds true for the comparison of the RS Copula and the Static Mixture Copula, but the maximum CVaR exceedances are identical for the Static and the RS Copulas. Overall, combining the Gaussian and Mixture Copulas in a RS framework improves the accuracy of the portfolio risk predictions compared to their single Static components.

In order to account for tail dependence in both regimes, I replace the Gaussian Copula with a Student's-t Copula. At first, I combine two Student's-t Copulas in the RS framework. Compared to the Gaussain|Gaussian RS Copula, this construct results more precise VaR hit ratios at the SL_5, whereas the maximum VaR predictions and the maximum CVaR exceedances are identical for both RS Copulas. Thus, the more precise VaR violation ratios in case of the Student's-t|Student's-t RS Copula are due to its ability to account for tail dependence during both regimes. Measuring the dependence via the Student's-t|Student's-t RS instead of the Static

Student's-t Copula improves the portfolio VaR violation ratios at the SL_5 and generates more distinct worst case VaR predictions, but the maximum CVaR exceedances are identical. The Student's-t|Canonical-Vine and the Student's-t|Mixture RS Copulas based VaR forecasts reveal very similar features. A comparison of the VaR violation ratios, the worst case VaR predictions and the maximum CVaR exceedances points out the more accurate representation of the dependence structure through the RS Copulas than through the Static Student's-t Copula. Only the Static Canonical-Vine Copula generates similarly accurate VaR forecasts and outperforms the RS Copulas in regards to maximum CVaR exceedances.

The conducted analyses show that the RS Copulas build a superior basis for portfolio VaR predictions than their single Static components. This conclusion is supported by the Kupiec test, which does not reject any RS Copula based VaR predictions as imprecise. However, the Static Canonical-Vine and Mixture Copulas predict more precise CVaR levels. This is due to their focus on extreme left tail dependence.

Next, I examine the VaR forecasts based on the Dynamic Copulas (Table 6.6). A first glance at the VaR violation ratios reveals similar elaborateness of any Dynamic Copula model. The Kupiec test supports this result. Only the Dynamic Gumbel Copula captures the dependence structure of the Stocks dataset imprecisely. This is in line with its characteristics; The dependence intensity is captured via a single parameter and its focus is on right tail dependence. In contrast, the Dynamic Clayton Copula represents the dependence structure most accurately, resulting the most precise VaR hit ratios and smallest CVaR exceedances. This clearly indicates left tail dependence in the G7 Stocks dataset and the Dynamic Clayton Copula's ability to comprise it accurately. Furthermore, the dominance of the Dynamic Mixture (containing one Elliptical and one Clayton) over the Dynamic Elliptical Copulas in regards to worst case VaR predictions amplifies the importance of considering left tail dependence in a multivariate setup. The Dynamic Mixture's superiority is due to its ability to shift the portions of symmetric and asymmetric Dynamic Copulas (Figure 4.6). The precision of the VaR predictions clearly indicate that Dynamic Copulas with asymmetric left tail features depict the empirical dependence structure of the Stocks dataset most accurately. In contrast, Dynamic Mixtures consisting of one Elliptical and one Gumbel Copula do not enhance the dependence measure compared to pure Dynamic Elliptical Copulas. This is in line with the Gumbel Copula which focuses on right tail dependence, whereas Stock indices are left tail dependent.

Table 6.5 – Regime-Switch Copula G7 Stocks Equally Weighted Portfolio VaR and CVaR. I predict one-week VaR and CVaR at the 1%, 5% and 10% significance levels (*SL*). This table presents the relative violation frequencies for the VaR and CVaR predictions (rel. Hit VaR, rel. Hit CVaR) during the backtest. The Kupiec test evaluates the null hypothesis ($H_0 = 0$) of correct VaR coverage against imprecise VaR coverage ($H_0 = 1$) at the 95% significance level. The Max. VaR reports the maximum predicted VaR and the Min. VaR reports the minimum predicted VaR, for the backtest procedure. The Max. VaR (CVaR) Excess denotes the maximum exceedance of the VaR (CVaR) forecasts during the backtest. The average absolute distance of the realized returns from the predicted CVaR levels in case of VaR violations is denoted by AAD CVaR. The RS Copulas are abbreviated: GA|GA is a Gaussian|Gaussian RS Copula. GA|St is a Gaussian|Student's-t RS Copula. GA|CV is a Gaussian|Canonical-Vine RS Copula. GA|M is a Gaussian|Mixture RS Copula. St|St is a Student's-t|Student's-t RS Copula. St|CV is a Student's-t|Canonical-Vine RS Copula. St|M is a Student's-t|Mixture RS Copula. The multivariate Mixture Copula consists of one Gaussian, one Clayton and one Gumbel Copulas.

		GA|GA	GA|St	GA|CV	GA|M	St|St	St|CV	St|M
rel. Hit VaR	SL_{99}	0.010	0.010	0.010	0.010	0.010	0.010	0.010
	SL_{95}	0.063	0.058	0.063	0.058	0.058	0.058	0.058
	SL_{90}	0.125	0.125	0.125	0.125	0.125	0.125	0.125
Kupiec Test	SL_{99}	0	0	0	0	0	0	0
	SL_{95}	0	0	0	0	0	0	0
	SL_{90}	0	0	0	0	0	0	0
Max. VaR	SL_{99}	-0.170	-0.172	-0.170	-0.176	-0.168	-0.169	-0.169
	SL_{95}	-0.110	-0.109	-0.110	-0.110	-0.109	-0.109	-0.109
	SL_{90}	-0.082	-0.081	-0.081	-0.083	-0.082	-0.082	-0.080
Min. VaR	SL_{99}	-0.033	-0.033	-0.032	-0.032	-0.032	-0.032	-0.033
	SL_{95}	-0.021	-0.021	-0.020	-0.021	-0.021	-0.020	-0.021
	SL_{90}	-0.015	-0.015	-0.015	-0.015	-0.015	-0.015	-0.015
Max. VaR Excess	SL_{99}	-0.058	-0.060	-0.057	-0.056	-0.057	-0.059	-0.057
	SL_{95}	-0.090	-0.091	-0.090	-0.089	-0.091	-0.091	-0.090
	SL_{90}	-0.106	-0.106	-0.106	-0.104	-0.106	-0.106	-0.106
rel. Hit CVaR	SL_1	0.010	0.010	0.010	0.010	0.010	0.010	0.010
	SL_5	0.019	0.019	0.024	0.019	0.019	0.019	0.019
	SL_{10}	0.048	0.048	0.048	0.053	0.048	0.048	0.053
AAD CVaR	SL_1	0.000	0.000	0.000	0.000	0.000	0.000	0.000
	SL_5	0.001	0.001	0.001	0.001	0.001	0.001	0.001
	SL_{10}	0.001	0.001	0.001	0.001	0.001	0.001	0.001
Max. CVaR Excess	SL_1	-0.042	-0.042	-0.041	-0.039	-0.042	-0.041	-0.039
	SL_5	-0.070	-0.069	-0.072	-0.069	-0.069	-0.070	-0.069
	SL_{10}	-0.084	-0.084	-0.086	-0.084	-0.084	-0.085	-0.084

Table 6.6 – Dynamic Copula G7 Stocks Equally Weighted Portfolio VaR and CVaR. I predict one-week VaR and CVaR at the 1%, 5% and 10% significance levels (*SL*). This table presents the relative violation frequencies for the VaR and CVaR predictions (rel. Hit VaR, rel. Hit CVaR) during the backtest. The Kupiec test evaluates the null hypothesis ($H_0 = 0$) of correct VaR coverage against imprecise VaR coverage ($H_0 = 1$) at the 95% significance level. The Max. VaR reports the maximum predicted VaR and the Min. VaR reports the minimum predicted VaR, for the backtest procedure. The Max. VaR (CVaR) Excess denotes the maximum exceedance of the VaR (CVaR) forecasts during the backtest. The average absolute distance of the realized returns from the predicted CVaR levels in case of VaR violations is denoted by AAD CVaR. The Dynamic Copulas are abbreviated: GU is a Dynamic Gumbel Copula. CL is a Dynamic Clayton Copula. GA is a Dynamic Gaussian Copula. St is a Dynamic Student's-t Copula. Mix is a Dynamic Mixture Copula. Mix1 combines a dynamic Gaussian and a dynamic Clayton Copula. Mix2 combines a dynamic Student's-t and a dynamic Clayton Copula. Mix3 combines a dynamic Gaussian and dynamic Gumbel Copula. Mix4 combines a dynamic Student's-t and a dynamic Gumbel Copula.

		GU	CL	GA	St	Mix1	Mix2	Mix3	Mix4
rel. Hit VaR	SL_{99}	0.029	0.010	0.010	0.010	0.010	0.010	0.010	0.010
	SL_{95}	0.106	0.058	0.058	0.058	0.058	0.058	0.058	0.063
	SL_{90}	0.135	0.120	0.125	0.125	0.125	0.125	0.125	0.125
Kupiec Test	SL_{99}	1	0	0	0	0	0	0	0
	SL_{95}	1	0	0	0	0	0	0	0
	SL_{90}	0	0	0	0	0	0	0	0
Max. VaR	SL_{99}	-0.139	-0.187	-0.177	-0.179	-0.183	-0.185	-0.180	-0.179
	SL_{95}	-0.098	-0.115	-0.113	-0.113	-0.116	-0.117	-0.114	-0.114
	SL_{90}	-0.077	-0.083	-0.083	-0.084	-0.085	-0.087	-0.084	-0.084
Min. VaR	SL_{99}	-0.023	-0.032	-0.032	-0.031	-0.030	-0.031	-0.031	-0.030
	SL_{95}	-0.016	-0.019	-0.020	-0.020	-0.019	-0.020	-0.020	-0.019
	SL_{90}	-0.012	-0.013	-0.015	-0.014	-0.014	-0.014	-0.014	-0.014
Max. VaR Excess	SL_{99}	-0.075	-0.048	-0.056	-0.056	-0.055	-0.055	-0.056	-0.057
	SL_{95}	-0.097	-0.087	-0.090	-0.090	-0.088	-0.090	-0.089	-0.090
	SL_{90}	-0.109	-0.107	-0.105	-0.106	-0.105	-0.105	-0.105	-0.106
rel. Hit CVaR	SL_1	0.019	0.010	0.010	0.010	0.010	0.010	0.010	0.010
	SL_5	0.053	0.019	0.024	0.024	0.014	0.014	0.024	0.024
	SL_{10}	0.087	0.043	0.043	0.043	0.043	0.043	0.043	0.043
AAD CVaR	SL_1	0.000	0.000	0.000	0.000	0.000	0.000	0.000	0.000
	SL_5	0.001	0.001	0.001	0.001	0.001	0.001	0.001	0.001
	SL_{10}	0.001	0.001	0.001	0.001	0.001	0.001	0.001	0.001
Max. CVaR Excess	SL_1	-0.061	-0.024	-0.038	-0.038	-0.037	-0.037	-0.038	-0.038
	SL_5	-0.081	-0.062	-0.069	-0.069	-0.069	-0.069	-0.069	-0.069
	SL_{10}	-0.092	-0.079	-0.084	-0.084	-0.084	-0.084	-0.084	-0.084

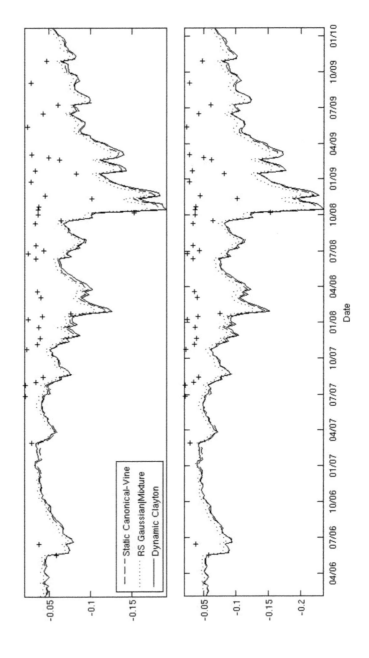

Figure 6.2 – G7 Stocks Portfolio VaR and CVaR Forecasts. The top figure plots the 1-week VaR forecasts and the bottom figure plots the 1-week CVaR forecasts based on the Dynamic Clayton, the RS Gaussian|Mixture and the Static Canonical-Vine Copulas at the SL_1 for the equally weighted Stocks portfolio. The Mixture Copulas consist of one Gaussian, one Clayton and one Gumbel Copulas. '+' represent the matching realized equally weighted returns $\bar{x}_t \le -0.02$. The backtest covers the timeframe 25.Jan.2006 to 20.Jan.2010.

In a second step, I compare the Dynamic Copulas to the Static Copulas on basis of the VaR and CVaR forecasts. Again, this examination is meaningful, because the portfolio VaR and CVaR forecasts based on the Dynamic and the Static Copulas rely on the same univariate volatility predictions but differ only in regards to their dependence structures. The risk predictions based on the Static Gumbel Copula are less precise than their counterparts relying on the Dynamic Gumbel Copula. Their VaR violation ratios differ by 0.01 at the SL_1 and 0.005 at the SL_5. The predicted maximum VaR levels differ by about the same magnitude and the Dynamic Gumbel Copula reduces the maximum CVaR exceedance by about 0.005 at the SL_1. Although both Gumbel Copulas represent the dependence structure of the Stock markets poorly, the Dynamic Copula's ability to change its parameter intensity is an advantage. The second Dynamic Archimedian Copula in the examination is the Clayton Copula. In the same manner as its Static counterpart, it focuses on left tail dependence what is an empirically observed feature in Stock markets. The Dynamic Clayton Copula improves the VaR predictions, tremendously. At the SL_1, the Dynamic and the Static models reveal the same VaR hit ratios, but the Dynamic model predicts a 0.008 greater maximum VaR and reports a 0.01 smaller maximum CVaR exceedance. At the SL_5, the VaR hit ratio of the Dynamic Clayton Copula based forecasts is at 0.058 what is 0.024 lower than its Static Copula based counterpart. Based on the Dynamic Clayton Copula, the predicted worst case VaR at the SL_5 is 0.011 greater and the maximum CVaR excess is 0.007 smaller than based on the Static Clayton. At the SL_{10}, the maximum portfolio VaR predictions differ by about 0.01 and the maximum CVaR exceedances by about 0.006. The superior performance of the Dynamic model clearly indicates the dependence structure of the Stocks dataset varies over time. Therefore, modeling the Clayton Copula parameter intensity dynamically is advantageous.

Further, I examine the Elliptical Copulas with dynamic correlation matrices and compare them to their Static counterparts. The Dynamic Gaussian Copula represents the dependence structure of the Stocks dataset much more precisely than its Static form. The differences are obvious for the VaR violation ratios. The Dynamic version reveals a very precise hit ratio of 0.01 at the SL_1 and 0.058 at the SL_5, 0.004 and 0.014 lower than the Static Gaussian Copula. An examination of the worst case VaR predictions amplifies the superiority of the Dynamic model. Its forecasts exceed the Static Copula's maximum VaRs by 0.017 at the SL_1, 0.009 at the SL_5 and 0.006 at the SL_{10}. The dynamic correlation parameters are able to capture correlation meltdowns, improving the portfolio VaR forecasts. A comparison of the maximum CVaR exceedances accentuates the Dynamic Copula's advantageous features. Measuring the dependence structure via the Dynamic model diminishes the maximum CVaR excesses by 0.004 at the SL_1, 0.003 at the SL_5 and 0.002 at the SL_{10}. The Dynamic Student's-t Copula models the correlation matrix via the same dynamic process as the Dynamic Gaussian Copula (Equation 3.17), but it accounts for tail dependence via its degree-of-freedom. Hence, the differences between the Dynamic Student's-t Copula and its Static version are similar to the differences between the Dynamic and the Static Gaussian Copulas.

Finally, I examine the efficiency of the VaR and CVaR forecasts based on the Dynamic Mixture Copulas. For simplicity I compare them to the Static Mixture Copulas consisting of one Elliptical, one Clayton and one Gumbel Copulas. First, I focus on the combinations containing one Dynamic Elliptical and one Dynamic Clayton Copulas. According to the VaR violation ratios, the Dynamic Mixtures deliver additional value only at the SL_5. However, the maximum VaR predictions vary according to the underlying dependence models. Due to their parameter flexibility, the Dynamic Mixture Copulas are able to comprehend the dependence structure of the data much more accurate than the Static Mixtures. Thus, the Dynamic Mixtures result more distinct worst case VaR predictions and slightly smaller maximum CVaR exceedances at any significance level. In a second step, I analyze the adaptability of the Dynamic Mixture Copula consisting of one Dynamic Elliptical and one Dynamic Gumbel Copulas to the Stocks dataset. Compared to their Static counterparts, they enhance dependence modeling, but due to their right tail dependence feature, they are less accurate than the Dynamic Mixtures containing a Clayton skeleton.

Overall, I find evidence that Dynamic Copulas capture the dependence structure of Stocks exacter than Static or RS Copulas. They enhance the portfolio VaR predictions, resulting more distinct worst case VaR predictions and more precise VaR hit ratios. Additionally, they reduce the maximum CVaR exceedances (Figure 6.2). The conducted analyses show that the Dynamic Clayton Copula captures and predicts Stock market dependencies most accurately, resulting the most accurate portfolio VaR and CVaR levels. This outcome supports the hypothesis of left tail dependent Stock markets. Hence, the proposed extension of the Dynamic Clayton Copula to multiple dimensions is a very powerful tool to model future Stock portfolio VaRs and CVaRs.

6.3 Multi Asset Classes Portfolio

Many empirical portfolios contain securities from multiple asset classes. Hence, the definition of a precise risk model for this portfolio type is especially important. Regardless of the asset classes, the main drivers of portfolio risk remain the same: the univariate volatilities and the multivariate dependence structure. In regards to volatility, many empirical studies prove GARCH models' adaptabilities to different time series. In contrast, only little research has been conducted on how to capture the dependencies of multiple asset classes, accurately. Therefore, I utilize various Copula functions to capture the dependencies of an equally weighted Multi Asset Classes portfolio. The according out-of-sample portfolio risk forecasts depict the Copula model which captures the dependencies most accurately.

At first, I measure the dependencies of the different asset classes via Static Copulas. During the backtest procedure they forecast overly stringent VaR levels which result in imprecise VaR violation ratios (Table 6.7). This outcome holds true for any Static Copula and indicates strong shifts in the dependence structure, which the Static skeletons are not able to comprise. The Archimedian Copula parameters insinuate independent time series (Table 4.8). The Elliptical and Mixture Copula parameters depict slightly positive and negative dependencies. Although any tested Copula models the securities as almost independent during the backtest, the predicted VaR levels overestimate the portfolio losses. Additionally, the predicted CVaR levels are only exceeded by a maximum of 0.005 at the SL_1, 0.014 at the SL_5 and 0.017 at the SL_{10}. The portfolio VaR overestimation and the insignificant portfolio CVaR exceedances indicate that any Static Copula overestimates the dependencies in the Multi Asset Classes portfolio. However, the conducted analyses also show that diversification among multiple asset classes is effective to protect portfolios against severe losses, even under imperfect dependence measures. The Static Copulas are not flexible enough to capture changes in the dependence structure and therefore overestimate Multi Asset Classes portfolio risks (Figure 6.3). In order to improve the accuracy of the Multi Asset Classes portfolio VaR forecasts, I implement RS Copulas to measure the dependence structures. In contrast to Static Copulas, the interaction of the securities is modeled either from the high or the low dependence regime. This introduces additional flexibility to model time-instable dependencies and significantly improves the portfolio VaR forecasts (Table 6.8). The VaR hit ratios at the SL_1 depict very precise forecasts, but they are less accurate at the SL_5 and SL_{10}. Nevertheless, they outperform the strike ratios of the Static Copula based predictions at any SL. This reveals the importance to account for time-instable dependence structures.

Figure 6.3 illustrates the time paths of the RS Gaussian|Gaussian and Static Student's-t Copula VaR forecasts. Obviously, the Static Copula predicts more distinct VaR levels than the RS model. The maximum VaR predictions document this difference. However, the VaR strike ratios at any SL indicate that the Static Copulas overestimate the dependencies and hence forecast overly stringent portfolio VaR levels. The low dependence regime RS Copula parameters in table 4.11 and the VaR strike ratios support the hypothesis that diversification among several asset classes is efficient.

On average, the maximum CVaR exceedances of the RS and the Static Copulas differ by about 0.003. This difference is neglectable and amplifies the superiority of the RS Copula approach. Among the RS Copulas, the Gaussian|Gaussian which does not account for tail dependence generates the most precise VaR predictions and its maximum CVaR exceedances are identical with those from other RS Copulas. In comparison to the Static and RS Copulas, the application of Dynamic Copulas generates the most precise portfolio VaR forecasts at the SL_5 and the SL_{10}. Compared to RS Copulas, they offer additional flexibility to measure the securities' interactions and hence improve the quality of the portfolio VaR predictions (Table 6.9). At the SL_1, the Dynamic Elliptical and Mixture Copulas slightly underestimate the dependencies resulting a portfolio VaR hit ratio of 1.4%. However, the exceedance of the extra hit is only 0.0013. Further, compared to any other Copula model the Mixture Copula, containing one Dynamic Student's-t and one Dynamic Clayton, predicts the most precise VaR levels at the SL_5. This is due to its parameter plurality and its ability to account for left tail dependence. The individual parameters change their intensities and the weights develop over time, resulting a very precise adaptation to the data and an accurate representation of the time-instable dependence structures (Figure 4.8). Nevertheless, the maximum VaR predictions and the maximum CVaR exceedances suggest the Dynamic Student's-t Copula is a similarly appropriate skeleton. In contrast, the VaR predictions based on the Dynamic Archimedian Copulas are less precise. This shows that the interactions of multiple asset classes change too individually to be captured via a single parameter. This conclusion is supported by the maximum portfolio CVaR exceedances. The Static Copulas predict CVaR levels which are exceeded by a maximum of 0.005, whereas the Dynamic Copulas predict CVaRs which are exceeded by a maximum of 0.008. This difference is neglectable, what is supported by the average absolute distance (AAD) from the predicted portfolio CVaRs in case of VaR violations. Figure 6.3 illustrates the distances of the maximum predicted portfolio VaRs and CVaRs from the according realized portfolio returns.

Table 6.7 – Static Copula Multi Asset Classes Equally Weighted Portfolio VaR and CVaR. I predict one-week VaR and CVaR at the 1%, 5% and 10% significance levels (*SL*). This table presents the relative violation frequencies for the VaR and CVaR predictions (rel. Hit VaR, rel. Hit CVaR) during the backtest. The Kupiec test evaluates the null hypothesis ($H_0 = 0$) of correct VaR coverage against imprecise VaR coverage ($H_0 = 1$) at the 95% significance level. The Max. VaR reports the maximum predicted VaR and the Min. VaR reports the minimum predicted VaR, for the backtest procedure. The Max. VaR (CVaR) Excess denotes the maximum exceedance of the VaR (CVaR) forecasts during the backtest. The average absolute distance of the realized returns from the predicted CVaR levels in case of VaR violations is denoted by AAD CVaR. F is a Frank Copula. GU is a Gumbel Copula. CL is a Clayton Copula. GA is a Gaussian Copula. St is a Student's-t Copula. Mix1 is a multivariate Mixture Copula which consists of one Gaussian, one Clayton and one Gumbel Copulas. CV is a Canonical-Vine Copula. Its pair-Copulas are presented in the parameter estimation section. Mix2 is a multivariate Mixture Copula which consists of one Student's-t, one Clayton and one Gumbel Copulas.

		F	GU	CL	GA	St	CV	Mix1	Mix2
rel. Hit VaR	SL_{99}	0.005	0.005	0.005	0.005	0.005	0.005	0.005	0.005
	SL_{95}	0.034	0.034	0.029	0.029	0.029	0.024	0.029	0.029
	SL_{90}	0.072	0.072	0.067	0.063	0.067	0.058	0.063	0.063
Kupiec Test	SL_{99}	0	0	0	0	0	0	0	0
	SL_{95}	0	0	0	0	0	0	0	0
	SL_{90}	0	0	0	0	0	0	0	0
Max. VaR	SL_{99}	-0.058	-0.058	-0.062	-0.061	-0.063	-0.062	-0.061	-0.062
	SL_{95}	-0.038	-0.037	-0.039	-0.039	-0.039	-0.040	-0.039	-0.039
	SL_{90}	-0.029	-0.029	-0.029	-0.030	-0.030	-0.031	-0.030	-0.029
Min. VaR	SL_{99}	-0.018	-0.018	-0.021	-0.020	-0.021	-0.021	-0.020	-0.021
	SL_{95}	-0.012	-0.012	-0.013	-0.013	-0.013	-0.013	-0.013	-0.013
	SL_{90}	-0.009	-0.009	-0.009	-0.009	-0.009	-0.010	-0.009	-0.009
Max. VaR Excess	SL_{99}	-0.014	-0.014	-0.012	-0.011	-0.011	-0.011	-0.012	-0.011
	SL_{95}	-0.019	-0.020	-0.019	-0.019	-0.019	-0.018	-0.019	-0.019
	SL_{90}	-0.023	-0.023	-0.023	-0.022	-0.022	-0.022	-0.022	-0.022
rel. Hit CVaR	SL_1	0.005	0.005	0.005	0.005	0.005	0.005	0.005	0.005
	SL_5	0.010	0.010	0.010	0.010	0.010	0.010	0.010	0.010
	SL_{10}	0.024	0.024	0.019	0.019	0.019	0.019	0.019	0.019
AAD CVaR	SL_1	0.000	0.000	0.000	0.000	0.000	0.000	0.000	0.000
	SL_5	0.000	0.000	0.000	0.000	0.000	0.000	0.000	0.000
	SL_{10}	0.000	0.000	0.000	0.000	0.000	0.000	0.000	0.000
Max. CVaR Excess	SL_1	-0.007	-0.009	-0.006	-0.005	-0.005	-0.004	-0.005	-0.005
	SL_5	-0.014	-0.015	-0.014	-0.014	-0.014	-0.014	-0.014	-0.014
	SL_{10}	-0.018	-0.018	-0.018	-0.017	-0.017	-0.017	-0.017	-0.017

Table 6.8 – Regime-Switch Copula Multi Asset Classes Equally Weighted Portfolio VaR and CVaR. I predict one-week VaR and CVaR at the 1%, 5% and 10% significance levels (*SL*). This table presents the relative violation frequencies for the VaR and CVaR predictions (rel. Hit VaR, rel. Hit CVaR) during the backtest. The Kupiec test evaluates the null hypothesis ($H_0 = 0$) of correct VaR coverage against imprecise VaR coverage ($H_0 = 1$) at the 95% significance level. The Max. VaR reports the maximum predicted VaR and the Min. VaR reports the minimum predicted VaR, for the backtest procedure. The Max. VaR (CVaR) Excess denotes the maximum exceedance of the VaR (CVaR) forecasts during the backtest. The average absolute distance of the realized returns from the predicted CVaR levels in case of VaR violations is denoted by AAD CVaR. The RS Copulas are abbreviated: GA|GA is a Gaussian|Gaussian RS Copula. GA|St is a Gaussian|Student's-t RS Copula. GA|CV is a Gaussian|Canonical-Vine RS Copula. GA|M is a Gaussian|Mixture RS Copula. St|St is a Student's-t|Student's-t RS Copula. St|CV is a Student's-t|Canonical-Vine RS Copula. St|M is a Student's-t|Mixture RS Copula. The multivariate Mixture Copula consists of one Gaussian, one Clayton and one Gumbel Copulas.

		GA|GA	GA|St	GA|CV	GA|M	St|St	St|CV	St|M
rel. Hit VaR	SL_{99}	0.010	0.010	0.010	0.010	0.010	0.010	0.005
	SL_{95}	0.034	0.034	0.034	0.034	0.034	0.034	0.034
	SL_{90}	0.082	0.077	0.077	0.072	0.077	0.067	0.072
Kupiec Test	SL_{99}	0	0	0	0	0	0	0
	SL_{95}	0	0	0	0	0	0	0
	SL_{90}	0	0	0	0	0	0	0
Max. VaR	SL_{99}	-0.057	-0.057	-0.057	-0.057	-0.057	-0.058	-0.057
	SL_{95}	-0.037	-0.037	-0.037	-0.037	-0.037	-0.037	-0.037
	SL_{90}	-0.028	-0.028	-0.028	-0.028	-0.028	-0.028	-0.028
Min. VaR	SL_{99}	-0.018	-0.018	-0.018	-0.018	-0.018	-0.018	-0.018
	SL_{95}	-0.012	-0.012	-0.012	-0.012	-0.012	-0.012	-0.012
	SL_{90}	-0.008	-0.008	-0.008	-0.008	-0.008	-0.008	-0.008
Max. VaR Excess	SL_{99}	-0.013	-0.014	-0.014	-0.013	-0.014	-0.014	-0.013
	SL_{95}	-0.020	-0.020	-0.020	-0.020	-0.020	-0.020	-0.020
	SL_{90}	-0.023	-0.023	-0.023	-0.023	-0.023	-0.023	-0.023
rel. Hit CVaR	SL_1	0.005	0.005	0.005	0.005	0.005	0.005	0.005
	SL_5	0.019	0.019	0.019	0.019	0.019	0.019	0.019
	SL_{10}	0.029	0.029	0.029	0.029	0.029	0.029	0.029
AAD CVaR	SL_1	0.000	0.000	0.000	0.000	0.000	0.000	0.000
	SL_5	0.000	0.000	0.000	0.000	0.000	0.000	0.000
	SL_{10}	0.000	0.000	0.000	0.000	0.000	0.000	0.000
Max. CVaR Excess	SL_1	-0.009	-0.009	-0.009	-0.008	-0.009	-0.009	-0.008
	SL_5	-0.016	-0.016	-0.016	-0.016	-0.016	-0.016	-0.016
	SL_{10}	-0.019	-0.019	-0.019	-0.019	-0.019	-0.019	-0.019

Table 6.9 – Dynamic Copula Multi Asset Classes Equally Weighted Portfolio VaR and CVaR. I predict one-week VaR and CVaR at the 1%, 5% and 10% significance levels (*SL*). This table presents the relative violation frequencies for the VaR and CVaR predictions (rel. Hit VaR, rel. Hit CVaR) during the backtest. The Kupiec test evaluates the null hypothesis ($H_0 = 0$) of correct VaR coverage against imprecise VaR coverage ($H_0 = 1$) at the 95% significance level. The Max. VaR reports the maximum predicted VaR and the Min. VaR reports the minimum predicted VaR, for the backtest procedure. The Max. VaR (CVaR) Excess denotes the maximum exceedance of the VaR (CVaR) forecasts during the backtest. The average absolute distance of the realized returns from the predicted CVaR levels in case of VaR violations is denoted by AAD CVaR. The Dynamic Copulas are abbreviated: GU is a Dynamic Gumbel Copula. CL is a Dynamic Clayton Copula. GA is a Dynamic Gaussian Copula. St is a Dynamic Student's-t Copula. Mix is a Dynamic Mixture Copula. Mix1 combines a dynamic Gaussian and a dynamic Clayton Copula. Mix2 combines a dynamic Student's-t and a dynamic Clayton Copula. Mix3 combines a dynamic Gaussian and dynamic Gumbel Copula. Mix4 combines a dynamic Student's-t and a dynamic Gumbel Copula.

		GU	CL	GA	St	Mix1	Mix2	Mix3	Mix4
rel. Hit VaR	SL_{99}	0.010	0.005	0.014	0.014	0.014	0.014	0.014	0.014
	SL_{95}	0.034	0.034	0.043	0.043	0.038	0.048	0.043	0.038
	SL_{90}	0.072	0.072	0.091	0.091	0.091	0.091	0.091	0.091
Kupiec Test	SL_{99}	0	0	0	0	0	0	0	0
	SL_{95}	0	0	0	0	0	0	0	0
	SL_{90}	0	0	0	0	0	0	0	0
Max. VaR	SL_{99}	-0.057	-0.058	-0.048	-0.048	-0.047	-0.047	-0.048	-0.047
	SL_{95}	-0.037	-0.037	-0.030	-0.030	-0.031	-0.030	-0.031	-0.029
	SL_{90}	-0.028	-0.028	-0.023	-0.022	-0.023	-0.022	-0.023	-0.023
Min. VaR	SL_{99}	-0.018	-0.020	-0.018	-0.019	-0.018	-0.019	-0.018	-0.019
	SL_{95}	-0.012	-0.012	-0.012	-0.012	-0.012	-0.012	-0.012	-0.011
	SL_{90}	-0.009	-0.009	-0.008	-0.008	-0.008	-0.008	-0.008	-0.008
Max. VaR Excess	SL_{99}	-0.013	-0.011	-0.013	-0.013	-0.014	-0.013	-0.014	-0.013
	SL_{95}	-0.020	-0.019	-0.020	-0.020	-0.020	-0.020	-0.020	-0.020
	SL_{90}	-0.023	-0.023	-0.023	-0.023	-0.023	-0.023	-0.023	-0.023
rel. Hit CVaR	SL_1	0.005	0.005	0.005	0.005	0.005	0.005	0.005	0.005
	SL_5	0.014	0.010	0.019	0.019	0.019	0.019	0.019	0.019
	SL_{10}	0.024	0.024	0.019	0.019	0.019	0.019	0.019	0.019
AAD CVaR	SL_1	0.000	0.000	0.000	0.000	0.000	0.000	0.000	0.000
	SL_5	0.000	0.000	0.000	0.000	0.000	0.000	0.000	0.000
	SL_{10}	0.000	0.000	0.000	0.000	0.000	0.000	0.000	0.000
Max. CVaR Excess	SL_1	-0.010	-0.008	-0.008	-0.008	-0.008	-0.008	-0.008	-0.008
	SL_5	-0.016	-0.015	-0.015	-0.015	-0.015	-0.016	-0.015	-0.015
	SL_{10}	-0.019	-0.018	-0.019	-0.019	-0.018	-0.019	-0.019	-0.019

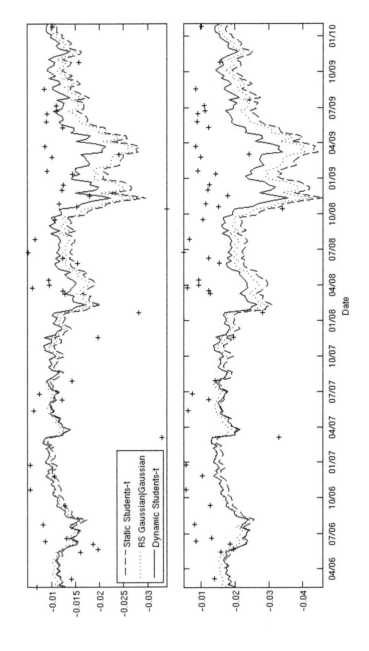

Figure 6.3 – Multi Asset Classes Portfolio VaR and CVaR Forecasts. The top figure plots the 1-week VaR forecasts and the bottom figure plots the 1-week CVaR forecasts based on the Dynamic Student's-t, the RS Gaussian|Gaussian and the Static Student's-t Copulas at the SL_{10} for the equally weighted Multi Asset Classes portfolio. '+' represent the matching realized equally weighted returns $\bar{x}_t \leq -0.005$. The backtest covers the timeframe 06.Feb.2006 to 01.Feb.2010.

6.4 Summary

This section shortly outlines the most important findings from the out-of-sample portfolio VaR backtests. I find evidence of right tail dependence among the G7 Bond yields, which is captured precisely by the Static Gumbel Copula. Nevertheless, the application of the Dynamic Gumbel Copula improves the portfolio VaR and CVaR forecasts, tremendously. This depicts severe right tail dependence among Bond yields and significantly changing dependence intensities. It also proves the Dynamic skeleton's ability to comprise fundamental shifts in the dependence structure and to accurately forecast future interactions. In contrast to the Dynamic Copulas, the RS Copulas characterize the interaction of the Bond yields via two dependence regimes. However, their poor portfolio VaR forecasts indicate that changes in the Bond yield dependencies are rather fundamental and permanent, but they do not follow a simple and recurring pattern.

The dependencies of the G7 Stock markets follow a simple pattern: they tighten during volatile and downturn phases and vice versa. Consequently, models which account for this simple and recurring pattern contribute to precise Stock portfolio VaR and CVaR forecasts. The Static Canonical-Vine Copula contains several bivariate Clayton Copulas, which explicitly account for left tail dependencies. Thus, its application generates the most precise portfolio risk predictions among the Static skeletons. The RS Copulas cluster the Stock markets into one high and one low dependence regimes. This is an exact representation of the Stock market dependence characteristics and results accurate portfolio VaR and CVaR forecasts. Nevertheless, the Dynamic Clayton Copula captures the interactions of the Stock markets most precisely. The underlying Copula skeleton accounts for left tail dependence and simultaneously the intensity of the Copula parameter swings over time. Its application results the most accurate Stocks portfolio VaR and CVaR predictions.

Finally, the dependencies of multiple asset classes are most difficult to comprise. In contrast to Stock markets, they do not follow a simple and recurring pattern, but they change fundamentally over time (Section 5.3). Hence, Static Copulas measure and predict them imprecisely, resulting inaccurate portfolio VaR predictions. In contrast, the RS Copulas cluster the multiple asset classes into one high and one low dependence regimes. Although they improve the portfolio VaR forecasts, they are not flexible enough to comprise the fundamental shifts in the dependence structure. The Dynamic Elliptical and Mixture Copulas capture the dependencies via multiple parameters which constantly adjust their intensities to shifts in the underlying data. Their superior flexibilities result the most precise VaR hit ratios during the backtest.

117

Chapter 7

Portfolio Allocation

Markowitz (1952) set the basis for modern portfolio theory. His work focuses on variance minimization for a selected target return. In this setup, the portfolio target return is simply the weighted expected returns of the assets. The according portfolio variance consists of two factors: the asset variances and their appendant covariances, respectively their correlations. This thesis focuses on time-instable and asymmetric dependencies, and proposes a parametric approach to properly comprise them. Well quantified dependencies are a key component for precise portfolio constructions. To amplify the impact of misspecified correlations, I simulate return datasets with equal univariate characteristics but different dependence structures. At first, I simulate four Bond yield datasets from the linear correlation matrix, the Static Gumbel, the RS Gaussian|Student's-t and the Dynamic Gumbel Copulas. In a second step, the simulated Bond yields are transformed into virtual Bond prices to allow for a meaningful portfolio allocation. In case of the G7 stocks, I simulate four datasets: The first dataset contains the dependence structure of linear correlation coefficients; The second to the fourth datasets contain the dependencies from the Static Canonical-Vine, the RS Gaussian|Mixture and the Dynamic Clayton Copulas. Finally, I simulate four Multi Asset Classes datasets with equal univariate characteristics but different dependence structures. In this case, the first simulated dataset comprises the dependence structure of the linear correlation matrix. The second to the fourth datasets are based on simulations from the Static Student's-t, the RS Gaussian|Gaussian and the Dynamic Student's-t Copulas.

Regardless of the dependence measure, the univariate simulations , $(u_1, ..., u_d) \sim U[0, 1]$, are transformed into return series via the univariate distributions. According to the Sklar theorem (1959) (Equation 3.1), this procedure results four simulated Bond returns datasets, four Stock returns datasets and four Multi Asset Classes returns datasets. Within each asset class, the four datasets reveal identical univariate characteristics but they differ in regards to their dependence structures. Allocating portfolios on basis of the four different datasets within each asset class, demonstrates the impact of the different dependence measures on the optimal portfolio shares. Additionally, I calculate higher moments for each portfolio to identify the characteristics of the utilized Copulas and their impacts on the joint distribution shapes.

I discuss two asset allocation procedures in this thesis to demonstrate the impact of dependence misspecification. At first, I allocate Mean-Variance efficient portfolios and calculate their third and fourth moments as well as their Conditional-Value-of-Risks (CVaR). The Mean-Variance optimizations are only approximations because neither the univariate nor the joint distributions are normal. Nevertheless, this is the most common portfolio allocation procedure and therefore I utilize it to demonstrate the impact of different dependence measures on the 2-Moment optimal portfolio shares. Second, I construct portfolios by minimizing the portfolio CVaRs for given target returns. Similar to the Mean-Variance framework, this procedure results Mean-CVaR efficient portfolios. Again, I compute the third and fourth moments of all portfolios to demonstrate the characteristics of the individual Copula functions and their impacts on the joint distribution shapes.

7.1   Algebra of Higher Moments

In this section I give a brief introduction to higher moments which set the basis for the portfolio allocations. Consider two random variables A and B. The expected values of both variables are denoted as $\mu_A = E[A]$ and $\mu_B = E[B]$. The expected variances of the variables are the quadratic deviations from the expected values. Commonly, the covariance describes the interaction between both variables. It is denoted as: $\Sigma_{A,B} = E[(A - E[A])(B - E[B])]$. The covariance matrix comprises the variances and the correlation of the random variables. The skewness and coskewness of both variables is defined, analogously:

$$cs_A \;=\; E[A - E[A]]^3 \tag{7.1}$$

$$cs_{A,B} \;=\; E[(A - E[A])^2 (B - E[B])] \tag{7.2}$$

$$cs_{B,A} \;=\; E[(A - E[A])(B - E[B])^2]. \tag{7.3}$$

Note that the coskewness of A and B, $cs_{A,B}$, differs from the coskewness of B and A, $cs_{B,A}$. Hence, there exist two coskewnesses for two random variables. This is due to the quadratic terms in the coskewness equations. In order to calculate the coskewnesses for more than two assets, its general form is given by:

$$cs_{A,B,C} = E[(A - E[A])(B - E[B])(C - E[C])]. \qquad (7.4)$$

The portfolio skewness is defined as $cs_p = w' \, \mathbf{CS}(w \otimes w)$, where $\otimes$ denotes the Kronecker product. All elements of the weights vector ($w^{d \times 1}$) are multiplied with each other, resulting a $d^2 \times 1$ vector. The matrix $\mathbf{CS}^{d \times d^2}$ contains all skewnesses and coskewnesses of the asset universe. This matrix is constructed from the three dimensional skewness/coskewness cube by transforming the matrices from the third dimension into the second dimension. After the transformation, common matrix calculations can be applied to higher moments - a great advantage.

In a similar manner, the fourth moment defines the kurtosis and cokurtosis. In order to calculate the portfolio kurtosis, the Kronecker product has to be applied twice to construct a weight vector which matches the four dimensional kurtosis/cokurtosis cube. In general, the cokurtosis for four assets is defined as:

$$ck_{A,B,C,D} = E[(A - E[A])(B - E[B])(C - E[C])(D - E[D])]. \qquad (7.5)$$

Similar to the three dimensional skewness cube, the four dimensional kurtosis cube can be transposed into a matrix $\mathbf{CK}^{d \times d^3}$. The portfolio kurtosis is then calculated as $ck_p = w' \, \mathbf{CK}(w \otimes (w \otimes w))$, but empirically observed cokurtoses are rather small. Moments higher than the fourth are empirically insignificant, but their calculation requires extensive computer power. Therefore, I calculate only the first four moments of each optimal portfolio.

Overall, the first four moments reveal the following characteristics: The distribution mean defines its position and the according variance characterizes the distribution dispersion. The skewness defines the asymmetry of the distribution. In general, a negative skewness implicates longer left and shorter right tails. The opposite holds true for positive skewness. The kurtosis describes the distribution concavity. The normal distribution reveals a kurtosis of 3. Any kurtosis larger than 3 implies a stronger concentration of the distribution around its mean and higher probabilities of extreme values on the distribution boundaries. Compared to the normal distribution, a kurtosis smaller than 3 implies a weaker concentration around the mean and smaller probabilities of realizations on the distribution boundaries. Throughout this thesis I always present the excess kurtosis. Most empirical works concerned with higher moments in portfolio theory standardize the previously described moments with the securities' standard deviations. I follow this method throughout this thesis. In general, the standardized moment (SM) of order o for the random variable A is calculated as:

$$SM_A^o = \frac{E\left[A - E[A]\right]^o}{\left(\sqrt{E[A - E[A]]^2}\right)^o} \tag{7.6}$$

Higher moments of portfolios characterize the joint distribution which defines the portfolio risks. Portfolios which are efficient in a 2-Moment framework might turn inefficient under conditions of higher moments. Nevertheless, standard risk measures, e.g. the covariance matrix, only account for the first two moments but neglect the skewness of the joint distribution. In contrast, empirical joint distributions of financial assets are often negatively skewed. The according long left tail is caused by asymmetric univariate distributions and by asymmetric dependencies. I explicitly account for asymmetric dependencies via Archimedian Copulas. According to the Sklar theorem (1959), the GARCH models define the univariate distribution shapes and the Copula impacts the shape of the joint distribution. Consequently, joint distributions which are constructed on basis of the covariance setup are symmetric, whereas joint distributions which are defined through Archimedian Copulas comprise asymmetries and higher moment characteristics, accurately. Constructing portfolios on basis of different joint distributions results different optimal shares. Asymmetric dependencies affect the optimal portfolio shares most severely in the Mean-CVaR procedure because it explicitly focuses on the left tail of the joint distribution.

7.2 Mean-Variance Efficiency

Markowitz (1952) questions how to structure an investor's portfolio to achieve an optimal risk-return tradeoff. He divides his work into two parts. The first part focuses on return expectations which most commonly are derived from historic data. The second part is dedicated to the portfolio risk which arises from the combination of multiple securities. Markowitz (1952) measures the portfolio risk via the covariance matrix of the individual assets. Consequently, an investor minimizes the variance/covariance matrix ($\Sigma^{d \times d}$) of a portfolio that satisfies his return expectations. The according optimization with respect to the portfolio shares ($w^{d \times 1}$) is denoted by:

$$\min_{w} \; w'\Sigma w \tag{7.7}$$
$$s.t. \quad w'\mu = \bar{\mu}_p,$$

where μ is the $d \times 1$ vector of expected returns. The application of the Lagrange methodology offers a solution to this quadratic optimization problem. Therefore, I denote the optimization problem and its constraints as:

$$L = w'\Sigma w - \Lambda_1(w'\mu - \bar{\mu}_p) - \Lambda_2(w'l - 1), \tag{7.8}$$

where l is a $d \times 1$ unit vector. The derivation of the Lagrange system and the according transformations result an analytical solution for the optimal portfolio weights:

$$w = \Sigma^{-1}(\mu \; l) \begin{pmatrix} \mu'\Sigma^{-1}\mu & \mu'\Sigma^{-1}l \\ l'\Sigma^{-1}\mu & l'\Sigma^{-1}l \end{pmatrix} \begin{pmatrix} \bar{\mu}_p \\ 1 \end{pmatrix} \tag{7.9}$$

Equation 7.9 calculates the optimal portfolio weights for the individual portfolio target returns, $\bar{\mu}_p$. Implementing the optimal portfolio weights into the portfolio variance equation results the according portfolio variance. The graphical illustration of all target returns and their according minimized variances in a risk-return diagram results the concave efficient frontier. Portfolios beneath the efficient frontier are inefficient and portfolios above are not realizable. In order to accomplish an optimal risk-return tradeoff, the investor has to pick a portfolio on the efficient frontier that matches his individual preferences. Nevertheless, this portfolio selection is only accurate under two conditions. First, the returns have to be normally or at least symmetrically distributed. Second, the investor has to reveal a quadratic utility function. If the returns are not symmetrically distributed, the Mean-Variance framework is only an approximation of the optimal portfolios. In order to overcome those restrictions, this work also considers higher moments in the allocation procedure.

7.3 Higher Moments Optimization

There exist a lot of different methodologies to account for higher moments in the portfolio selection process. Section 7.2 describes portfolio selection via the classical Mean-Variance approach, in this section I discuss an extension of the classic Mean-Variance framework to the third moment. Arditti (1967) examines portfolio selection procedures for the first three moments and concludes that this extension enhances the portfolio selection. Levy (1969) analyzes the effect of the first four moments on the optimal portfolio constellation and finds significant impact of all moments. Further empirical work presents evidence that moments greater than the fourth do not significantly enhance the portfolio selection, but dramatically increase the computational effort.

Considering the skewness and any higher moments in the portfolio allocation procedure requires additional constraints in the optimization. Those additional constraints might lead to optimal portfolios that might not match the classical Mean-Variance efficient frontier, but instead might be found somewhere beneath it. Vice versa, mean-variance optimal portfolios might not be optimal under conditions of the third and fourth moments. For example, a 3-Moment efficient portfolio might reveal a lower mean than its 2-Moment optimal counterpart, but the same variance. In return, the 3-Moment efficient portfolio would offer more positive skewness.

In contrast to the 2-Moment optimization, the 3-Moment optimization explicitly accounts for the skewness/coskewness of the securities. In the same manner as in the Mean-Variance optimization, consider d risky assets. Those are characterized by their means ($\mu^{d \times 1}$), their covariances ($\Sigma^{d \times d}$) and their coskewnesses cube ($\mathbf{CS}^{d \times d \times d}$). $\mathbf{CS}$ is transformed into a matrix ($\mathbf{CS}^{d \times d^2}$) to allow simple matrix calculations during the optimization. The portfolio weights are denoted as a $d \times 1$ vector ($w^{d \times 1}$) and the first four moments of the portfolio are defined as:

$$\mu_p = w'\mu \tag{7.10}$$

$$\sigma_p^2 = w'\Sigma w \tag{7.11}$$

$$cs_p = w'\,\mathbf{CS}(w \otimes w) \tag{7.12}$$

$$ck_p = w'\,\mathbf{CK}(w \otimes (w \otimes w)), \tag{7.13}$$

where $\otimes$ denotes the Kronecker product. The optimization of the Mean-Variance setup is analytically possible, because it is only a quadratic problem. The extension of the optimization to higher moments results a multi-dimensional setup. Thus, an analytical solution does not exist, but I can simply minimize the variance for given return and higher moment targets. For the 3-Moment optimization, those constraints result the following optimization problem:

$$\min_{w} \; w'\Sigma w \tag{7.14}$$

$$s.t. \quad \bar{\mu}_p = w'\mu$$

$$\overline{cs}_p = w' \, \Sigma(w \otimes w)$$

The problem from equation 7.14 is transformed into the following Lagrange function:

$$L = w'\Sigma w + \Lambda_1 (\bar{\mu}_p - w'\mu) + \Lambda_2 (\overline{cs}_p - w'\mathbf{CS}(w \otimes w)). \tag{7.15}$$

In the next step, the Lagrange function is differentiated and its derivatives are set equal to zero. This results the following system of equations with respect to the asset weights, w, and the Lagrange factors, Λ_1 and Λ_2:

$$\frac{\partial L}{\partial w} = 2\Sigma w - \Lambda_1 \mu - 3\Lambda_2 \mathbf{CS}(w \otimes w) = 0 \tag{7.16}$$

$$\frac{\partial L}{\partial \Lambda_1} = \bar{\mu}_p - w'\mu = 0 \tag{7.17}$$

$$\frac{\partial L}{\partial \Lambda_2} = \overline{cs}_p - w' \, \mathbf{CS}(w \otimes w) = 0 \tag{7.18}$$

This system of equations describes the exact solutions with respect to w. In contrast to the Mean-Variance optimization, an analytical solution is not possible. Hence, numerical methods are necessary to minimize the variance under the given constraints. The calculation of the minimum variance portfolios for given target returns and target skewnesses result in an efficient area. Similar to the Mean-Variance framework, the choice of the optimal portfolio depends on the investor's individual preferences. The portfolio optimization for higher moments is executed in the same manner. Any additional moment requires an additional constraint and an extra Lagrange factor.

A very efficient alternative to capture higher moments is the Value-at-Risk (VaR) methodology (Equation 6.1). Instead of minimizing the variance for a target return, Roy (1952) constructs portfolios via shortfall minimization under the same conditions. Similar to the Mean-Variance procedure, there exists an analytical solution for the portfolio selection problem if the returns are normally distributed. His "safety first" principle minimizes investors' left tail risk for a given target return. Hence, his model is closely related to the newer VaR approach, which calculates the worst lower boundary for a given confidence level. Alexander and Baptist (2002) implement the VaR concept into the Mean-Variance framework, resulting a Mean-VaR concept. This defines risk as the probability to exceed a certain threshold. Minimizing the VaR for a target return results the optimal portfolio. In case of normally distributed returns, the authors find matching Mean-Variance and Mean-VaR efficient frontiers. This result does not surprise; If the returns are normally distributed, one can easily calculate the VaR parametrically from the expected returns and the variance/covariance matrix (Σ) as:

$$VaR_{SL}(w) = \Phi^{-1}(SL)w'\Sigma w - w'\mu, \tag{7.19}$$

where Φ^{-1} represents the quantile function of the univariate standard normal distribution and SL denotes the significance level.

Unfortunately, the VaR concept is incapable of handling losses that might occur beyond the indicated threshold amount and turns unstable in an asymmetrically distributed framework. Therefore, I enhance from the VaR concept to the Conditional-Value-at-Risk (CVaR) (Equation 6.2). The CVaR's greatest advantages over the VaR are its ability to account for losses beyond the threshold, Ξ, on the left distribution tail, its numerical speed and its mathematically defined adaptability to any distribution shape rather than only to the Gaussian distribution. Additionally, the optimization of Mean-CVaR portfolios implicitly accounts for higher moments but does not require additional constraints. I apply Rockafellar's and Uryasev's (2002) algorithm to minimize the CVaR under stable conditions and to preserve convexity. Consequently, the minimization of the loss associated with w over all $w \in W$ is equivalent to maximizing $CVaR_{SL}(w)$ over all $w \in W \times \mathbb{R}$, resulting:

$$\underset{w \in W \times \mathbb{R}}{\text{argmax}} \; CVaR_{SL}(w), \tag{7.20}$$
$$s.t. \quad w'\mu = \bar{\mu}_p.$$

The algorithm calculates portfolio weights w which minimize expected losses beyond the threshold Ξ.

7.4 Portfolio Allocation with higher Moments

In this section I empirically apply the previously mentioned methods to allocate Bond, Stocks and Multi Asset Classes portfolios on basis of the complete data samples. Bond yields are not an investable asset class and therefore I transform the yield simulations into Bond prices to construct optimal portfolios. I construct Mean-Variance and Mean-CVaR optimal portfolios, but the weights are constrained to:

$$-1 \leq w_j \leq 1 \text{ for } j = 1, ..., d \qquad (7.21)$$
$$\sum_{j=1}^{d} w_j = 1.$$

In case of the 2-Moment portfolio selection, the variance is minimized for a given target return. In case of the Mean-CVaR portfolio selection, the constraints remain the same but the portfolio CVaR is minimized for a given target return. Of course, only a certain portion of those portfolios is practically applicable due to asset splitting problems or liquidity issues. The primary objective of this section is to demonstrate the impact of correlation misspecification on the optimal portfolio shares. Thus, I simulate return datasets from the linear correlation matrix and the Copulas which perform best during the VaR and CVaR backtests. This results four Stocks datasets with equal univariate characteristics but different dependence structures. Each simulated Stocks dataset contains seven indices. The same procedure results four simulated Multi Asset Classes datasets which contain four indices, each. Again, the same procedure is repeated to simulate four Bond yield datasets containing seven indices each with the same univariate characteristics but different dependence structures. Tereafter, the yield simulations are transformed into Bond prices. For each index, 50000 simulations are generated. Finally, the Mean-Variance and Mean-CVaR optimizations are exercised on basis of the twelve simulated datasets.

At first, I allocate portfolios based on the Bond yield simulations with reference maturity (rm) 10 years. Although Bond yields are not directly investable, there exists a well defined relation between Bond yield-to-maturity (YTM) and virtual Bond prices (BP):

$$\frac{BP_t}{BP_{t-1}} = \frac{(1 + YTM_{t-1})^{rm}}{(1 + YTM_t)^{rm}} \qquad (7.22)$$

According to equation 7.22, the simulated Bond yields are transformed into virtual Bond price returns for the allocation procedures. Thus, right tail dependent Bond yields translate into left tail dependent Bond prices. In Chapter 6, the Static and Dynamic Gumbel and the RS Gaussian|Student's-t Copulas were identified as the most adequate skeletons within their categories to model the dependencies of the G7 Bond yields. Consequently, transforming the right tail dependent Static and Dynamic Gumbel Copula yield simulations results in left tail dependent virtual Bond prices. In contrast, Bond yields which are simulated via the correlation matrix and the RS Copula are symmetrically dependent, resulting in symmetrically dependent transformed Bond prices. Figure 7.1 presents the Mean-Variance efficient and figure 7.2 the Mean-CVaR efficient virtual G7 Bond portfolios.

Due to the fact that neither all univariate nor the multivariate Bond return distributions are symmetric, the Mean-Variance optimization is only an approximation. The $\mu_p - \sigma_p$ efficient frontiers are similar for any Copulas and the linear correlation matrix because at the end of the observation period, any model framework measures similar dependence intensities. However, the differences caused by the four dependence models are obvious for the portfolio skewness levels (second row in Figures 7.1 and 7.2). The Static and the Dynamic Gumbel Copulas simulate right tail dependent Bond yields, resulting in left tail dependent virtual Bond prices. In contrast, the linear correlation matrix and the RS Gaussian|Student's-t Copula are symmetric dependence models. Consequently, Bond portfolios allocated on basis of the yield simulations from the Static and Dynamic Gumbel Copulas reveal a much greater negative portfolio skewness amplitude, although any portfolios' $\mu_p - \sigma_p$ tradeoff is almost identical. Of course, the third moment greatly influences the portfolio CVaR levels, as they are directly derived from the joint distributions. Therefore, the four $\mu_p - CVaR_p$ curves reveal greater dispersions than their according $\mu_p - \sigma_p$ efficient frontiers.

Comparing the two-moment efficient portfolios with the Mean-CVaR optimal portfolios, amplifies the impact of the asymmetric Copulas on the optimal portfolio shares. Minimizing the portfolio CVaR does not solely focus on variance minimization, but it considers the portfolio skewness and kurtosis, as well. The Static and Dynamic Gumbel Copulas cause more intensely skewed joint distributions than the symmetric correlation matrix and the symmetric RS Copula, although the univariate parameters are identical. Consequently, the Mean-Variance and Mean-CVaR optimal $\mu_p - \sigma_p$, $\mu_p - cs_p$, $\mu_p - ck_p$ and $\mu_p - CVaR_p$ curves differ more significantly if the optimizations are executed based on simulations from the asymmetric Copulas. Allocating Mean-CVaR optimal virtual Bond portfolios based on simulations from the "best-fit" Dynamic Gumbel Copula results the least attractive $\mu_p - \sigma_p$ combinations. In contrast, the symmetric dependence frameworks severely underestimate the portfolio skewness of a virtual Bond port-folio, resulting in overly optimistic $\mu_p - \sigma_p$ curves. Thus, the simulation study emphasizes the necessity to consider asymmetric dependencies and higher moments of risk for an effective Bond portfolio allocation.

Figure 7.3 presents the Mean-Variance efficient G7 Stocks portfolios. Note that the Mean-Variance optimization is only an approximation because the univariate and joint return distri-butions are non-normal. The shapes of the efficient frontiers are similar for any dependence models. Increasing return expectations are attended by increasing volatilities. In Chapter 6, the Dynamic Clayton Copula was identified as the most adequate skeleton to model the depen-dencies of the G7 Stocks dataset. Therefore, I use it as the dependence structure benchmark in this section. The linear covariance matrix models symmetric dependencies and reveals the least attractive return-variance combinations what is due to correlation underestimations. This interpretation is counterintuitive, but remember the investor is not restricted from short selling assets (Equation 7.21). Thus, significant positive correlations are utilized for diversification by holding negative shares in one asset and positive shares in another. Consequently, the RS Cop-ula indicates the most attractive return-variance combinations because it simulates data from the high dependence regime via the symmetric Gaussian Copula.

Similar to the Dynamic Clayton, the Static Canonical-Vine Copula is an asymmetric de-pendence model and captures left tail dependencies which cause negatively skewed joint dis-tributions. The second plot in figure 7.3 denotes the skewnesses of the 2-Moment efficient portfolios. Of course, they are most distinct for the two asymmetric Copulas, what illustrates their impact on the joint distribution shapes. However, those asymmetries are neglected by the 2-Moment optimization what explains the similar shapes of the four efficient frontiers. In con-trast to the efficient frontiers, the four $\mu_p - cs_p$ plots are shaped very differently and do not follow a unique pattern. The $\mu_p - cs_p$ curves of the two asymmetric Copulas reveal positive gradients, whereas the symmetric dependence models suggest the opposite. This amplifies the impact of asymmetric dependencies on the portfolio risk/return characteristics and illustrates the necessity to account for this feature during the portfolio allocation procedure. Additionally, the negative portfolio skewnesses clearly indicate that the 2-Moment efficient portfolios turn inefficient under conditions of higher moments.

Figure 7.1 – G7 Bonds Mean-Variance efficient Portfolios: The first row presents the 2-Moment efficient portfolios. The second row presents the according return-skewness combinations. The third row presents the according portfolio kurtoses. The fourth row presents the according return-CVaR combinations at SL_1. The linear correlation matrix and the three Copula models are estimated on basis of the complete G7 Bond yields dataset. The complete dataset covers the time-frame 06.March.1991 to 03.Feb.2010. In the graphics, the dependence models are represented via: '.' Linear Covariance Matrix; '*' Static Gumbel Copula; '+' RS Gaussian|Student's-t Copula; 'o' Dynamic Gumbel Copula. The returns on the y-axis and the volatilities are annualized. The skewnesses, kurtoses and CVaRs are presented as weekly data.

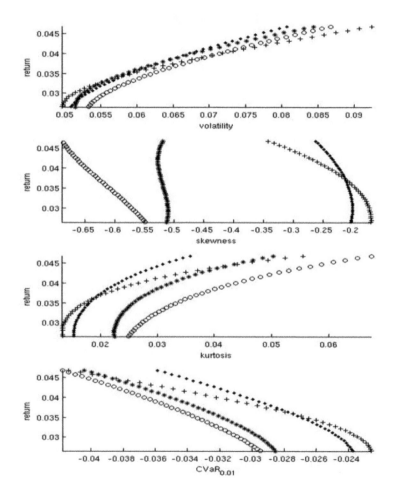

Figure 7.2 – G7 Bonds Mean-CVaR efficient Portfolios: The fourth row presents the Mean-CVaR efficient portfolios at SL_1. The first row presents the resulting Mean-Variance tradeoffs. The second row presents the according return-skewness combinations and the third row presents the according portfolio kurtoses. The linear correlation matrix and the three Copula models are estimated on basis of the complete G7 Bond yields dataset. The complete dataset covers the time-frame 06.March.1991 to 03.Feb.2010. In the graphics, the dependence models are represented via: '.' Linear Covariance Matrix; '*' Static Gumbel Copula; '+' RS Gaussian|Student's-t Copula; 'o' Dynamic Gumbel Copula. The returns on the y-axis and the volatilities are annualized. The skewnesses, kurtoses and CVaRs are presented as weekly data.

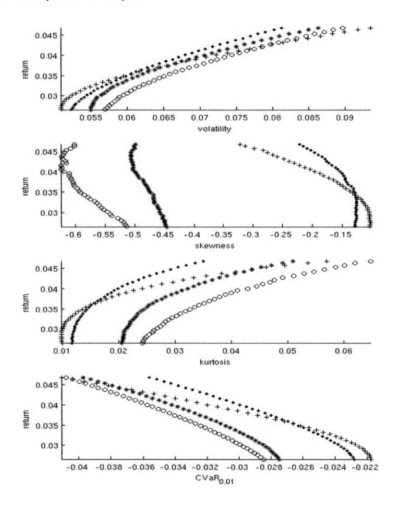

Constructing portfolios on basis of simulations from the Dynamic Clayton Copula results the most distinct kurtoses. This is due to the Clayton Copula's shape and its parameter intensity at the end of the observation period when the 2-Moment optimal portfolios are allocated. Nevertheless, the $\mu_p - ck_p$ plots follow a unique pattern. Increasing return expectations require more distinct portfolio kurtoses. High levels of kurtoses define narrow density shapes with more distinct tails which increase severe shortfall risks. The $\mu_p - \sigma_p$ allocation procedure neglects this aspect as it only considers the first two moments.

The CVaRs of the 2-Moment efficient portfolio are presented in the fourth row of figure 7.3. Again, portfolios allocated on basis of the linear covariance matrix offer the least attractive return-CVaR characteristics. This is due to the correlation underestimation which restricts the investor from diversifying through short sales. A comparison of the $\mu_p - CVaR_p$ and $\mu_p - \sigma_p$ curves based on simulations from the Dynamic Clayton and the Gaussian|Mixture RS Copulas depicts a very interesting feature. Both $\mu_p - \sigma_p$ curves are shaped almost identical but shifted on the x-axis. In contrast, the two according $\mu_p - CVaR_p$ curves differ significantly. The RS Copula based curve requires increasingly negative CVaR levels for annual returns greater than 0.015. In contrast, the Dynamic Clayton based curve suggests decreasing CVaR levels as the annual returns rise from 0.005 to 0.04. The opposite gradients of both curves are due to different joint distribution shapes, whose left tails define the CVaR. Again, differences in the joint distribution shapes are solely caused by the applied Copulas, because any simulations feature the same univariate characteristics. The Archimedian Copulas model asymmetric dependencies, resulting in negatively skewed portfolio distributions with long left tails. In contrast, the dominant high dependence regime of the RS Copula is modeled via a Gaussian Copula resulting in a symmetric joint distribution. This feature explains the significant differences of the two $\mu_p - CVaR_p$ curves. For the two respective $\mu_p - \sigma_p$ curves, only the first two moments of the joint distributions are relevant what explains their similar shapes.

In contrast to the 2-Moment optimization, the Mean-CVaR procedure accounts for higher moments. The left tail of the joint distribution defines the portfolio CVaR and therefore the distribution shape significantly impacts the optimal portfolio weights. In contrast to the Mean-Variance optimization, the Mean-CVaR procedure minimizes the expected losses beyond a threshold. Hence, the optimization procedure focuses on the left tail of the portfolio return distribution, whereas the right tail is neglected. Figure 7.4 presents the Mean-CVaR efficient portfolios at the SL_1. Portfolios constructed on basis of the RS Copula simulations offer the most attractive $\mu_p - CVaR_p$ combinations whereas the linear covariance matrix suggests the least favorable tradeoffs. This outcome is similar to the Mean-Variance efficient portfolio allocation. However, the differences of the Mean-Variance and the Mean-CVaR efficient portfolios are most distinct for the asymmetric dependence models. This outcome is due to the different joint distribution shapes. The asymmetric Copulas simulate data which contains severe left tail dependence what causes long left tails in the according joint return distributions. In contrast, the linear correlation matrix and the high dependence regime Gaussian Copula model symmetric dependence structures. This significantly reduces the skewnesses of their joint distributions. Any skewnesses in their joint distributions are due to the univariate model characteristics. The Mean-CVaR allocation measures risk via the portfolio distribution quantiles and hence distinct negative skewness and positive kurtosis increase the riskiness. In contrast, the 2-Moment optimization neglects these features. As the asymmetric Copulas simulate the most negatively skewed joint distributions, their $\mu_p - CVaR_p$ optimal portfolios differ most severely from their $\mu_p - \sigma_p$ optimal portfolios. The symmetric dependence models cause less joint distribution skewnesses and hence their Mean-Variance and Mean-CVaR optimal portfolios differ less.

A comparison of the second to the fourth moments of the $\mu_p - CVaR_p$ and $\mu_p - \sigma_p$ efficient portfolios (Figures 7.3, 7.4) amplifies the necessity to account for higher moments during the portfolio selection process. It also demonstrates the impact of accurate asymmetric Copulas on the optimal portfolio shares. The first graph of Figure 7.4 presents the $\mu_p - \sigma_p$ combinations for the Mean-CVaR efficient portfolios. Based on simulations from the symmetric dependence models, the possible combinations are slightly less attractive than those from the 2-Moment optimization. The Mean-CVaR optimal portfolios based on the linear correlation matrix require about 1.5% more variance for the same returns than the according 2-Moment efficient portfolios. For the RS Copula the difference is only about 0.7%. In contrast, the Mean-Variance and Mean-CVaR optimal $\mu_p - \sigma_p$ combinations differ significantly if the allocation procedures are executed on basis of simulations from the Static Canonical-Vine or from the Dynamic Clayton Copulas. The Mean-CVaR optimal portfolios accept 10% and 6% higher levels of variance for the same expected returns than the according 2-Moment optimal portfolios. Those differences are due to the additional negative skewnesses of the joint distributions which are caused by the asymmetric dependencies. Severe negative portfolio skewness increases the CVaR levels and thus the Mean-CVaR allocation does not solely focus on variance but also on skewness reduction.

Figure 7.3 – G7 Stocks Mean-Variance efficient Portfolios: The first row presents the 2-Moment efficient portfolios. The second row presents the according return-skewness combinations. The third row presents the according portfolio kurtoses. The fourth row presents the according return-CVaR combinations at SL_1. The linear correlation matrix and the three Copula models are estimated on basis of the complete G7 Stocks dataset. The complete dataset covers the time-frame 31.Dez.1997 to 18.Jan.2010. In the graphics, the dependence models are represented via: '.' Linear Covariance Matrix; '*' Static Canonical-Vine Copula. The pair-Copulas within the Canonical-Vine are denoted in table 4.7; '+' RS Gaussian|Mixture Copula. The Mixture contains one Gaussian, one Clayton and one Gumbel Copulas; 'o' Dynamic Clayton Copula. The returns on the y-axis and the volatilities are annualized. The skewnesses, kurtoses and CVaRs are presented as weekly data.

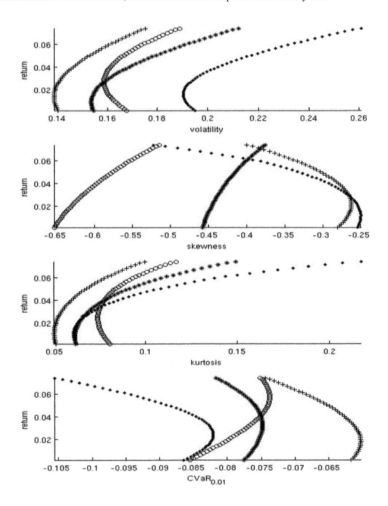

Figure 7.4 – G7 Stocks Mean-CVaR efficient Portfolios: The fourth row presents the Mean-CVaR efficient portfolios at SL_1. The first row presents the resulting Mean-Variance tradeoffs. The second row presents the according return-skewness combinations and the third row presents the according portfolio kurtoses. The linear correlation matrix and the three Copula models are estimated on basis of the complete G7 Stocks dataset. The complete dataset covers the time-frame 31.Dez.1997 to 18.Jan.2010. In the graphics, the dependence models are represented via: '.' Linear Covariance Matrix; '*' Static Canonical-Vine Copula. The pair-Copulas within the Canonical-Vine are denoted in table 4.7; '+' RS Gaussian|Mixture Copula. The Mixture contains one Gaussian, one Clayton and one Gumbel Copulas; 'o' Dynamic Clayton Copula. The returns on the y-axis and the volatilities are annualized. The skewnesses, kurtoses and CVaRs are presented as weekly data.

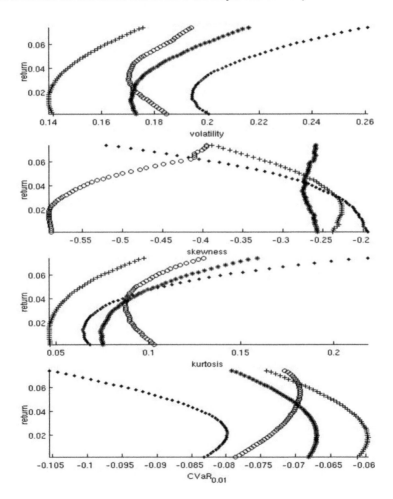

The asymmetric Copulas cause much more negative portfolio skewnesses than the symmetric dependence models, and therefore their Mean-Variance and Mean-CVaR optimal portfolio shares differ more significantly. In addition, lower levels of portfolio kurtosis reduce the tail probabilities. Decreasing the portfolio kurtosis is an effective method to reduce the CVaR levels, especially if the underlying joint distribution is negatively skewed. However, reducing the portfolio skewness is the most effective method to reduce the portfolio CVaR levels and therefore, the Mean-CVaR allocation procedure accepts more kurtosis for less negative skewness. This effect is most pronounced for simulations from the asymmetric Copulas which cause the most severe negative skewnesses in the joint distributions. Compared to the Mean-Variance optimal portfolios, the Mean-CVaR algorithm, based on the asymmetric Copulas, increases the portfolio kurtosis by 0.014. The increase for the symmetric dependence models is only about 0.002 and 0.005. Overall, the comparison of the Mean-Variance and Mean-CVaR optimal G7 Stocks portfolios amplifies the importance to account for asymmetric dependencies and for higher moments in the portfolio selection.

Next to Stocks only portfolios, I allocate Multi Asset Classes portfolios via the Mean-Variance and the Mean-CVaR algorithms. Again, both allocation algorithms are executed on basis of simulations from the linear correlation matrix and the "best-fit" Copulas. In case of the Multi Asset Classes data, the VaR backtests identify the Static Student's-t, the Dynamic Student's-t and the RS Gaussian|Gaussian as the most appropriate Copula skeletons within their categories. Figure 7.5 presents the characteristics of the 2-Moment optimal portfolios. The first plot in this graphic presents the $\mu_p - \sigma_p$ optimal combinations for each dependence model. In contrast to the G7 Stocks dataset, the optimal Multi Asset Classes portfolio shares differ less significantly with respect to the underlying dependence models, resulting similar efficient frontiers. This is due to the similar characteristics of the dependence models and the insignificant correlations among different asset classes (Chapter 4). Again, the univariate models are identical for any simulated dataset and hence the observable differences in the $\mu_p - \sigma_p$ optimal frontiers are solely due to dependence misspecification. The VaR backtests identify the Dynamic Student's-t Copula as the most appropriate dependence model for the Multi Asset Classes dataset. Consequently, I utilize its efficient frontier as the benchmark for the other dependence models. 2-Moment efficient portfolios which are allocated on basis of simulations from the linear correlation matrix, reveal the greatest distance from the benchmark. Thus, I conclude that the linear correlation matrix represents the interactions of the multiple asset classes most inaccurately.

The second plot in figure 7.5 presents the according portfolio skewnesses for the 2-Moment efficient portfolios. Of course, simulating data from the symmetric Copulas and transforming them via univariate Gaussian distributions (Table 4.5) results portfolio skewness levels of $cs_p = 0$. The portfolio CVaRs are defined through the joint distribution shape. The variance dictates the dispersion, the skewness and kurtosis influence its shape and characterize its tails. Thus, differences in the simulated portfolio CVaR levels are only due to different dependence intensities which are incorporated into the simulations via the linear correlation matrix and the "best-fit" Copulas. The $\mu_p - CVaR_p$ curves behave oppositely to the $\mu_p - \sigma_p$ curves what is in line with the theoretical foundations. In order to generate higher returns, the investor has to accept stronger levels of volatility. Hence, increasing returns require more distinct CVaR levels. Again, the CVaR levels calculated on basis of simulations from the linear correlation matrix reveal the greatest distance from the benchmark (Dynamic Student's-t Copula). This outcome amplifies the impact of misspecified dependencies on the optimal portfolio choice.

In the same manner as for the two previous datasets, I allocate Mean-CVaR efficient Multi Asset Classes portfolios. However, the Mean-CVaR and the Mean-Variance efficient portfolios are identical because the simulations are based on univariate Gaussian distributions (Table 4.5) and symmetric "best-fit" Copulas. Hence, the resulting joint distributions are shaped symmetrically and the minimization of the portfolio variance and portfolio CVaR results in the same optimal portfolio shares. This leads to the conclusion that the Multi Asset Classes Mean-Variance efficient portfolios are also efficient under higher moments of risk.

Figure 7.5 – Multi Asset Classes Mean-Variance efficient Portfolios: The first graph presents the 2-Moment efficient portfolios. The second graph presents the according return-skewness combinations. The third graph presents the according portfolio kurtoses. The fourth graph presents the according return-CVaR combinations at SL_1. The linear correlation matrix and the three Copula models are estimated on basis of the complete Multi Asset Classes dataset. The complete dataset covers the time-frame 02.Jan.1989 to 01.Feb.2010. In the graphics, the dependence models are represented via: '.' Linear Covariance Matrix; '*' Static Student's-t Copula; '+' RS Gaussian|Gaussian Copula; 'o' Dynamic Student's-t Copula. The returns on the y-axis and the volatilities are annualized. The skewnesses, kurtoses and CVaRs are presented as weekly data.

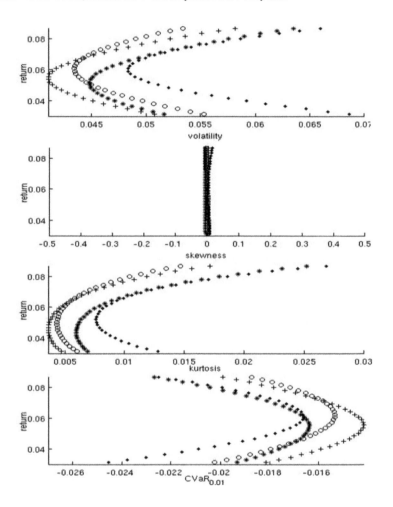

Chapter 8

Conclusion

This thesis focuses on the interaction of financial markets and provides evidence that their dependence structure changes severely over time. The most common approach to measure multivariate dependencies of time series is the linear correlation matrix, which models only symmetric dependence and is not able to comprise shifts in the dependence structure. Copulas are an advantageous concept to capture asymmetric dependencies and to improve the representation of the interaction of financial markets. Nevertheless, Copulas are not flexible enough to comprise fundamental changes in the dependence structure. To enhance the flexibility of this concept, I examine two extensions to the Static Copula approach. First, Regime-Switch Copulas which split the dataset into one high and into one low dependence regimes which are represented through different Copula functions. This setup introduces additional flexibility to capture shifting interactions of financial markets. Second, this thesis proposes various multivariate Dynamic Copulas. They utilize the Static Copula frameworks but allow the Copula parameters to follow well defined stochastic processes. Thus, the Copula parameter intensities adapt to changes in the dependence structure at each observation and are able to detect fundamental changes. This setup is more flexible than the Regime-Switch Copulas because the individual Copula parameters are not limited to jump between two regimes but they evolve over time.

The empirical examinations of the dependence models prove the Dynamic Copula framework's superiority to capture the interaction of financial markets most precisely. This thesis utilizes three different datasets for the empirical analysis. The G7 Bond yields to demonstrate each Copula's ability to capture right tail dependencies. The G7 Stocks to analyze each Copula's ability to capture left tail dependence. One Multi Asset Classes dataset to examine the preciseness of the various Copulas to measure the interaction of different asset classes and to capture changes in their dependence structure. Realistic portfolios often consist of multiple asset classes and quantifying their interactions precisely is a key factor for modern risk and portfolio management. Below, I shortly summarize the key findings from the empirical examinations.

Chapter 4 estimates the univariate GARCH models and the multivariate Copulas. The GARCH parameter estimates indicate sudden and abrupt jumps from low to high volatility levels. The reduction of high volatilities to lower levels is rather smooth. This pattern holds true for any examined financial asset. Additionally, those estimates support previous findings that high and low volatility levels occur in clusters and that negative returns have a stronger impact on volatility than positive returns of the same amplitude. Any utilized Copula model indicates right tail dependent Bond yields. This insinuates that joint Bond yield increases are more probable than joint Bond yield decreases. The Dynamic Copulas identify two fundamental shifts in the Bond yield dependence structure. In 1999, the Euro introduction significantly tightens the comovements of the European Bond yields. In contrast, the solvency issues of several South European countries in 2009 decrease the dependencies of the global Bond markets. The G7 Stock markets reveal left tail dependence and their interactions follow a recurring pattern. Joint Stock market depreciations are more likely than joint appreciations and the dependencies tighten significantly during volatile phases. The dependencies between different asset classes change most distinctly over time. They are driven by fundamental changes in the underlyings and do not follow a recurring pattern. Nevertheless, diversification among several asset classes is more efficient in regards to loss avoidance than global diversification within the same asset class.

Chapter 5 examines the interactions of the dependence structure with the univariate returns and volatilities. Additionally, it analyzes the impact of the univariate returns on the univariate volatility levels. The univariate G7 Bond yield changes cannot explain the occurrence of the regimes filtered from the Regime-Switch Copulas. In the same manner, the univariate volatilities are not the drivers for the high or low dependence regimes. Hence, the hypothesis that the high dependence regime would occur during Bond yield increases which would be accompanied by high volatilities is rejected. In contrast, the time-paths of the Dynamic Copula parameters are strongly linked to the univariate returns and volatilities. While the average Bond yields shrink, their dependencies tighten. This pattern is due to the Euro introduction which tightens the comovements of the G7 Bond yields while the yields drop throughout the observation period. Most of the univariate Bond yield volatilities are positively correlated with their according Dynamic Copula parameters. Thus, volatility accessions tighten the G7 Bond yield dependencies. The same holds true for the G7 Stock markets. The Dynamic Copula parameters and the univariate volatility levels are significantly positively correlated. Thus, Stock market dependencies tighten significantly during volatile phases. Additionally, the analyses show that negative return drifts accrue with tightening Stock market dependencies. Overall, Stock market dependencies tighten during volatile downturn phases. This combination destroys diversification effects when they are needed the most and therefore is most hazardous to financial wealth. Those findings show that global diversification among Stock markets is inefficient to protect portfolios from severe losses. The Multi Asset Classes dataset offers the greatest diversification potential. There is no evidence for tightening dependencies during volatile phases. In addition, the conducted analyses indicate no joint market downturns. Therefore, diversification among multiple asset classes offers protection against severe financial losses.

Chapter 6 conducts one week portfolio Value-at-Risk (VaR) and Conditional-Value-at-Risk (CVaR) forecasts. According to the Sklar theorem (1959), this is a two-step procedure. At first, the univariate volatilities are forecasted independently from the Copula model. A battery of goodness-of-fit tests guarantees their accuracies. In a second step, 50000 random paths are generated from the selected Copula. In a third step, the same univariate volatility forecasts are nested with the simulations from different Copulas. This guarantees that the resulting return simulations only differ in regards to their dependence structure, but are equal in regards to their univariate features. Finally, equally weighted portfolios are constructed and their according portfolio VaRs and CVaRs are calculated. This procedure ensures that the differences in the portfolio VaR and CVaR forecasts are only due to differences in the Copula models. Hence, a direct comparison of the portfolio VaR and CVaR forecast accuracies depicts the Copula skeleton which represents the dependence structure most precisely. The Dynamic Gumbel Copula captures the dependencies of the G7 Bond yields most accurately, resulting in the most exact portfolio VaR hit ratios and smallest CVaR exceedances. This result is in line with the previous findings because the Dynamic Gumbel Copula focuses on right tail dependence. In the case of the G7 Stocks, the Dynamic Clayton Copula measures their interactions most accurately. In return, the predicted portfolio CVaR levels are the least exceeded and the VaR hit ratios indicate precise quantile forecasts. In contrast to the Gumbel skeleton, the Clayton Copula focuses on left tail dependence, a previously detected feature in the G7 Stocks dataset. The only other

Copula predicting similarly exact Stock portfolio VaRs and CVaRs is the Static Canonical-Vine framework which combines several bivariate Clayton Copulas in its hierarchical structure. The interactions of the Multi Asset Classes dataset are described most concisely by the Dynamic Student's-t Copula. Its application results in very accurate VaR predictions at any significance level and in very small CVaR excesses. In contrast to the G7 Bond yields and the G7 Stocks, the interactions of multiple asset classes change more individually. Hence, the Dynamic Student's-t Copula's parameter plurality, its parameters' abilities to follow individual time paths and its ability to account for tail dependence are advantageous features to comprise the time-instable dependencies.

Chapter 7 demonstrates the impact of misspecified dependencies by allocating Mean - Variance and Mean - CVaR efficient portfolios for the G7 Bond yields, the G7 Stocks and the Multi Asset Classes datasets. Bond yields are non-investable and therefore I transform the yields into Bond prices to perform the allocation procedures. Both allocations are executed on basis of simulations from a linear covariance matrix and the "best-fit" Static, RS and Dynamic Copulas, resulting in four simulated Bond, four simulated Stocks and four simulated Multi Asset Classes datasets. Within each asset class, the four simulated datasets are equal in regards to their univariate features but comprehend different dependence structures. The Mean-Variance portfolio allocation results in four different efficient frontiers for each asset class. The dispersions of the four efficient frontiers are solely caused by the variations in the dependence models. However, the Mean-Variance optimization focuses solely on the first two moments and therefore neglects the skewness of the joint distribution which is caused by asymmetric Copulas. The Mean-CVaR allocation amplifies the impact of time-instable and asymmetric dependencies among Bond and Stock markets on the optimal portfolio shares because it explicitly accounts for the third and fourth moments of the joint distributions. Those results demonstrate the inability of the linear correlation matrix to quantify Bond and Stock market interactions precisely. In contrast, any "best-fit" Copulas for the multiple asset classes reveal a symmetric character, but measure different dependence amplitudes. Consequently, differences in the optimal portfolio shares are solely caused by variations in the measured dependence intensities. Again, the optimal portfolio shares indicate that the linear correlation matrix misspecifies the dependence structure most severely. Due to the univariate Gaussian distributions and the symmetric dependence models, the execution of the Mean-Variance and Mean-CVaR procedures results in identical multi asset classes optimal portfolios.

Overall, the conducted analyses show that the interactions of financial markets are time-instable. Compared to Static skeletons, the proposed Dynamic Copulas comprise changing dependencies more accurately and contribute to detect future portfolio risks. However, introducing additional flexibility to the dependence frameworks is computationally expensive. The computer resources required to estimate the Dynamic Copulas grow exponentially with additional dataset dimensions.

Nevertheless, Dynamic Copulas could contribute to the solution of a broad range of practical issues. For instance, the evaluation of basket options or the construction of accurate hedges. Furthermore, Dynamic Copulas can also contribute to enhance the evaluation of structured products which contain multiple financial assets. Additionally, the existing theoretical constructs could be enhanced to improve multivariate time-instable dependence modeling. I propose dynamic extensions for the basic multivariate Archimedian and Elliptical as well as for the Mixture Copulas. However, the stochastic processes could easily be integrated into the hierarchical Canonical-Vine Copulas. This would allow to combine several different bivariate Dynamic Copulas to comprise multivariate dependencies. The additional flexibility should further advance the accuracy of multivariate dependence representation.

Appendix A

Filtered Volatilities

Figure A.1 – G7 Bond yields filtered Volatility Levels.

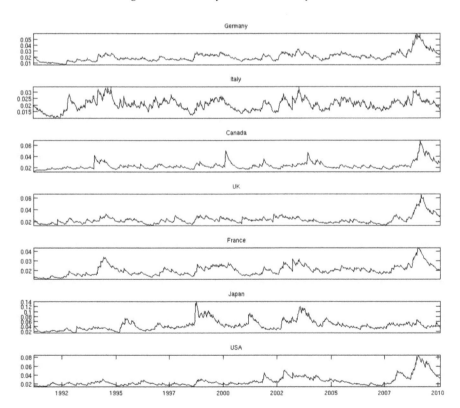

Figure A.2 – G7 Stocks filtered Volatility Levels.

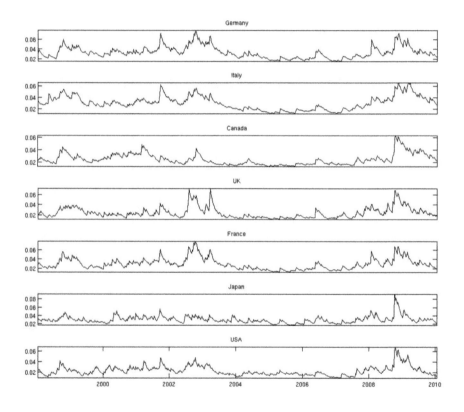

Figure A.3 – Multi Asset Classes filtered Volatility Levels.

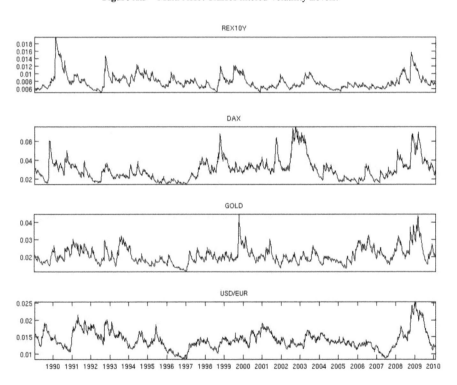

Appendix B

Returns and Volatilities

Figure B.1 – G7 Bond yields. The figures present the yield changes (solid line) and the according yield changes during their low volatility clusters (dashed line). The volatility clusters are estimated for each return series individually. The graphics cover the time frame 06.Mar.1991 to 03.Feb.2010.

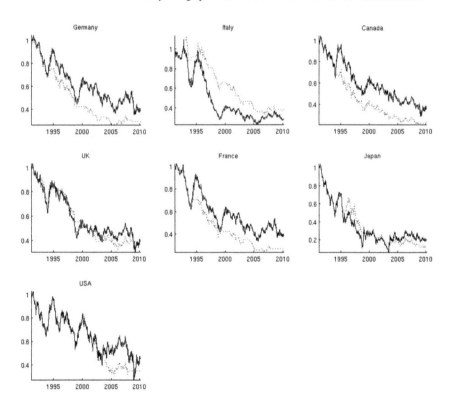

Figure B.2 – G7 Stocks. The figures present the return indices (solid line) and the according returns during their low volatility clusters (dashed line). The volatility clusters are estimated for each return series individually. The graphics cover the time frame 31.Dec.1997 to 20.Jan.2010.

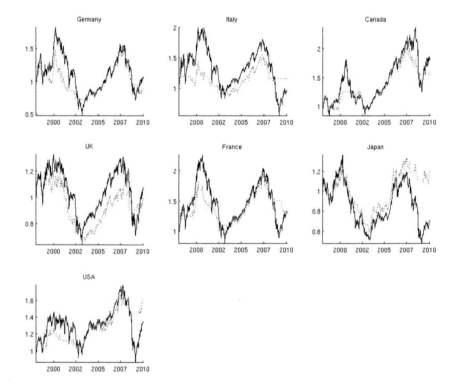

Figure B.3 – Multi Asset Classes. The figures present the return indices (solid line) and the according returns during their low volatility clusters (dashed line). The volatility clusters are estimated for each return series individually. The graphics cover the time frame 02.Jan.1989 to 01.Feb.2010.

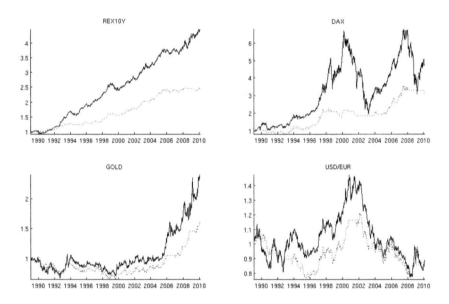

References

Aas, K. & Czado, C. & Frigessi, A. & Bakken, H. (2009): Pair-Copula Constructions of Multiple Dependence; in: Insurance: Mathematics and Economics, Vol. 44, pp. 182–198.

Akaike, H. (1974): Fitting Autoregressive Models for Prediction; in: Ananals of the Institute of Statistical Mathematics, Vol. 19, pp. 364-385.

Alexander, G. & Baptist, A. (2002): Economic Implications of Using a Mean-VaR model for Portfolio Selection: A Comparison with Mean-Variance Analysis; in: Jounal of Economic Dynamics and Control, Vol. 26, pp. 1159-1193.

Ang, A. & Bekaert, G. (2002): International Asset Allocation with Regime Shifts; in: The Review of Financial Studies, Vol. 15, pp. 1137-1187.

Ang, A. & Chen, J. (2002): Asymmetric Correlations of Equity Portfolios; in: Journal of Financial Economics, Vol. 63, pp.443-494.

Bae, K. & Karolyi, A. & Stulz, R. (2003): A new Approach to Measuring Financial Contangion; in: The Review of Financial Studies, Vol. 16, pp. 717-763.

Baillie, R. & Myers, R. (1991): Modeling commodity price distributions and estimating the optimal futures hedge; in: Journal of Applied Econometrics, Vol. 6, pp. 109-124.

Bedford, T. & Cooke, R. (2002): Vines - A New Graphical Model for Dependent Random Variables. , in: Annals of Statistics, Vol. 30, pp. 1031–1068.

Bernoth, K. & von Hagen, J. & Schuknecht, L. (2004): Sovereign Risk Premia in the European Government Bond Market; in: Working Paper.

Bollerslev, T. (1986): Generalized Autoregressive Conditional Heteroskedasticy; in: Journal of Econometrics, Vol. 31, pp. 307-327.

Bollerslev, T. & Chou, R. & Kroner, K. (1992): ARCH modeling in finance: A review of the theory and empirical evidence; in: Journal of Econometrics, Vol. 52, pp. 5-59.

Bouye, E. & Durrleman, V. & Nikeghbali, A. & Riboulet, G. & Roncalli, T. (2000): Copulas for Finance: A Reading Guide and some Applications; in: Working Paper.

Bouye, E. & Durrleman, V. & Nikeghbali, A. & Roncalli, T. (2001): Copulas: An open Filed for Risk Management; in: Working Paper.

Brandt, M. & Kang, Q. (2004): On the relationship between the conditional mean and volatility of stock returns: a latent VAR approach; in: Journal of Financial Economics 72, 217–257.

Brown, S. & Warner, J. (1985): Using daily Stock Returns – The Case of Event Studies; in: Journal of Financial Economics, Vol. 14, pp. 3-31.

Cappiello, L. & Engle, R. & Sheppard, K. (2006): Asymmetric Dynamics in the Correlations of Global Equity and Bond Returns; in: Journal of Financial Econometrics, Vol. 4, pp. 537-572.

Chollete, L. & Heinen, A. & Valdesogo, A. (2009): Modelling International Financial Returns with a Multivariate Regime-Switching Copula; in: Journal of Financial Econometrics, Vol. 7, pp. 437-480.

Christie, A. (1982): The stochastic behavior of common stock variance: Value, leverage and interest rate effects; in: Journal of Financial Economics, Vol. 10, pp. 407-432.

Das, S. & Uppal, R. (2004): Systemic Risk and international Portfolio Choice; in: The Journal of Finance, Vol. 59, pp. 2809-2834.

Durrleman, V. & Nikeghbali, A. & Roncalli, T. (2000): Which Copula is the right one?; in: Working Paper.

Embrechts, P. & Lindskog, F. & McNeil, A. (2003): Modelling Dependence with Copulas and Applications to Risk Management; in: Handbook of Heavy Tailed Distributions in Finance, Amsterdam.

Enders, W (2003): Applied Econometric Time Series; 2nd Edition, Wiley.

Engle, R. (1982): Autoregressive Conditional Heteroskedasticy with Estimates of the Variance of the U.K. Inflation; in: Econometrica, Vol. 50, pp. 987-1008.

Engle, R. & Ng, V. (1993): Measuring and testing the Impact of News on Volatility; in: The Journal of Finance, Vol. 48, pp. 1749-1778.

Engle, R. & Susmel, R. (1993): Common Volatility in International Equity Markets; in: Journal of Business & Economic Statistics, Vol. 11, pp. 167-176.

Engle,R. & Sheppard, K. (2001): Theoretical and Empirical properties of Dynamic Conditional Correlation Multivariate GARCH; in: working paper.

Fama. E (1976): Foundations of Finance; Basic Books.

Forbes, K. & Rigobon, R. (2003): No Contagion, only Interdependence: Measuring Stock arket Comovements; in: The Journal of Finance, Vol. 57, pp., 2223-2261.

French, K. & Schwert, G, & Stambaugh, R. (1987): Expected stock returns and volatility; in: Journal of Financial Economics, Vol. 19, pp. 3-29.

Garcia, R & Tsafak, G. (2007): Dependence Structure and Extreme Comovements in International Equity and Bond Markets with Portfolio Diversification Effects; in: Techinal Report, Cirano.

Granger, W. (1969): Investigating Casual Relations by Econometric and Cross-Spectral Models; in: Econometrica, Vol. 37, pp. 424-438.

Guidolin, M. & Timmermann, A. (2007): Asset Allocation under multivariate Regime Switching; in: Journal of Economic Dynamics & Control, Vol. 31, pp. 3503-3544.

Hafner, C. & Manner, H. (2009): Dynamic Stochastic Copula Models: Estimation, Inference and Applications; in: Working Paper.

Hamilton (1989): A new Approach to the Economic Analysis of nonstationary Time Series and the Business Cycle; in: Econometrica, Vol. 57, pp. 357-384;

Hansen, B. (1994): Autoregressive Conditional Density Estimation; in: International Economic Review, Vol. 35, pp. 705–730.

Hoermann, W. & Leydold, J. & Derflinger, G. (2004): Automatic Nonuniform Random Variate Generation; Springer Verlag, Berlin.

Hong, Y. & Tu, J. & Zhou, G. (2007): Asymmetries in Stock Returns: Statistical Tests and Economic Evaluation; in: The Review of Financial Studies, Vol. 20, pp. 1547-1581.

Hu, L. (2006): Dependence Patterns across financial Markets: a mixed Copula Approach; in: Applied Financial Economics, Vol. 16, pp. 717-729.

Hult, H. & Lindskog, F. (2002): Multivariate Extremes, Aggregation and Dependence in Elliptical Distributions; in: Advances in Applied Probability, Vol. 34, pp. 587-608.

Jin, X. (2009): Large Portfolio Risk Management with Dynamic Copulas; in: Working Paper.

Joe, H. (1997): Multivariate Models and Dependence Concepts; Chapman & Hall, London.

Joe, H. & Xu, J. (1996): The Estimation Method of Inference Functions for Margins for Multivariate Models; in Department of Statistics, University of British Columbia, Technical Report, Vol. 166.

Karolyi, G. & Stulz, R. (1996): Why do Markets move together? An Investigation of U.S.-Japan Stock Return Comovements; in: The Journal of Finance, Vol. 51, pp. 951-986.

Kimberling, C. (1974): A probabilistic Interpretation of complete Monotonicity; in: Aequationes Mathematicae, Vol. 10, pp. 152-164.

King, M. & S. Wadhwani (1990): Transmission of Volatility between Stock Markets; in: Review of Financial Studies, Vol. 3, pp.5-33.

Kofman, P. & Martens, M. (1997): Interaction between Stock Markets : an Analysis of the common Trading Hours at the London and New York Stock Exchange; in: Journal of International Money and Finance, Vol. 16, pp. 387-414.

Kole, E. & Koedijk, K. & Verbeek, M. (2006): Selecting Copulas for Risk Management; in: Journal of Banking & Finance, Vol. 31, pp. 2405-2423.

Kupiec, P. (1995): Techniques for Verifying the Accuracy of Risk Measurement Models; in: Journal of Derivatives, Vol. 3, pp. 73-84.

Levy, H. (1969): A Utility Function dependending on the First Three Moments; in: The Journal of Finance, Vol. 24, pp. 715-719.

Lintner, J (1965): The Selection of Risk Assets and the Selection of Risky Investments in Stock Portfolios and Capital Budgets; in: The Review of Economics and Statistics, Vol. 47, pp. 13-37.

Liu, J. (2007): Portfolio Selection in Stochastic Environment; in: The Review of Financial Studies, Vol. 20, pp. 1-39.

Lo, A. & MacKinlay, C. (1988): Stock Market Prices do not follow Random Walks: Evidence from a simple Specification Test; in: The Review of Financial Studies, Vol. 1, pp. 41-66.

Longin, F. & Solnik, B. (2001): Extreme Correlation of international Equity Markets; in: The Journal of Finance, Vol. 56, pp. 649-676.

Markowitz, H. (1952): Portfolio Selection; in: Journal of Finance, Vol. 7, pp. 77-91.

Marshall, A. & Olkin, I. (1988): Families of Multivariate Distributions; in: Journal of the American Statistical Association, Vol. 83, pp. 834-841.

Mele, A. (2007): Asymmetric Stock Market Volatility and the Cyclical Behavior of Expected Returns; in: Journal of Financial Economics, Vol. 86, pp. 446-478.

Mendes, B & Souza, R. (2004): Measuring financial Risk with Copulas; in: International Review of Financial Analysis, Vol. 13, pp. 27-45.

Merton, R. (1980): On estimating the expected return on the market: An exploratoryinvestigation; in: Journal of Financial Economics, Vol. 8, pp. 323-361.

Nelsen, R. (2006): An Introduction to Copulas; 2nd Edition, Springer, New York.

Nelson, D. (1991): Conditional Heteroskedasticy in Asset Returns: A new Approach; in: Econometrica, Vol. 59, pp. 347-370.

Newey, W. & McFadden, D. (1994): Large Sample Estimation and Hypothesis Testing; in: Handbook of Econometrics, Vol. 4, Amsterdam.

Ng, W. (2008): Modeling Duration Clusters with Dynamic Copulas; in: Finance Research Letters, Vol. 5, pp. 96-103.

Patton, A (2006): Modelling Asymmetric Exchange Rate Dependence; in: International Economic Review, Vol. 47, pp. 527-556.

Patton, A. (2007): Copula based Models for Financial Time Series; in: Working Paper.

Pelletier, D. (2006): Regime switching for dynamic correlations; in: Journal of Econometrics, Vol. 131, pp. 445-473.

Rockafellar, T. & Uryasev, S. (2002): Conditional Value-at-Risk for general Loss Distributions; in: Journal of Banking and Finance, Vol. 26, pp. 1443-1471.

Rodriguez, J. (2007): Measuring Financial Contagion: A Copula Approach; in: Journal of Empirical Finance, Vol. 14, pp. 401-423.

Roy, A. (1952): Saftey First and the Holding of Assets; in: Econometrica, Vol. 20, pp. 431-449.

Schwert, G. (1989): Why does stock market volatility change over time?; in: Journal of Finance, Vol. 44, pp. 1115–1153.

Schwert, G. (1990): Stock volatility and the Crash of 87; in: Review of Financial Studies Vol. 3, pp. 77-102.

Schwert, G. & Seguin, P. (1990): Heteroskedasticity in stock returns; in: The Journal of Finance, Vol. 45, pp. 1129-1155.

Sharpe, W. (1964): Capital Asset Prices: A Theory of Market Equilibrium under Conditions of Risk; in: The Journal of Finance, Vol. 19, pp. 425-442.

Sklar, A. (1959): Fonctions de repartition a n dimensions et leurs marges; Publ. Inst. University Paris, Vol. 8, p. 229-231.

Statman, M. & Scheid, J. (2008): Correlation, Return Gaps, and the Benefits of Diversification; in: The Journal of Portfolio Management, Vol. 3, pp. 132-139.

Tsay, R. (2005): Analysis of Financial Time Series; Second Edition, Wiley.

White, H. (1982): Maximum Likelihood Estimation of misspecified Models; in: Econometrica, Vol. 50, pp. 1-25.

QUANTITATIVE ÖKONOMIE

Herausgegeben von Prof. Dr. Eckart Bomsdorf, Köln, Prof. Dr. Wim Kösters, Bochum, Prof. Dr. Winfried Matthes †, Wuppertal, Prof. Dr. Mark Trede, Münster, Prof. Dr. Ansgar Belke, Essen, und Prof. Dr. Markus Pütz, Lahr

Band 161
Tobias Wintz
Neuproduktprognose mit Wachstumskurvenmodellen –
Prognoseprozess, Modellauswahl und Schätzung
Lohmar – Köln 2010 ◆ 344 S. ◆ € 63,- (D) ◆ ISBN 978-3-89936-915-1

Band 162
Philippe Wittmann
Das Testen der Martingaleigenschaft
Lohmar – Köln 2010 ◆ 140 S. ◆ € 43,- (D) ◆ ISBN 978-3-89936-956-4

Band 163
Stephan Scholze
Kurzfristige Prognose von Tageszeitreihen mit Kalendereffekten
Lohmar – Köln 2010 ◆ 196 S. ◆ € 49,- (D) ◆ ISBN 978-3-8441-0000-6

Band 164
Sue Man Fan
Multiple Tests für die Evaluation von Prognosemodellen –
Eine Analyse am Beispiel der Prognose von Vermögenspreisen
Lohmar – Köln 2010 ◆ 192 S. ◆ € 49,- (D) ◆ ISBN 978-3-8441-0001-3

Band 165
Martin Meermeyer
Prognose von betriebswirtschaftlichen Zeitreihen auf Basis von Splineregressionsmodellen – Mit einem empirischen Anwendungsbeispiel aus der Warenwirtschaft
Lohmar – Köln 2011 ◆ 168 S. ◆ € 47,- (D) ◆ ISBN 978-3-8441-0036-5

Band 166
Valentin Braun
Dynamic Copulas for Finance – An Application to Portfolio Risk Calculation
Lohmar – Köln 2011 ◆ 176 S. ◆ € 48,- (D) ◆ ISBN 978-3-8441-0040-2

Lightning Source UK Ltd.
Milton Keynes UK
UKHW020908050522
402542UK00009B/832